BROOKLANDS
BOOKS

CHEVY BLAZER
1969-1981

Compiled by
R.M. Clarke

ISBN 1 85520 0465

Distributed by
Brooklands Book Distribution Ltd.
'Holmerise', Seven Hills Road,
Cobham, Surrey, England
Printed in Hong Kong

BROOKLANDS BOOKS

BROOKLANDS ROAD TEST SERIES

AC Ace & Aceca 1953-1983
Alfa Romeo Alfasud 1972-1984
Alfa Romeo Alfetta Coupes GT. GTV. GTV6 1974-1987
Alfa Romeo Giulia Berlinas 1962-1976
Alfa Romeo Giulia Coupes 1963-1976
Alfa Romeo Spider 1966-1987
Allard Gold Portfolio 1937-1958
Alvis Gold Portfolio 1919-1969
American Motors Muscle Cars 1966-1970
Aston Martin Gold Portfolio 1972-1985
Austin Seven 1922-1982
Austin A30 & A35 1951-1962
Austin Healey 100 & 100/6 Gold Portfolio 1952-1959
Austin Healey 3000 Gold Portfolio 1959-1967
Austin Healey 'Frogeye' Sprite Col No.1 1958-1961
Austin Healey Sprite 1958-1971
Avanti 1962-1983
BMW Six Cylinder Coupes 1969-1975
BMW 1600 Col. 1 1966-1981
BMW 2002 1968-1976
Bristol Cars Gold Portfolio 1946-1985
Buick Automobiles 1947-1960
Buick Muscle Cars 1965-1970
Buick Riviera 1963-1978
Cadillac Automobiles 1949-1959
Cadillac Automobiles 1960-1969
Cadillac Eldorado 1967-1978
High Performance Capris Gold Portfolio 1969-1987
Chevrolet Camaro SS & Z28 1966-1973
Chevrolet Camaro & Z-28 1973-1981
High Performance Camaros 1982-1988
Camaro Muscle Cars 1966-1972
Chevrolet 1955-1957
Chevrolet Impala & SS 1958-1971
Chevrolet Muscle Cars 1966-1971
Chevelle and SS 1964-1972
Chevy Blazer 1969-1981
Chevy EL Camino & SS 1959-1987
Chevy II Nova & SS 1962-1973
Chrysler 300 1955-1970
Citroen Traction Avant Gold Portfolio 1934-1957
Citroen DS & ID 1955-1975
Citroen 2CV 1949-1988
Shelby Cobra Gold Portfolio 1962-1969
Cobras & Replicas 1962-1983
Corvair 1959-1968
Chevrolet Corvette Gold Portfolio 1953 1962
Corvette Stingray Gold Portfolio 1963-1967
High Performance Corvettes 1983-1989
Datsun 240Z 1970-1973
Datsun 280Z & ZX 1975-1983
De Tomaso Collection No.1 1962-1981
Dodge Charger 1966-1974
Dodge Muscle Cars 1967-1970
Excalibur Collection No.1 1952-1981
Ferrari Cars 1946-1956
Ferrari Cars 1973-1977
Ferrari Dino 1965-1974
Ferrari Dino 308 1974-1979
Ferrari 308 & Mondial 1980-1984
Ferrair Collection No.1 1960-1970
Fiat-Bertone X1/9 1973-1988
Fiat Pininfarina 124 + 2000 Spider 1968-1985
Ford Automobiles 1949-1959
Ford Bronco 1966-1977
Ford Bronco 1978-1988
Ford Cortina 1600E & GT 1967-1970
Ford Fairlane 1955-1970
Ford Falcon 1960-1970
Ford GT40 Gold Portfolio 1964-1987
Ford RS Escorts 1968-1980
High Performance Escorts Mk1 1968-1974
High Performance Escorts Mk II 1975-1980
High Performance Mustangs 1982-1988
Honda CRX 1983-1987
Hudson & Railton 1936-1940
Jaguar Cars 1957-1961
Jaguar Cars 1961-1964
Jaguar Mk2 1959-1969
Jaguar E-Type Gold Portfolio 1961-1971
Jaguar E-Type 1966-1971
Jaguar E-Type V-12 1971-1975
Jaguar XKE Collection No.1 1961-1974
Jaguar XJ6 1968-1972
Jaguar XJ6 Series II 1973-1979
Jaguar XJ6 & XJ12 Series III 1979-1985
Jaguar XJ12 1972-1980
Jaguar XJS Gold Portfolio 1975-1988
Jaguar XK120.XK140.XK150 Gold Portfolio 1948-1960
Jeep CJ5 & CJ6 1960-1976
Jeep CJ5 & CJ7 1976-1986
Jensen Cars 1946-1967
Jensen Cars 1967-1979
Jensen Interceptor Gold Portfolio 1966-1986
Jensen Healey 1972-1976
Lamborghini Cars 1964-1970
Lamborghini Cars 1970-1975
Lamborghini Countach Col No.1 1971-1982
Lamborghini Countach & Urraco 1974-1980
Lamborghini Countach & Jalpa 1980-1985
Lancia Stratos 1972-1985
Land Rover 1948-1973 - A Collection
Land Rover Series II & IIa 1958-1971
Land Rover Series III 1971-1985
Land Rover 90 & 110 1983-1989
Lincoln Gold Portfolio 1949-1960
Lincoln Continental 1961-1969
Lotus and Caterham Seven Gold Portfolio 1957-1989
Lotus Cortina Gold Portfolio 1963-1970
Lotus Elan Gold Portfolio 1962-1974
Lotus Elan Collection No.2 1963-1972
Lotus Elite 1957-1964
Lotus Elite & Eclat 1974-1982
Lotus Turbo Esprit 1980-1986
Lotus Europa 1966-1975
Lotus Europa Collection No.1 1966-1974
Lotus Seven Collection No.1 1957-1982
Marcos Cars 1960-1988
Maserati 1965-1970
Maserati 1970-1975

Mazda RX-7 Collection No.1 1978-1981
Mercedes 190 & 300SL 1954-1963
Mercedes 230/250/280SL 1963-1971
Mercedes Benz SLs & SLCs Gold Portfolio 1971-1989
Mercedes Benz Cars 1949-1954
Mercedes Benz Cars 1954-1957
Mercedes Benz Cars 1957-1961
Mercedes Benz Competion Cars 1950-1957
Mercury Muscle Cars 1966-1971
Metropolitan 1954-1962
MG TC 1945-1949
MG TD 1949-1953
MG TF 1953-1955
MG Cars 1959-1962
MGA Roadsters 1955-1962
MGA Collection No.1 1955-1982
MGB Roadsters 1962-1980
MGB GT 1965-1980
MG Midget, 1961-1980
Mini Moke 1964-1989
Mini Muscle Cars 1961-1979
Mopar Muscle Cars 1964-1967
Mopar Muscle Cars 1968-1971
Morgan Three-Wheeler Gold Portfolio 1910-1952
Morgan Cars 1960-1970
Morgan Cars Gold Portfolio 1968-1989
Morris Minor Collection No.1
Mustang Muscle Cars 1964-1973
Oldsmobile Automobiles 1955-1963
Old's Cutlass & 4-4-2 1964-1972
Oldsmobile Muscle Cars 1964-1971
Oldsmobile Toronado 1966-1978
Opel GT 1968-1973
Packard Gold Portfolio 1946-1958
Pantera Gold Portfolio 1970-1989
Plymouth Barracuda 1964-1974
Plymouth Muscle Cars 1966-1971
Pontiac Tempest & GTO 1961-1965
Pontiac GTO 1964-1970
Pontiac Firebird 1967-1973
Pontiac Firebird and Trans-Am 1973-1981
High Performance Firebirds 1982-1988
Pontiac Fiero 1984-1988
Pontiac Muscle Cars 1966-1972
Porsche 356 1952-1965
Porsche Cars in the 60's
Porsche Cars 1960-1964
Porsche Cars 1964-1968
Porsche Cars 1968-1972
Porsche Cars 1972-1975
Porsche Turbo Collection No.1 1975-1980
Porsche 911 1965-1969
Porsche 911 1970-1972
Porsche 911 1973-1977
Porsche 911 Carrera 1973-1977
Porsche 911 Turbo 1975-1984
Porsche 911 SC 1978-1983
Porsche 914 Gold Portfolio 1969-1976
Porsche 914 Collection No.1 1969-1983
Porsche 924 Gold Portfolio 1975-1988
Porsche 928 1977-1989
Porsche 944 1981-1985
Range Rover Gold Portfolio 1970-1988
Reliant Scimitar 1964-1986
Riley 11/2 & 21/2 Litre Gold Portfolio 1945-1955
Rolls Royce Silver Cloud 1955-1965
Rolls Royce Silver Shadow 1965-1981
Rover P4 1949-1959
Rover P4 1955-1964
Rover 3 & 3.5 Litre 1958-1973
Rover 2000 + 2200 1963-1977
Rover 3500 1968-1977
Rover 3500 & Vitesse 1976-1986
Saab Sonett Collection No.1 1966-1974
Saab Turbo 1976-1983
Shelby Mustang Muscle Cars 1965-1970
Stubebaker Gold Portfolio 1947-1966
Stubebaker Hawks & Larks 1956-1963
Sunbeam Tiger & Alpine Gold Portfolio 1959-1967
Thunderbird 1955-1957
Thunderbird 1958-1963
Thunderbird 1964-1976
Toyota MR2 1984-1988
Triumph 2000. 2.5. 2500 1963-1977
Triumph GT6 1966-1974
Triumph Spitfire 1962-1980
Triumph Spitfire Col No.1 1962-1982
Triumph Stag 1970-1980
Triumph Stag Collection No.1 1970-1984
Triumph TR2 & TR3 1952-60
Triumph TR4-TR5-TR250 1961-1968
Triumph TR6 1969-1976
Triumph TR6 Collection No.1 1969-1983
Triumph TR7 & TR8 1975-1982
Triumph Vitesse & Herald 1959-1971
TVR Gold Portfolio 1959-1988
Volkswagen Cars 1936-1956
VW Beetle Collection No.1 1970-1982
VW Golf GTi 1976-1986
VW Karmann Ghia 1955-1982
VW Kubelwagen 1940-1975
VW Scirocco 1974-1981
VW Bus. Camper. Van 1954-1967
VW Bus. Camper. Van 1968-1979
VW Bus. Camper. Van 1979-1989
Volvo 120 1956-1970
Volvo 1800 1960-1973

BROOKLANDS ROAD & TRACK SERIES

Road & Track on Alfa Romeo 1949-1963
Road & Track on Alfa Romeo 1964-1970
Road & Track on Alfa Romeo 1971-1976
Road & Track on Aston Martin 1962-1984
Road & Track on Auburn Cord and Duesenburg 1952-1984
Road & Track on Audi & Auto Union 1952-1980
Road & Track on Audi 1980-1986
Road & Track on Austin Healey 1953-1970
Road & Track on BMW Cars 1966-1974
Road & Track on BMW Cars 1975-1978
Road & Track on BMW Cars 1979-1983

Road & Track on Cobra, Shelby & GT40 1962-1983
Road & Track on Corvette 1953-1967
Road & Track on Corvette 1968-1982
Road & Track on Corvette 1982-1986
Road & Track on Datsun Z 1970-1983
Road & Track on Ferrari 1950-1968
Road & Track on Ferrari 1968-1974
Road & Track on Ferrari 1975-1981
Road & Track on Ferrari 1981-1984
Road & Track on Fiat Sports Cars 1968-1987
Road & Track on Jaguar 1950-1960
Road & Track on Jaguar 1961-1968
Road & Track on Jaguar 1968-1974
Road & Track on Jaguar 1974-1982
Road & Track on Jaguar 1983-1989
Road & Track on Lamborghini 1964-1985
Road & Track on Lotus 1972-1981
Road & Track on Maserati 1952-1974
Road & Track on Maserati 1975-1983
Road & Track on Mazda RX7 1978-1986
Road & Track on Mercedes 1952-1962
Road & Track on Mercedes 1963-1970
Road & Track on Mercedes 1971-1979
Road & Track on Mercedes 1980-1987
Road & Track on MG Sports Cars 1949-1961
Road & Track on MG Sprots Cars 1962-1980
Road & Track on Mustang 1964-1977
Road & Track on Peugeot 1955-1986
Road & Track on Pontiac 1960-1983
Road & Track on Porsche 1961-1967
Road & Track on Porsche 1968-1971
Road & Track on Porsche 1972-1975
Road & Track on Porsche 1975-1978
Road & Track on Porsche 1979-1982
Road & Track on Porsche 1982-1985
Road & Track on Porsche 1985-1988
Road & Track on Rolls Royce & B'ley 1950-1965
Road & Track on Rolls Royce & B'ley 1966-1984
Road & Track on Saab 1955-1985
Road & Track on Toyota Sports & GT Cars 1966-1984
Road & Track on Triumph Sports Cars 1953-1967
Road & Track on Triumph Sports Cars 1967-1974
Road & Track on Triumph Sports Cars 1974-1982
Road & Track on Volkswagen 1951-1968
Road & Track on Volkswagen 1968-1978
Road & Track on Volkswagen 1978-1985
Road & Track on Volvo 1957-1974
Road & Track on Volvo 1975-1985
Road & Track - Henry Manney at Large and Abroad

BROOKLANDS CAR AND DRIVER SERIES

Car and Driver on BMW 1955-1977
Car and Driver on BMW 1977-1985
Car and Driver on Cobra, Shelby & Ford GT 40 1963-1984
Car and Driver on Corvette 1956-1967
Car and Driver on Corvette 1968-1977
Car and Driver on Corvette 1978-1982
Car and Driver on Corvette 1983-1988
Car and Driver on Datsun Z 1600 & 2000 1966-1984
Car and Driver on Ferrari 1955-1962
Car and Driver on Ferrari 1963-1975
Car and Driver on Ferrari 1976-1983
Car and Driver on Mopar 1956-1967
Car and Driver on Mopar 1968-1975
Car and Driver on Mustang 1964-1972
Car and Driver on Pontiac 1961-1975
Car and Driver on Porsche 1955-1962
Car and Driver on Porsche 1963-1970
Car and Driver on Porsche 1970-1976
Car and Driver on Porsche 1977-1981
Car and Driver on Porsche 1982-1986
Car and Driver on Saab 1956-1985
Car and Driver on Volvo 1955-1986

BROOKLANDS PRACTICAL CLASSICS SERIES

PC on Austin A40 Restoration
PC on Land Rover Restoration
PC on Metalworking in Restoration
PC on Midget/Sprite Restoration
PC on Mini Cooper Restoration
PC on MGB Restoration
PC on Morris Minor Restoration
PC on Sunbeam Rapier Restoration
PC on Triumph Herald/Vitesse
PC on Triumph Spitfire Restoration
PC on VW Beetle Restoration
PC on 1930s Car Restoration

BROOKLANDS MOTOR & THOROGHBRED & CLASSIC CAR SERIES

Motor & T & CC on Ferrari 1966-1976
Motor & T & CC on Ferrari 1976-1984
Motor & T & CC on Lotus 1979-1983

BROOKLANDS MILITARY VEHICLES SERIES

Allied Mil. Vehicles No.1 1942-1945
Allied Mil. Vehicles No.2 1941-1946
Dodge Mil. Vehicles Col. 1 1940-1945
Military Jeeps 1941-1945
Off Road Jeeps 1944-1971
Hail to the Jeep
US Military Vehicles 1941-1945
US Army Military Vehicles WW2-TM9-2800

BROOKLANDS HOT ROD RESTORATION SERIES

Auto Restoration Tips & Techniques
Basic Bodywork Tips & Techniques
Basic Painting Tips & Techniques
Camaro Restoration Tips & Techniques
Custom Painting Tips & Techniques
Engine Swapping Tips & Techniques
How to Build a Street Rod
Mustang Restoration Tips & Techniques
Performance Tuning - Chevrolets of the '60s
Performance Tuning - Ford of the '60s
Performance Tuning - Mopars of the '60s
Performance Tuning - Pontiacs of the '60s

BROOKLANDS BOOKS

CONTENTS

BROOKLANDS BOOKS

ACKNOWLEDGEMENTS

Brooklands Books publish source books. There is nothing original within their covers and their purpose is to make available to today's owners the road tests and other technical stories that were printed about a marque when it was in production.

Amongst our 350 titles are a number of others on Chevrolet. They include four separate books on Camaro, three on Corvette and individual titles on Chevelle, Corvair, Impala, Chevy II and Nova and the most recent which deals with Chevys stylish El Camino pickup.

We are guided in our choice of subjects by popular demand and have recently produced a number of 4x4 titles. They include three on Land Rover, two on CJ Jeeps and one of our larger Gold Portfolios on Range Rover. In the pipeline are two Ford Bronco titles which report on the first 22 years production of these popular vehicles.

Our books are printed in small numbers as works of reference for those that indulge in the automotive hobby. We exist firstly because there is a need by owners for this information and secondly because the publishers of the world's leading motoring journals generously assist by allowing us to include their copyright road tests and other stories. We are indebted in this instance to the management of Autocar, Car and Driver, 4WD, HR 4-Wheel & Off Road ,Mechanix Illustrated, Motor Trend, Off Road Australia, Off Road Fun Cars, Overlander, Petersen Publications, PV4, and Speed Age for their ongoing support.

R.M. Clarke

BY ED ORR

Cross-country desert testing
shows that Chevrolet has an off-road
winner in its

4WD BLAZER

Chevrolet's long-awaited four-wheel drive Blazer proves to be an exceptionally good off-road vehicle. Though longer and wider than competitive bob-tailed rigs, it's quite nimble in back country use and, with power steering and an automatic transmission, very easy to drive. The basic Blazer structure and sheet metal are taken from the full-size Chevrolet pickup and bring a new standard of style to the four-wheel drive field. The fiberglass wagon-style roof shown here is an option and can be removed. Desert testing showed that the roof is tight fitting and rattle-free.

There are three basic types of commercially produced off-road vehicles. The average off-roader rarely sees the first for they are the pure boondock machines that never run on pavement and most of them couldn't if they tried. These include the experimental military machines such as the Lockheed "Terra Star" and the "Archemides" screw-propelled troop carrier.

Of more concern to those interested in getting as far away from it all as possible are the second and third group. These are similar in that they are both dual-purpose cars. The difference lies in the emphasis. There are off-road/*on-road* cars and *off-road*/on-road rigs. Ford's Bronco is an example of the first category. It is essentially a highway car that can be made to perform fairly well in the dirt. An example of the second type is the subject of this month's Speed Age scrutiny—the new Chevrolet Blazer.

Here is a machine that performs creditably on the freeway, but its shine really comes through when the dust begins to fly. And it should. It has been long enough getting here.

Ever since FoMoCo pranced into the off-road scene, the year's hottest rumur was that Chevy was not far behind. As the months rolled by it would become obvious that this would not be the year so the rumor was updated 12 months and recirculated with fresh vigor.

When the announcement finally came, it caught most of the off-road fraternity a bit off guard like the villagers who had heard the little boy cry "Wolf!" too often.

The first impression one receives is, "Look at the size of that Mutha!" Climbing into the driver's seat evokes the same kind of thrill you got from sitting behind the wheel of the local fire engine on a grammar school field trip. The altitude seems similar, but it is just an illusion as the Blazer is no taller than most four-wheel drives.

But the rig is big. There is room enough in front for three people and a small hound dog. It is from two to six inches wider than the other four-wheel drives and all of it is used for people. This could prove to be a real boon on long trips when passengers, whose tempers are already rubbing on each other, hardly need to add elbows to the list.

Size is not without sacrifice and in some respects the Blazer's bulk would seem a handicap. In bright red trunks the Blazer's curb weight is listed as 3875 pounds which is exceeded only by the long wheelbase Toyota at 4075. And it is nearly 700 pounds heavier than the Bronco. Front and rear overhang, too, seem long at 33.3 inches and 40.2 inches respectively. This limits the departure angle to 25 degrees and the approach angle to 35.2 degrees, which is steeper than it sounds. If there is steep highway hill near where you live, the kind that say "Trucks use low gear," chances are the angle is no greater than eight degrees. And I can guarantee you the first time you look over the edge of a 60-degree sand shear you'll swear it is vertical.

Power plants for the Blazer include the 250 cubic-inch six or the 307 or 350 inch V-8's. Our test car was equipped with the 307 mill and with four adults aboard we never wanted for power. There were other goodies too. It was equipped with optional automatic trans and power steering.

Road testing or, more accurately, off-road testing a machine like this would seem to be all but impossible in freeway-planted Los Angeles, and it is, so we didn't even try. We headed for desert country, instead.

On the long drive to escape the far-reaching city we had a chance to evaluate the Blazer's highway performance and all the drivers had the same complaint.

Starting into a mild turn, the Blazer heeled over at an alarming rate. Notice I said rate, not distance. The body leans through the first few degrees of arc with no more resistance than a hippy girl at a love-in. Abruptly the lean stops, the car stabilizes and from there on it feels so rock solid you get the distinct impression it would spin out before rolling over. We suspect that some firmer shocks would help as would wider tires. The stock rubber on the Blazer is so narrow it would look more at home on a '49 Studebaker.

Once in the rough, the Blazer really comes into its own. For a beastie that big, the ride is remarkably good, much better than its competition, and that power steering makes negotiating tight turns as easy as dialing a telephone. The brakes are another surprise.

You'd think that with all that weight and the skinny skins, the car would slide clear into the next county trying to stop. But not so. Standing hard on the pedal brings the Blazer up so short you feel like getting out to see what you hit.

It takes a few miles getting used to the extra width and in the process of learning we donated the radio antenna to a passing bush. A spring loaded antenna mount, such as the CB operators use, might help. But it would be picking nits to complain as that was the only failure in the entire trip.

Another piece of optional equipment on the test car was the fiberglass top. Word is that perfecting the manufacturing technique for this top gave Chevrolet its biggest headache of the project. But they hung in there and the top's fit and workmanship cannot be faulted. On the personal side it did a great job of keeping the desert sun from scorching our skulls.

Of course, in a few miles the spare tire mount began to rattle but they *all* do that and this should hardly be taken to mean the Blazer isn't sturdy. Witness their performance in the recent Baja 500 where, in their first competition appearance, they took sixth and seventh in class.

With the optional bench seat in the rear, there is still plenty of room for sleeping bags, camp stove and tent stakes. There should be. It is only two inches shy of six feet from the top back of the driver's seat to the tailgate. This makes the car a natural for families as well as hunter-fisher types who want a rig that can really carry the load.

While highway handling may not be as stable as that of a conventional truck, rough surface maneuverability (above) is remarkably good. With the 307 inch Chevy V-8 engine, the Blazer has plenty of power to leap tall obstacles at a single bound (right). Exhaust system dangles precariously below the vehicle (below) but never struck the ground during 150 miles of rugged desert travel. Test was conducted by a party of four, all of whom had plenty of room to stretch within the Blazer's roomy passenger compartment.

Chevy Heads for the Hills

Ol' Number One is now involved, so
there must be something to this
four-wheel-drive, off-the-road epidemic

by Julian G. Schmid

Chevrolet's Blazer is an open top with optional hardtop. Most revolutionary feature is four-wheel-drive (opposite, right center) with two-speed plus four-speed gearbox and power takeoff. (Below left) Power steering is not necessary but is desirable for both maneuverability and ease. (Right) suspension and chassis may be a bit outmoded by current suspension standards, but you're assured of having more durability with tough leaf springs and wide tires.

Step aside, folks, just outside the mainstream of time, and watch how it all happens. Round and round, a familiar phenomenon... Man passes by covered with hair, gradually loses it along with the elongation of his limbs, and just about the time it's all gone, a bit of primordial fuzz grows slightly visible and he's right back where he started.

There's such a thing as being too basic, too refined. And if nature doesn't have it, he pads and automates until comfort is his. But when his Frankenstein rises — larger than himself — he beats it back to submission in the arena of his origin.

It keeps him honest, creating his own challenge, while it keeps him safe, meeting it with his own creation rather than himself.

So Man still climbs mountains on weekends, and fords streams and cuts through underbrush, but now he does it cushioned comfortably within a new form of transportation module known commonly as the "four-wheel-drive, off-the-road vehicle."

Interestingly, this thing has been around since the Jeep, but then the pendulum was in the opposite swing and

sensual pleásure wasn't fashionable... until someone eventually noticed that sensual pleasure was becoming extinct.

So Jeep had a boom, Ford's Bronco had a boom, International Harvester, Rover and Toyota had booms, and now the swing shall be complete: Chevrolet's new K-5 Blazer will have a boom.

Success off the road is an admirable achievement for Detroit designers, because the thinking required is diametrically opposed to customary concepts. Where plastics and styling changes are primary in passenger cars, off-the-road vehicles must be virtually invulnerable. And where multiple model choices are offered in cars, simplicity is the foremost virtue off the road.

Likewise, the Blazer. Order one and you get a four-wheel-drive open utility base — single unit body integrated with a pickup box — and one seat for the driver. No doubletalk superselling, no hidden extras. Just meat. Sure, you can tailor it considerably after that, but you can't double the price of the Blazer with extras like a passenger car. Most important is its basic, adequate utility. There's a front driver's seat and a heater. Period. Stop. Even the dash is simple — speedometer and fuel gauges, with the rest of the information handled by idiot lights.

All of which has a purpose. Strength. Box and side panels are welded to door pillar structures, and the pickup box steel floor to the cab floor.

The hardtop roof option, probably necessary in most of the Blazer's natural habitat, is a one-piece item made entirely of reinforced glass fiber so that it weighs only 151 pounds. The back of the top is fitted with a lockable lift gate, but the rest is secure — side windows are not movable and doors seal tightly to the top. The top is available in only two colors — white or black textured paint.

If you're irreconcilably committed to copping out, you can add the usual "stuff" to the interior: passenger seat and buckets, three-passenger rear seat, armrests, vinyl bucket seats, console between the two front seats, and color-keyed carpeting is included when you order the hardtop.

While all else is identical, Chevy has felt the need — from habit if no other reason — to designate two different model numbers based solely on two dif-

ferent engines. The KS10 has, as a base powerplant, a 250 cubic inch six rated at 155 gross hp at 4200 rpm (120 net hp at 3800) and 235 lbs.-ft. gross torque at 1600 rpm (210 net torque at 2000 rpm). The 307 cubic inch V-8 model — KE10 — delivers 200 gross hp at 4600 rpm (150 net at 4000) and 300 gross torque at 2400 (255 at 2000). Both of these are with the base transmission of an all-synchro three-speed connected to a two-speed Dana transfer case and a standard axle ratio of 3.73:1.

Optional power teams include two engines — a 350 cubic inch, 255-hp V-8 (195 hp net at 4000 rpm, 305 net torque at 2400 rpm), with either a four-speed manual gearbox or Turbo Hydra-Matic, optional 3.07 rear axle ratio, and Positraction.

Distinctly aware that perhaps their largest market will be in the West, Chevy has made air conditioning available to ease the occupants' transition from metropolis to mountains. Of course, with the work required for the Blazer under its normal conditions of usage, the air conditioning unit will probably be best handled by the V-8 engine.

If you're concerned with comfort, you won't be off the road in the first place, so Chevrolet has sacrificed a soft ride for basic strength in the Blazer by installing leaf springs both front and rear. Each of the front springs has a rating of 1450 pounds, and the rear springs, 1800 pounds each. Tires are 7.35x15. This suspension may be a throwback to the Conestoga-like durability of old, but it possesses some qualities on which the Blazer's competitors compromised at the beginning, and for which they suffered miserably. The Blazer will not suffer the same humiliation. Proof of this is the Blazer's ability to carry more than 1200 pounds over its 3844-pound curb weight.

Power brakes and steering are both available, and the steering is, in fact, desirable in order to increase maneuverability over the 24:1 ratio of the manual unit. Turning diameter is 36.66 feet curb-to-curb, and 38.78 feet wall-to-wall.

With its 104-inch wheelbase, the Blazer is quite agile, and stability is excellent with a track of 64 inches front and 61 inches rear. Total length is only 177.5 inches, and ground clearance is eight inches. **/MT**

FOUR-WHEELERS

CHEVY BLAZER

Chevrolet's 4-wheel-drive vehicle, the Blazer, is the newest in the field. There is little that is in any way revolutionary about it, but it does possess one very definite advantage over the other 4-wheelers in its class. It is built more to pickup truck dimensions, and this gives it both a wider track and a longer box length behind the rear seats. It is the only one of the Jeep-types that can take a full-length mattress with everything buttoned up. The Blazer has 78¼ inches of box length at floor level as against 43 in the British Land-Rover, 54 in the CJ6 Jeep, 55¼ in the Ford Bronco, and 60 in the International Scout. This could be a critical factor for the 4-wheel-drive buyer who wants to equip his vehicle for all-around use. In most other areas of consideration —power, cost, looks—there is not a great deal of difference between the American big four: Blazer, Bronco, Scout and Jeep.

The Chevy Blazer was introduced last year, and has only superficial changes for 1970. This is an accepted practice both here and abroad. The "truck lines" do not follow the model-year practice used for passenger vehicles, and major changes occur only when there is a good reason for them. As with the other American 4-wheel-drive vehicles, the base price can be a little deceiving, too. If you buy a Blazer, you have a very spartan piece of machinery for your $3000 or so. It has a driver's seat . . . period. Passenger seats are extra-cost options. A few of the other options you may want to add are the fiberglass hardtop, bucket seats, passenger arm rest, air conditioning, power steering, power brakes, radio, heavy-duty springs and shock absorbers, free-wheeling hubs, auxiliary battery and front towing hooks. All of these add up.

The less-expensive standard engine for the Blazer is Chevy's old and reliable 250-cubic-inch straight-6, with 155 hp. For economical and non-sporty use, this regular-grade gasoline engine is more than adequate. The standard V-8, for about $95 more, is the 307-cubic-inch, 200-hp V-8, still on regular gas. For only about $40 more than this, you can have the big quad-throat 350-cubic-inch V-8 with 255 hp, but there goes your gas mileage and your economy. If you do a lot of high-speed highway driving on your way to the boonies, either of the V-8's would be a better choice than the straight-6.

The standard transmission in the base Blazer is a 3-speed fully synchronized manual. Options include a 4-speed for $95 and a 4-speed Turbo Hydra-Matic for $226. Many drivers still enjoy doing their own shifting, and prefer the manual box. There is an increasing swing to the automatic, though, as it saves a great deal of work, particularly in slow, heavily-loaded situations. The transfer case, which allows the front wheels to be powered, is a Dana #20 2-speed (high and low 4-wheel drive, with high 2-wheel drive when not in use) with a slightly different ratio for the automatic transmission.

Suspension on the Blazer 4-wheel-drive models is by leaf springs front and rear. The new 2-wheel-drive version uses coil springs. For really rough going, or for competition, heavy-duty shock absorbers and front leaf springs are available, and are recommended.

The standard clutch on the inline-6 Blazer is 10-inch, with 100 square inches of surface; standard on the 307-cubic-inch V-8 is an 11-inch, with 124 square inches. Optional for these engines, and standard with the 350-cubic-inch optional engine, is a 12-inch, 150-square-inch clutch. It's recommended with any of the engines for any kind of sporty driving.

Standard wheels are 5½-inch rims, with E78x15-B tires. Optional rims go to 6 inches, and in 15- and 16½-inch diameter. These larger wheels allow factory optional tires in 8.75- and 10-inch widths, which are certainly the minimum anyone would want for serious off-road driving. The 10-inchers will cost about $480 the set of five, so it would be well to check the independent wheel and tire suppliers to make certain you end up with the best setup for your particular needs. It may save you quite a bit of money to buy your Blazer with standard wheels and tires, saving these for towing and for around town, then investing in four really good off-road super-wienies for the rugged trips.

For family or winter use, Chevy's fiberglass top is almost a necessity. It can be bought outright for under $270, and this includes the windows, upper lift gate on the rear, and front doors with rollup windows and quarter vents. For $358 you can have the top, with or without extra rear seats, plus the whole "Custom Sport Truck" package. This includes various items of body and interior trim, color-keyed carpeting, interior vinyl door and body padding, bucket seats, console, and chrome trim for just about everything on the beggar. If you intend to use your Blazer for all-around use, and more on the street than for off-road, this CST package is a good investment. The power brakes at $44 and power steering at $132 are of questionable value if you are going to drive the Blazer strictly as a fun car. They are definitely worth considering if you are going into rugged country with the box heavily loaded with camping gear or with a camper unit.

Our evaluation, then, of the 1970 Chevrolet Blazer is that it is certainly as good as, but no better than, the Bronco, Scout or Jeepster in its overall specifications and performance. The added length in the rear certainly is a very strong plus in the Blazer's favor for anyone who wants to be able to live inside, in any kind of weather. The 104-inch wheelbase is roughly the same as that of the Scout, the Jeepster and the Toyota Land Cruiser Wagon, and a foot or so longer than that of the Bronco, Land-Rover and standard Land Cruisers. In other words, it should be able to go anywhere the first group can, but might get hung up in some places that wouldn't stop the shorter wheelbased members of the group.

The fully equipped Blazers we have tested, at around $4500 total cost, have been neat and easy to drive on the pavement, and a ball to drive off-road. If you're a Chevy fan, by all means try a Blazer.

SPECIFICATIONS	
Wheelbase	104.0
Overall length	177.5
Width	79.0
Height	68.5
Front tread	64.0
Rear tread	62.5
Ground clearance	7.33
Box length—floor	78.25
Box length—top	70.0
Box width—floor	72.0
Box width—tailgate	65.0
Box depth	19.25
Max. gross vehicle wt.	5000

3

4

1. GMC-built version of Blazer is called the "Jimmy," utilizes same engines, options as Blazer, but base price is slightly higher.

2. Blazer with top, a factory option, makes a handy ready-to-roll camper.

3. Pickup with rear seat installed is one of the handiest multi-purpose vehicles available.

4. Blazer chassis complete. Engine is 350-cu.-in. V-8 with 4-barrel carb. Leaf springs are used front and rear, with progressive-load type in rear. Before you turn the page, look at that frame. There is nothing about the Blazer that appears puny or underdesigned.

MI Tests the Chevy Blazer

By Tom McCahill

CHEVY BLAZER rides on 104-in. wheelbase. Rig has truck chassis and heavy-gauge ladder-type frame plus wide track for stability.

BLAZER ride, great and flat on highway, becomes a rugged experience off the road.

A S Squirrel-Head O'Finnegan once pointed out, "Keepin' up with the Kellys can be a loathsome, tiresome and lousy job." The Blazer, Chevrolet's answer to Tarzan, the PTA of East Little Rock and the Bronco, is such a vehicle.

While I can't be positive, I feel certain that when Henry's Bronco started to appear in casual numbers the boys at Chevy decided a "me too" course should be seriously considered. As a general purpose smasheroo for over hill and dale the tough Blazer isn't the best through-out rig by a moonshot or two, though it has some real goodies to recommend it. It seems certain, however, that the overall concept wasn't bolted together by a guy who was a real off-the-road enthusiast. Before I dull my little hatchet a few for instances are overdue. Here they are.

When we tested the 4x4 Chevy half-ton pickup truck on a wild boar hunt back in '64, we reported that it was an ideal rig for a farmer who happened to be a pole vaulter if he wanted to get into the front seat. We suggested that the truck should have a step for getting aboard as that front seat was way off the ground. Well, the Blazer needs a step, too, especially where the opposite sex is con-

cerned. Another spot Chev goofed up, in my opinion, was in sticking the 350-cu.-in. V8 in our test rig. The engine is great but Chevy should have shaved the compression ratio so that the Blazer could run comfortably on the lowest type of low-octane fuel. The book in our Blazer said to use only high-test gasoline. Now anybody who has strayed more than a few dozen miles from Times Square could tell you that in the hinterlands genuine high-test gas can be rare stuff. And if you do any border crossing, like into Mexico, the best fuel available is at times called kerosene. A vehicle of this type should be able to run on nearly anything, including lamp oil.

The interior of our test job was cluttered up with a spare tire of such tremendous size (10x16.5) that it obstructed the rear-view mirror, plus two skimpy non-tilt bucket seats (a bench seat would make a lot more sense), and a badly-placed rear seat that can't be folded. There is amazingly little space in this job after two hunters climb aboard with two dogs.

The Blazer could have been a great job but I don't feel the fellow who drew up the plans really had his heart in the project.

(Note to John De Lorean, Chevy's headman: Dear John, the next time you go on one of these wild tangents, how about contacting somebody who knows the field you are just entering. For a box of cookies and a framed picture of Rutherford B. Hayes we'd have been only too glad to check you out.)

Back to the test. A fire-engine-red Blazer ended up on my doorstep just as the hunting season in Florida opened. We drove it many miles across swamps matic transmission, was a nose tweak over 90.

The ground clearance of the Blazer was 8 in. and our tires were the deep-cleated, lug-type, not the greatest for high-speed running. The legroom in front was ample for anyone under 6'5" and the miserable rear seat also had plenty of legroom. The Blazer sported vent windows and visibility, except through the rear-view mirror, was excellent. The upholstery was vinyl and the steering was quick. The turning radius was the best I have found in any four-wheel-drive jungle buster. The ease of getting in and out was similar to climbing into an orange tree. Though air conditioning is an available option our test car didn't have it.

In summing up, this is almost a great rig. The wheelbase is about 5 in. too short and the same could be said of the overall length. The curb weight of 3,844 lbs. is good and so is the glove compartment.

In summing up the summing up, when you jump into someone else's field, John, old boy, make sure you have all the bases covered. The original, and you know who I mean, should have been the one to copy, not Lee Iacocca's little backbreaker. Amen. •

trieve when Tom-Tom, resembling a rocket out of Cape Kennedy, threw a block on Jimbo which sent him sprawling. To make matters even more insulting, he stepped on the pointer's head without missing a stride to make the retrieve. Tom-Tom got all four birds and the pointers didn't want any part of this mad, black demon so after that we had to lock him in the Blazer every time the bird dogs got on point.

When we returned home we had racked up just under 300 mi. of travel plus three hours of hard hunting and were thoroughly sold that the Blazer, with its truck chassis and heavy-gauge ladder-type frame plus its wide track for stability, was quite a torpedo. Incidentally, the front tread is 64 in. wide, which tops most passenger cars; there is 61 in. between the wheels at the rear.

We made our performance runs after the quail hunt at the Daytona Speedway. At first the performance seemed surprising but not after considering that the power plant was the optional 350-cu.-in. V-8 mill, sporting 355 ft. lbs. of torque and 255 hp. Zero to 30 averaged 4.4 seconds, 0 to 50 took 8.3 and 0 to 60 was 12 seconds flat. Top speed, due to the fact that we were twirling a 3.73 drag-type rear with auto-

HUGE spare tire's placement obstructed the rear-view mirror scene, reports McCahill.

didn't think I'd ever be able to make. One day during these tests Brooks Brender, Tom-Tom (my Lab) and I headed for Florida's West Coast 100 and some miles away. At the Riverside Villas Hunting Preserve at Homosassa my old friend B.J. Dixon—posing with me in the lead photo of this article—a great bird dog trainer, was waiting for us. B.J. had several young pointers he wanted me to see in action, which was no thrill at all to Tom-Tom. As we've written before on these pages, this is just about the best quail-shooting spot in the south and in following the dogs in the Blazer we drove over logs, thick stands of palmetto, through swamp holes and some fairly deep water. The Blazer took this tough terrain with the ease of a Sherman tank going over a field of cabbage. In less than three hours we had over 20 quail and B.J.'s new dog, Jimbo, not only proved he had a great nose but was steady as a rock. Tom-Tom was extremely unhappy about the whole performance, so once when Brooks and I had four birds down I gave him the signal to go—which almost proved disastrous. B.J.'s dogs all retrieve, too, and Jimbo was loping over to make a re-

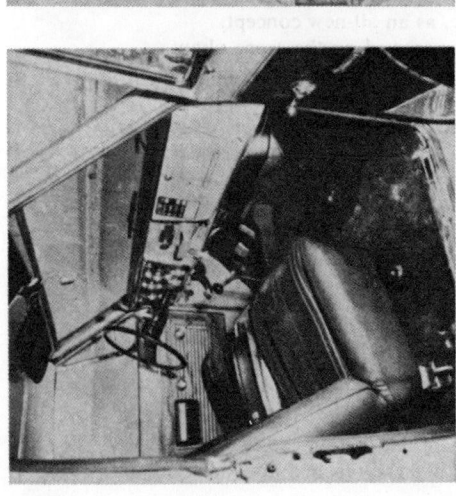
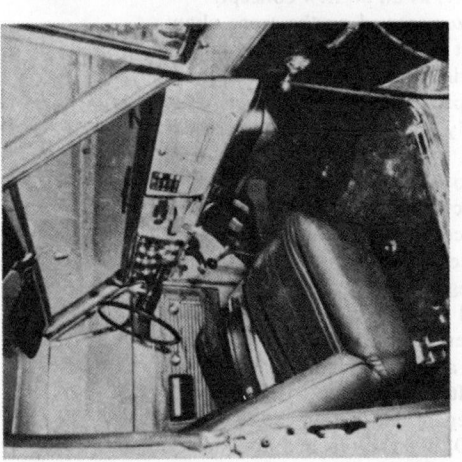

UP FRONT Blazer has two non-tilt buckets. McCahill would have preferred bench seat.

TEST CAR SPECS

Model Tested: Chevrolet Blazer	**Ground Clearance:** 8 in.
Engine: V8	**Front Tread:** 64 in.
Displacement: 350 cubic in.	**Rear Tread:** 61 in.
Brake hp: 255	**Curb Weight:** 3,844 lb.
Torque: 355 ft-lbs.	**Gas Tank Capacity:** 23.5 gallons
Compression: 9.0:1	**Turning Circle Diameter:** 36.66 ft.
Bore: 4 in.	**Tire Size:** 10x16.5
Stroke: 3.48 in.	**Base Price:** $2,947
Axle Ratio: 3.07	**As Tested:** $4,782.30
Wheelbase: 104 in.	**0 to 30 mph:** 4.4 sec.
Length: 177.5 in.	**0 to 50 mph:** 8.3 sec.
Height: 74 in.	**0 to 60 mph:** 12 sec.
Width: 79 in.	**Top Speed:** 90+ mph

All times recorded on corrected speedometer.

and rugged fields in pursuit of little birds. Before the first day was half over one thing became apparent. The ride, which is great and flat on interstate highways, quickly becomes as rugged as a prison matron's face when off the road. After a few miles your backbone will feel like a strand of spaghetti that has done time in a Waring blender and your tailbone will have aches in spots you never knew you had. If anything, the Blazer is over-suspended, a statement I

CHEVROLET BLAZER 350

FINALLY SOMEONE HAS DISCARDED THE IDEA
THAT FOUR-WHEEL-DRIVE VEHICLES CAN ONLY BE OPERATED
BY EX-TANK COMMANDERS AND VETERAN TRUCK DRIVERS

Think of it as a beginning. Nobody really understands the dimension of the recreational vehicle market, and Chevrolet has to be forgiven for not working harder with the Blazer. After all, no one else inside the industry has done much to exploit this area of enthusiasm—which may very well overwhelm all other forms of vehicular fancy—and therefore Chevrolet can share no more of the guilt than Ford and Chrysler, which have sold their Broncos and Dodge camper vans, etc., rather diffidently. American Motors has a chance to steal a march on the others with its recent acquisition of Willys, but with its lackluster record for trail-blazing, one can only hope the AMC will seize the initiative.

Everybody in Detroit is starting at ground zero with recreational vehicles. They look at their sales figures and see vitality with their pickup trucks and small vans; they can see a rising popularity in 4-wheel-drive vehicles, they are aware of the booming dune buggy scene, and they know millions of Americans are hung up on camping, skiing, boating and a multitude of outdoor sports that are abetted by solid utility vehicles that are half-car, half-truck. Some also see that the coming slump in the Super Car market may shunt a sizeable number of car nuts into the recreational vehicle field, boosted along by such free-form competitions as the Baja 1000 and the Mint 400. All of these trends bode well for this concept, but none of the major manufactur-

ers have really screwed up their courage enough to plunge in with a specially-designed machine. Their jeep-types, pickups and vans notwithstanding, nobody this side of Bruce Meyers and his beautifully zany Manxes have really assaulted this brand of vehicle with any sort of serious design intent. The market is presently clogged with compromises—spinoffs of pure utility machines like pickup trucks with vinyl upholstery or delivery vans with V-8 engines or jeep types with automatic transmissions that signify an awareness on the part of their builders but something less than a commitment to anything as radical, or expensive, as an all-new concept.

The Chevrolet Blazer arrived on the scene about one year ago in what seemed like the first undercover sales campaign in history. With a preliminary sales estimate of approximately 15,000 per year, the Blazer was hardly intended as a replacement for the Impala, but a mixture of circumstances caused the vehicle to be introduced in an atmosphere of semi-secrecy. By the time the modest press previews were completed, a few perfunctory press releases had been ground out and a limited schedule of advertising had been run, the new Blazer was about as well known among the American public as the Chrysler Airflow. To make matters worse, the St. Louis assembly plant in which the Blazer was being built plunged into a strike shortly after production began, and within the first four months less than 400 Blazers reached the dealer

THE PRESENT
4WD MARKET
IS CLOGGED WITH
COMPROMISES—
VEHICLES THAT
REPRESENT AN
AWARENESS ON
THE PART OF
THE MAKER, BUT
NOT A COMMITMENT

showrooms. This miniscule output caused even greater apathy on the part of the sales staff, and by the time production returned to normal, the vehicle had dropped near the bottom of Chevrolet's advertising and promotion priorities. In the first year, 5000 Blazers were sold, with another 10-15,000 expected to reach the public in the 1970 model year—hardly overwhelming numbers when thinking within the Detroit sales syndrome.

Like a vast majority of its competition, the Blazer is engineering compromise. It has been whacked together from existing components designed for Chevrolet's line of light trucks, and so it can hardly be described as a daring new concept in recreational vehicles. It is larger than the Bronco, Jeep, Scout genre, although its available cargo space is anything but impressive. On the other hand, the drivetrain pieces are well-designed, rugged and long-proved by use in Chevy's light trucks. So what one might give up in the way of new concepts, he might gain in the way of durability.

The Blazer is one tall machine. That is the central visual message that confronts any first-time witness, and it is directly traceable to the vehicle's truck heritage. Creating a low profile in a 4-wheel-drive vehicle is difficult, simply because the conventional solid axle suspension forces the engineers to mount the engine above the axle, rather than between wheels, as can be done with an independent setup. Given little choice about using solid axles fore and aft, doubtlessly because of cost considerations, the Chevy engineering department apparently decided to make a complete commitment to quaintness and fitted the Blazer with longitudinal leaf springs on all four corners. This gives the machine a suspension system first employed some-

time during the Spanish Inquisition. Despite its primitive layout, the Blazer is not as erratic a handler as one might expect. Its straight-line performance is quite satisfactory, and one can maintain 70-80 mph turnpike speeds with ease after certain compensations are made for a slight yawing motion and its spooky behavior in brisk sidewinds. One simply does not consider thundering around corners in a vehicle that is over six feet tall with a track slightly in excess of five feet, no matter if the suspension was designed by Eric Broadley. The Blazer is not a sports car, and never will be as long as it stands as tall as it does, but that does not mean its height is all to the bad. Its jacked-up suspension gives it a minimum ground clearance of seven inches (at the rear differential housing), which is satisfactory for off-road or snow work. What's more, a tall driver has an eye-level sight line almost five-and-a-half feet above the ground, which is beautiful for thundering through tall weeds or drifting snow. We initially tested our Blazer in some of the foulest winter weather to hit the Northeast since the Big Blizzard of '88 and found that driver height is a tremendous advantage when probing through wind-blown snow that cuts visibility to zero at ground level.

And the Blazer will pull. So far your Friendly C/D Snow Extraction service has removed 14 cars from various states of immobility, including three 4-wheel-drive Jeep snowplows (much to their owners' chagrin). Our test machine is equipped with four, studded Goodyear Polyglas 78-series snow tires that produce tremendous traction in heavy snow or glare-ice, and, with their ability to claw through the tough spots, the Blazer becomes a really neat winter machine.

The entire problem of traction is helped by the Blazer's driveline setup, which includes a 3-speed Turbo-Hydramatic transmission driving through a transfer case that feeds power fore-and-aft. This automatic is extremely smooth and easy-shifting, which means that sensitive applications of power can be made without slipping the clutch, as would have to be done with standard 4wd vehicles. Added to this advantage is the 4wd activation mechanism. While the automatic shift lever is mounted conventionally on the steering column, a stubby lever to operate the 4wd stands next to the driver's right knee in the customary position for a floor-mounted manual shifter. The Blazer can be driven in normal 2-wheel range without touching the floor lever. However, if a stretch of slippery pavement, mud or sand is encountered where extra traction is needed, one merely yanks back on the lever and pops everything into 4wd. (This is presuming the front hub lock-outs, which disengage the front differential when running for long periods in normal drive, have been locked in position.) A very neat setup indeed, because many 4wd vehicles require slowdown or complete stop before a change from 2wd to 4wd can be completed. However, 4wd is often needed in short bursts, especially in ice and snow, and the Blazer is particularly well-suited to this sort of application. In addition to the normal 4wd range, a low range is also provided, which does require a full stop and a careful selection of gears with the big floor shifter. This range is needed only for pulling freight trains or toppling buildings and therefore has limited applications for the normal Blazer driver.

Our Blazer is equipped with Chevrolet's 4-barrel, 300-hp, 350 cubic inch V-8, which gives plenty of torque and adequate performance in combination with the automatic transmission. One might think an engine of this size would turn the Blazer into a genuine fire-breather until it is recalled that the vehicle weighs in excess of 4000 pounds, and when the engine is called upon to operate accessories like power steering, power brakes and air conditioning, as it is on our deluxe "CST" model (an interior trim package designation meaning "Custom Sport Truck"), 300 horsepower is hardly superfluous. Adequate seems a proper description for the performance (0-60 in 11-12 secs) and this is reasonable, because any greater acceleration capacity, coupled with the Blazer's suspension and brakes (drums) could get someone in trouble on the highway and be of little value in heavy going.

The CST trim package elicits mixed reactions. Its complete instrumentation, including a tachometer, console with a giant storage bin and comfortable, vinyl bucket seats, are definitely noteworthy. However, fillips like exterior chrome trim panels (that tend to get scraped off) and floor carpeting (that refuses to stay clean with hard usage) are dubious benefits in a presumably functional machine. Another questionable asset is the rear seating arrangement, which has a large bench seat plunked practically in the middle of the six-foot-long storage area. This seat can be removed, although a wrench is required to accomplish the job. With the seat in place, the rear-end station wagon-type door opens up to a space only 30 inches deep. This is less than overwhelming storage capacity for a vehicle of this size. A few more bolts remove the fiberglass top which does nothing to increase the cargo capacity, unless one plans on carrying a giraffe. This is a mildly interesting feature in that the machine can be given a Jeep-like top-down configuration, but getting there is hardly half the fun. The top is heavy and bulky and no less than a pair of full grown men could handle the job of removing or installing the unit. What's more, the top did not fit particularly well on our test Blazer and was given to leaking in heavy rainstorms. However, any breezes that might enter during cold weather (and the machine has operated efficiently in below zero temperatures on several occasions) are overwhelmed by a hefty heater that operates in conjunction with the air-conditioning unit. There are certain no-nonsense parts about the Blazer that are most appealing and certainly one of them is the environmental controls that make the interior liveable in the most extreme weather conditions. In so many cases, recreational vehicles have rather sparse heating-cooling systems that flag in the face of day-long, 100° desert environs or windblown, sub-zero mountaintops, but the Blazer is adequately equipped in this department.

Despite the attempts to tame it, the Blazer remains more truck than car, with things like the bulky, oversize steering wheel and difficult entry (especially for children, women in minis or the elderly) standing out in stark relief to the fripperies. Being more truck than car wouldn't be so bad in the Blazer's case if it did what a truck is supposed to do—carry a big load. But the Blazer won't carry much more than a normal sedan. If the Blazer is to have a back seat at all, which it should, the thing should fold flat to provide a full six feet of cargo area which, in conjunction with the 5'4" width of the rear compartment, would provide room for more than a spare tire.

CONTINUED ON PAGE 82

CARS ACTING LIKE TRUCKS OR TRUCKS THAT ARE PRETENDING TO BE CARS IS NOT THE ULTIMATE SOLUTION TO A GROWING DEMAND FOR 4WD VEHICLES

PHOTOGRAPHY: HUMPHREY SUTTON

CHEVROLET BLAZER

4 WD TEST

A S THE CHEVROLET Blazer was only introduced in early 1969, it's something of a newcomer among 4wd recreation vehicles, the newest model in the field. It's probably accurate to say that Chevrolet took a good long look at the market before they decided where they should put their efforts and then, when they were sure what they wanted to do, they came in with a vehicle they felt sure was going to be a winner.

And the Blazer is a winner, too. It starts out with a good, rugged package and with a long list of practical options, it is indeed one of those 4wd recreation vehicles that can fit into every class from basic utility to full luxury.

The basic Blazer ($3234 for the 6, $3355 for the 307-cu.in. V-8) comes with an open-top utility body, a 3-speed all-synchro-manual transmission, a driver's seat, one sun visor and, except for the engine, that's about all. If you want the full-length fiberglass top, that comes to an additional $321. And if you opt for the "CST" package, which includes bucket seats, bright trim and a host of other items (see data panel), that'll be another $364. The rear bench seat is an additional $118 and so on. So it is very easy to get the delivered price up over $4000 before even getting into the bigger engines and other options. So if there's one thing the Blazer isn't, it's an economy model.

There are two basic engines; a 250-cu-in., 145-horsepower Six and a 307-cu-in., 200-bhp V-8. You can also order the 350-cu-in., 250-hp V-8 as an option on the 307 V-8 basic model and it comes to only $44 extra.

There are three transmissions for the Blazer. The 3-speed all-synchromesh manual comes standard with the 6 or the 307 V-8 but if you order the 350 V-8, you must then pay extra for either the Chevrolet heavy duty 4-speed manual or the Turbo Hydra-Matic 3-speed automatic transmission.

Chevrolet is the only manufacturer to offer front disc brakes on their recreation vehicles and these, which are power assisted to keep the pedal effort down to a reasonable level, are standard on all Blazers. Power steering is also available on the option list.

There is little choice of final drive ratios with the Blazer. You get a 3.73:1 with the Six or the 307 V-8 and a 3.07:1 with the 350 V-8. The only option is that you can also specify the 3.73:1 ring and pinion with the 350. The familiar (we almost said dreaded) Dana 20 2-speed transfer case with the U-shaped shift pattern is standard with the 3-speed manual transmission and a New Process 205, which has a straight-through gate, comes with the optional gearboxes.

In overall size, the Blazer is just about the bulkiest of the standard 4wd machines. It is wide (79 in.) and it is long (177 in.). This is a full step larger than Ford's Bronco (which is 68.8 and 152.1 in the same dimensions) and while this adds up to a larger interior package, the sides will reach out a lot further when the track is narrow and the rocks and vegetation encroach on the path.

As Chevrolet's Blazer and Ford's Bronco are the products of the two largest automobile manufacturers, perhaps some side-by-side comparisons of the two vehicles would be appropriate. For engines, the Bronco has two, a 100-hp six and a 205-hp V-8, while the Blazer has three, a 145-hp six, a 200-hp V-8 and a 250-hp V-8. In the transmission department, the Bronco has a 3-speed manual, period, while the Blazer has a 3-speed manual, a 4-speed manual and a 3-speed automatic. The Bronco does not offer power steering, the Blazer does. The Bronco has drum brakes, the Blazer has power discs in front. With the Bronco you can get a limited slip differential at both ends while the Blazer offers it only at the rear. Both offer free-running front hubs. The Blazer can be ordered with factory air conditioning, the Bronco cannot. Bucket seats and a bench rear seat are available for both. The Blazer will accept oversize tires without enlarging the rear fender cutouts, the Bronco will not. The Bronco's full-length top is metal, the Blazer's is fiberglass.

In almost every department, then, the Blazer has the larger list of options and consequently may be more likely to appeal to those who seek the ultimate in luxurious 4wd motoring. On the Bronco's side, however, is the fact that it is smaller in bulk and though the slow steering reduces this advantage because of the wheel-twirling required to maneuver it, it is shorter, has a smaller turning circle and it will go through holes that are 10 inches narrower than the Blazer.

Driving Impressions

OUR TEST Blazer was just about as much Blazer as you can buy from the factory. It had the 350-cu-in. V-8, automatic transmission, power steering, air conditioning, radio, deluxe seats and trim, numerous other little goodies such as the extra gauges, plus almost $500 worth of optional 10 x 16.5 6-ply Firestone Duplex tires with appropriately wide-rimmed wheels. The delivered price for our vehicle on the west coast is over $6100. And that's a lot for a 4wd recreation vehicle.

We found little worth complaining about with our Blazer but there are a few things that need mentioning. The 10 x 16.5 Firestone Duplex tires were hard-riding on the highway and sang as loudly as any off-on pavement tires we've ever encountered. They worked great off the pavement, however, we should add. Also, the driver's seat is too close to the steering wheel for our tastes and the ledge that runs behind the seat, kicking up about four inches to the cargo area, would make it difficult to relocate the seat to the rear. With power steering and a tiltable wheel we were able to live with it but another four inches to the rear would make the taller driver happy. Ingress may also be inconvenient for the shorter driver as the seat is over a yard off the ground. We had no complaints about the fiberglass top except that the tailgate window is heavy and you're probably going to have to have to develop muscles like a weightlifter if you use it regularly. As a side remark, we need to point out that the battery has no hold-down bracket and will fall off its shelf on steep upgrades.

It seems almost superfluous to add that the Blazer conquered all four of our test hills without even breathing hard. And it did this in spite of a flat spot in the carburetion that caused the engine to falter on the way up the steeper hills. That 350 V-8 has so much power in reserve that it simply went up anyway.

The 3-speed Turbo Hydra-Matic is excellently suited to the 350 V-8, behaving perfectly in every circumstance. The downshifting is quick and positive and even though there is an absence of engine braking with the automatic, the disc brakes kept everything securely under control on long downgrades where lesser braking systems would have begun losing their effectiveness from fade.

In our on-pavement tests at Orange County International Raceway, the Blazer breezed through our 6-stops-from-60 fade test with no loss of braking efficiency and only a very little change in pedal pressure. These stops were all smooth and straight, a testimonial to how much better Chevrolet has done in the braking department than anyone else in the field.

The transfer case in our test Blazer was the New Process 205. This also worked right and being located in the center of the transmission hump, it is in the right position for convenient operation.

The power steering makes the Blazer easy to drive off the pavement and the steering is quick enough to make up for some of the vehicle's bulk. On narrow trails, however, there are places where there isn't room to drive around those bushes and tree branches and where, ultimately, you're going to wince as a sharp branch scrapes down the side of the vehicle.

On a trip to Anza Borrego Desert State Park near San Diego, we thoroughly enjoyed driving the Blazer over their "jeep trails"

CHEVROLET BLAZER

PRICES

Basic list, FOB Detroit:
6-cyl with utility body $3234
V-8 with utility body 3355

Standard equipment: 4wd, power front disc brakes, painted bumpers, driver seat only, 3-spd manual transmission

"CST" model ($364) includes fiberglass top, bucket seats, console, armrest, RH sun visor, extra insulation, chrome bumpers, undercoating, bright trim, spare tire cover, color keyed carpeting.

Other prices for options are included in data below.

ENGINES

Standard 6-cyl engine . . . . . . ohv inline 6
Bore x stroke, in 3.875x3.50
Displacement, cu in 250
Compression ratio 8.5:1
Bhp @ rpm . . . . 145 @ 4200
Torque @ rpm, lb-ft . . . . . . 230 @ 1600
Type fuel required . . . . regular
Air cleaner type . . . . paper

Standard V-8 engine . . . . ohv V-8
Bore x stroke, in 3.875x3.50
Displacement, cu in 307
Compression ratio 8.5:1
Bhp @ rpm . . . . 200 @ 4600
Torque @ rpm, lb-ft . . . . . . 300 @ 2400
Type fuel required . . . . regular
Air cleaner type . . . . paper

Optional 350 instead of 307 V-8, $44, (also requires optional transmission)
Bore x stroke, in 4.00x3.50
Displacement, cu in 350
Compression ratio 8.5:1
Bhp @ rpm . . . . 250 @ 4600
Torque @ rpm, lb-ft . . . . . . 350 @ 3000
Type fuel required . . . . regular
Air cleaner type . . . . paper
Optional oil bath type $11

CHASSIS & BODY

Body/frame: steel ladder frame with separate steel body

Brakes: 11.9-in. dia disc front, 11 x 2-in. drum rear
Swept area, sq. in. 379
Power brakes . . . . std

Steering type . . . . ball-gear
Steering ratio 24:1
Turning circle, ft 36.6
Power steering $147

Wheel size, std 15x6
Optional wheel sizes: 16x5, 16x8.25
Tire size, std E78-15
Optional tires: G78-15, m&s, $39; 6pr 6.50-16, $69; E78-15 wsw, $26; E78-15, m&s, $11; H78-15 m&s, $60; 6pr 10-16.5, $478; 6pr 10-16.5 m&s, $480.

Front axle capacity, lb 3300
Optional . . . . .none
Front spring rating (at pad), lb 1450
Optional 1750 lb $33

Rear axle capacity 3300
Optional . . . . .none
Rear spring rating, lb (at pad) 1800
Optional 2000 lb $19

Additional suspension options: HD shocks, f/r, $16

ACCOMMODATION

Standard seat . . . . driver only
Optional: passenger seat, $80; bucket for driver & passenger, $188; rear bench, $118.
Headroom, front/rear, in 41.0/36.0
Pedal to seatback, max 37.0
Seat to ground 38.0
Heater & defroster . . . . std
Tinted glass $31
Air conditioning (V-8 only), $411 (includes HD cooling & 42-amp generator)
Load space (with seats in place), cu ft: 10
With rear seat folded/removed 78

INSTRUMENTATION

Instruments: 100-mph speedometer, 99,999.9 odometer, fuel level
Warning lights: generator, oil pressure, water temperature, brake on
Optional: Ammeter, temp & oil pressure, $13.
Above plus tachometer $58

DRIVE TRAIN

Transfer case 2-spd Dana 20 (with 3-spd), New Process 205 (4-spd & automatic)
Transfer case ratio: 2.03 & 1.00:1 (Dana 20); 1.96 & 1.00:1 (NP 205)
Free-running front hubs $77
Limited slip differential (rear) . . . . . $65.

Rear axle type . . . . . semi-floating hypoid
Final drive ratio: 3.73:1 (6 cyl & 307 V-8), 3.07:1 (350 V-8).
Optional final drive ratios: 3.73:1 (with 350 V-8), $13.

Standard transmission . . . . . 3-spd manual
Clutch dia., in . . . 10.0 (6-cyl), 11.0 (V-8)
Transmission ratios: 3rd 1.00:1
2nd 1.68:1
1st 2.85:1
Overdrive . . . . not available

Optional transmission: 3-spd automatic. Turbo Hydra-Matic, $242 (includes HD cooling)
Transmission ratios: 3rd 1.00:1
2nd 1.52:1
1st 2.52:1
Converter stall ratio 2.3:1

Optional transmission: 4-speed manual, $111.
Clutch dia., in: 12.0
Transmission ratios: 4th 1.00:1
3rd 1.44:1
2nd 1.80:1
1st 2.54:1

GENERAL

Curb weight, lb (test model) 4900

Maximum laden weight 5000
With HD suspension 5400

Wheelbase, in 104.0
Track, front/rear 64.0/62.5
Overall length 177.5
Height 68.8
Width 79.0
Overhang, front/rear 33.3/40.3

Approach angle, degrees 40
Departure angle, degrees 28
Ramp breakover angle 21

Ground clearance: front differential, in: 9.0.
At rear differential . . . .-. 9.0
At oil pan 17.0
At transfer case 11.0
At fuel tank 14.5

Fuel tank capacity, U.S. gal 21

MAINTENANCE

Service intervals, normal use:
Oil change, mi 6000
Filter change 6000
Chassis lube 6000
Minor tuneup 6000
Major tuneup 12,000
Warranty, months/miles 12/12,000

OTHER OPTIONS

Auxiliary battery $47
HD Battery $16
Chrome bumpers (included in CST package): $32.
Hub caps (15 in. only) $14
HD cooling (included with A/C or automatic transmission): $24.
42-amp generator (included with A/C): $23.
61-amp generator $32
Door-edge guards $6.35
Towing hooks, front (not available with chrome bumpers): $19
Bright trim (incl in CST pkg) $47
Cargo partition $53
Skid plate, fuel tank $48
Radio & antenna, AM $66
Same, AM/FM $149
Tilt steering wheel $58
Manual throttle $13
Auxiliary top (included in CST package): $321.

PERFORMANCE DATA

Note: All performance data taken with maximum rated payload on board.

Test model: Equipped with 350 V-8, automatic transmission, power steering, free-running front hubs, limited slip, CST pkg, 10x16.5 tires, air conditioning, HD battery, tilt steering wheel, extra gauges. HD shocks, rear seat, radio, camper mirrors. List price, $6126, West Coast.

DRY PAVEMENT

Acceleration, time to speed, sec:
```
0-30 mph . . . . . . . . . . . . . . . . . . . . 5.4
0-45 mph . . . . . . . . . . . . . . . . . . . . 9.0
0-60 mph . . . . . . . . . . . . . . . . . . . . 14.9
0-70 mph . . . . . . . . . . . . . . . . . . . . 21.1
```

Maximum speed in gears:
```
High range, 3rd (3600 rpm) . . . . . . 98.0
2nd (4500) . . . . . . . . . . . . . . . . . . 78.0
1st (4500) . . . . . . . . . . . . . . . . . . 43.0
Low range,.4th (3600 rpm) . . . . . . 48.2
2nd (4500) . . . . . . . . . . . . . . . . . . 37.9
1st (4500) . . . . . . . . . . . . . . . . . . 21.0
```

Cruising speed at 3000 rpm 79

BRAKE TESTS

Pedal pressure to achieve 1/2-g deceleration rate from 60 mph: 50.

Fade: Percentage increase in pedal pressure for 6 successive stops from 60 mph: nil.

Overall brake rating. . . . . . . .very good

OFF PAVEMENT

Hillclimbing ability:
Climb test hill no. 1 (47% grade) . . . . . yes
Climb test hill no. 2 (56% grade) . . . . . yes
Climb test hill no. 3 (63% grade) . . . . . yes
Climb test hill no. 4 (69% grade) . . . . . yes

Maneuverability . . . . .good
Turnaround capability . . . . .good

Comments: width limits maneuverability in tight quarters.

GENERAL

Heater rating . . . . .excellent
Defroster effectiveness . . . . . . .excellent
Wiper coverage . . . . .adequate

FUEL CONSUMPTION

Normal driving, mpg 10-12
Off-pavement, test conditions, mpg . . 5.4
Range, normal driving, mi 250
Range, off-pavement 113

but twice we came to narrow passages where a Jeep, Jeepster, Scout, Toyota or Bronco could have slithered through without endangering the sheet metal but with the Blazer, we simply had to give up and turn around. These were admittedly specialized jeep trails, however, and no doubt tailored to that vehicle's narrow width. In many trips to Baja California, which is generally considered to be about as rough as any country you can find for driving, we've never encountered any passage that a Blazer couldn't squeeze through on any road or track shown on any of the standard maps.

On the highway the Blazer is nothing less than excellent. The ride (our vehicle had standard springs but heavy duty shocks) was very good, the seats comfortable and the handling such that you feel perfectly secure cruising at 75 mph. As a mark of how easy the fully equipped Blazer is to drive, we put a 5 ft 1 in., 110-lb girl in the driver's seat and except that she complained of the steering wheel being too high, she managed it without the least strain or anxiety.

You don't get all this easy performance without paying for it, of course, so it will probably not come as any surprise to know that we averaged only 10-12 mpg in normal on-pavement driving and as little as 5 mpg in the slow, mostly low-range driving during our off-pavement tests. The fuel tank, which holds 21 gal, seems pretty big when you're filling it but the cruising range is not impressive and no auxiliary fuel tank is available.

So that's the Blazer, a big hunk of attractive machinery. We'd sum it up by saying that our test Blazer was effective, efficient—and expensive. 🔽WD

The Great RV Binge

Muscle Cars are out and Recreational Vehicles are in. We test three of the prime movers — the Chevrolet Blazer — Ford Bronco — AMC Jeepster — and find out why

By Chuck Koch

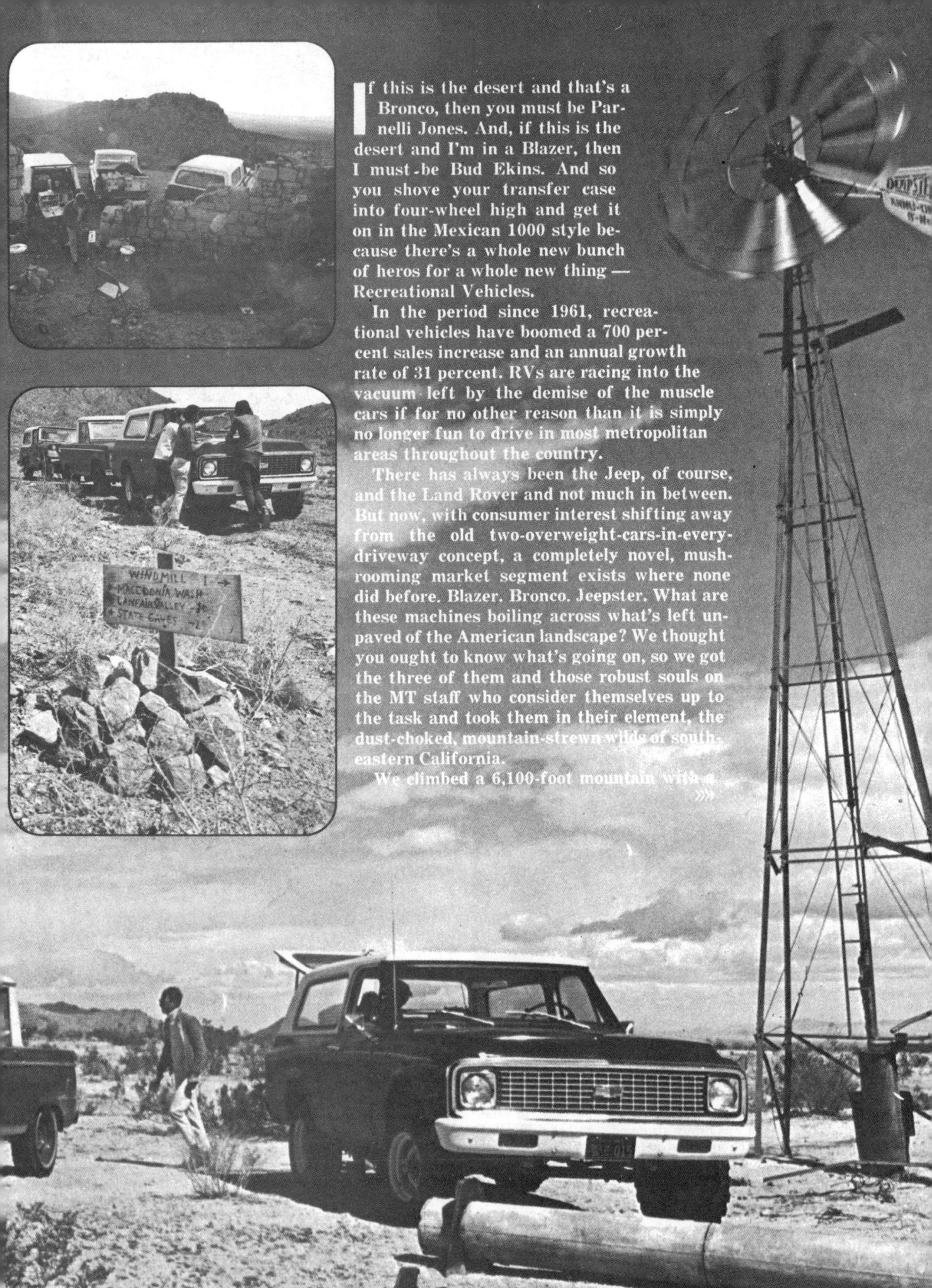

If this is the desert and that's a Bronco, then you must be Parnelli Jones. And, if this is the desert and I'm in a Blazer, then I must be Bud Ekins. And so you shove your transfer case into four-wheel high and get it on in the Mexican 1000 style because there's a whole new bunch of heros for a whole new thing — Recreational Vehicles.

In the period since 1961, recreational vehicles have boomed a 700 percent sales increase and an annual growth rate of 31 percent. RVs are racing into the vacuum left by the demise of the muscle cars if for no other reason than it is simply no longer fun to drive in most metropolitan areas throughout the country.

There has always been the Jeep, of course, and the Land Rover and not much in between. But now, with consumer interest shifting away from the old two-overweight-cars-in-every-driveway concept, a completely novel, mushrooming market segment exists where none did before. Blazer. Bronco. Jeepster. What are these machines boiling across what's left unpaved of the American landscape? We thought you ought to know what's going on, so we got the three of them and those robust souls on the MT staff who consider themselves up to the task and took them in their element, the dust-choked, mountain-strewn wilds of southeastern California.

We climbed a 6,100-foot mountain with a »»»

The Great RV Binge

vertical rise of 5,000 feet in only eight miles. We raced down a river wash at 60 mph hoping to avoid John Lamm who was somewhere up ahead, at a particularly vulnerable corner taking pictures. Two nights we spent at abandoned gold mines listening to Art Director Terry Bratcher sing the trucker songs and explain who "Bruce's Riders" were. But those are other stories.

To go off-roading you need certain logistical support equipment. Camping gear it's called. Sleeping bags, stoves, coolers, and gasoline cans all supplied by the good folks at Sears; and bikes, two from American Honda and one from Yamaha International. By the time we had hit a few rocks and ruts, it became apparent that if you plan to

Double opening tailgate in the Jeepster aids loading cargo; and carrying capacity is adequate.

Hills, rocks, and whatever else was encountered by the Blazer was easily conquered, as the vehicle's far superior horsepower and automatic transmission made off-road driving very simple.

Full fiberglass top on Blazer served equally to protect supplies and people from the elements. Wide track hurts car's maneuverability.

Narrow rear stance and short wheelbase increased Bronco's maneuverability in tight places. Pickup version offered no protection.

Photography: John Lamm

take bikes, you better take bumper racks on which to mount them. We put the Hondas inside the Blazer and then watched helplessly as the bikes quickly battered themselves and the vehicle every time any roughness was encountered. The Yamaha was firmly strapped in the Bronco's rear bumper and suffered no greater damage than a heavy coating of dust and a fouled plug from too much joy riding.

As for the vehicles, we ran into some problems here because the cars varied

from the all-out off-roader — Chevrolet calls theirs Blazer K5 — to the Jeepster, a casual blend of a street and dirt machine, with a price differential of $1,000, making an across-the-board comparison to the stock Ford Bronco, rather difficult. But we did discover the long and short points of each vehicle and also the excitement which is off-road driving. And that, of course, was the reason for the trip.

Perhaps best known among 4WD vehicles, for its record-setting perfor-

mances in the Baja, is Ford's Bronco. We had hoped to test the Bill Stroppe-prepared Baja Bronco but this model was unavailable, so we settled for a more or less standard pickup version and immediately decided that if you're planning to do any serious off-roading, the wagon is preferable. Not only does the hardtop allow more space to stack supplies, but also protects them against the elements and the insidious dust. In its way, the Bronco is a pioneer among

The Great RV Binge

4WD vehicles in that it introduced V8 power to the species and our test car was equipped with the 302-2v engine which had been tuned to run on premium gas, although the showroom models are designed for regular grade fuel.

Coupled to the engine is a three-speed manual transmission and the ever-present transfer case. The purpose of the transfer case is to distribute power to the wheels and allow the driver to select which drive configuration he wants to be in: two-wheel high, four-wheel high or low, depending on the type of terrain the car is traversing. While the Bronco's transfer case shift pattern was simple, a straight fore and aft movement of the lever, it took a lot of muscle power to shift. The car also had free-running front hubs, limited slip front axle and a traction-lok rear axle. Other specialized off-road items included skid plates, auxiliary gas tank, a heavy-duty cooling package, and tube-type 6.50 x 16.6 ply rated tires. In test form, the Bronco priced out at $4,125.13.

Chevrolet's Blazer, rapidly gaining in popularity among 4WD fans to the point where dealers cannot stock enough of them to meet the demand, is simply a

Bronco's 302-2v engine supplied enough power to get the car over most obstacles.

shortened version of a half-ton pickup. Of the three cars we tested, it was the largest, the most powerful and the most expensive, sporting a list of $5,560.10. Standard engine in the Blazer is the 307 V8 but ours had the 350-2v, which runs on low lead gas and produces 245 hp at 4800 rpm. It came with the full fiberglass top and when the rear seat was removed, the amount of cargo space was so phenomenal that we used the car as a catch-all for supplies which did not fit in the other vehicles. One problem with the setup, though, was lack of a proper storage location for the spare tire once the seat was out. Chevrolet

should definitely consider offering a swing-away tailgate tire carrier option, like the one you can get from Vic Hickey, to alleviate this shortcoming.

In addition to its superior power, the Blazer was also equipped with an automatic transmission, a decided advantage over the Bronco. Now, don't get us wrong. We like to shift gears as much as the next guy, but when you're in deep sand, a manual shift is about the last thing you want and it is a shame that

Above: Blazer's high clearance results from heavy front leaf springs and shock absorbers.

Above: Composed of coil springs, shocks, and a stabilizer bar, the Bronco's front suspension was good for adequate ground clearance height. Note shock absorber, which helps ease steering. Below: The Jeepster's suspension, a compromise between that of off-road and street machines, did not provide sufficient clearance to climb over the more difficult obstacles.

Ford has yet to offer an automatic in the Bronco, except in the expensive Baja version. The reason behind the automatic's superiority is in its torque converter, which more than doubles the low range torque production of the engine. This allows the driver to more precisely control the amount of power delivered to the wheels, making it possible to turn them without losing traction and digging a hole in the sand. The only way to

The Great RV Binge

approximate this process with a manual shift is to slip the clutch and this, naturally, reduces clutch life and does not guarantee full traction on starting. With the automatic it's just a matter of gently stepping on the accelerator and gradually applying pressure as you begin to move to multiply torque while the manual requires engaging the clutch, adding power, and finally hoping that those shovels you packed won't have to be used.

The Blazer was an all-out off-roader, equipped to go anywhere with skid plates, huge 10.00 x 16.5 six-ply tires, heavy-duty suspension and generator, power steering, disc brakes, auxiliary battery, a 3.73:1 axle, two hooks, and free running front hubs. It costs more than the other cars and really must be considered apart from the others.

Although the name Jeep is synonymous with four-wheel drive, the Jeepster Commando was more of a combination street/dirt car, not really suited for really rough off-roading. Its suspension

disengages the axle shaft from the hub, makes it possible to save needless wear on the front end when driving on paved roads. There is one catch; you must remember to lock or unlock the hubs when shifting in or out of four-wheel drive. They are advantageous, however, since they make adjusting brakes easier and there are those who claim that the locking hubs help slow the car when driving downhill.

The Jeepster also lacked sufficient ground clearance and the protective skid plates (which resulted in a few dents to the gas tank) but did have a full top

former. Not because it went where the others wouldn't; it didn't, but because of the ease with which it got there.

As tested, the Blazer was built for the dirt, making it somewhat obnoxious to drive on the road but pure delight in the boondocks. In addition to the powerful 350 engine and oversize tires, it was equipped with heavy-duty front and rear shock absorbers and the optional front springs with a rating of 1,750 pounds. Combine these with 5 leaf rear springs rated at 1,800 pounds each and you have a towering ground clearance of 8¾ inches. Then consider the added

Top: The Jeepster's lack of power led to its inability to climb hills. Above Left: Bucket seats in Jeepster made the car comfortable, even if legroom was not outstanding. Above Center: Bench seats made Bronco least comfortable. Above Right: Firm buckets made the Blazer best.

is too soft and ground clearance not sufficient to surmount large obstacles. On our trip, though, it did go where the Blazer and Bronco went but with more difficulty. Despite its rather calm personality, the Jeepster had a rugged OHV V6 engine with a four main bearing crankshaft. This motor is extremely light, to save front suspension wear, yet very durable and fairly powerful; displacing 225 c.i. and producing 160 hp at 4200 rpm. While the engine tended to strain traversing steep inclines, we could not fault the 13.5 mpg fuel economy, a factor to be appreciated when you're in the desert, miles from a gas station.

Like the Blazer, it was equipped with power steering and automatic transmission but lacked the free running hubs. Most serious off-road drivers will not be caught without these hubs. Their reasons vary but the basic thought is that there is no need to work the front axle machinery while traveling down a highway. The free running hubs, which consist of a dog clutch that engages or

and sufficient cargo space when the rear seat was folded down. For safety sake we had a power winch installed, at a cost of $330.62, just in case one of the cars became inextricably mired along the way. Luckily, this didn't happen but the winch did give us a facade of security. Minus the winch, the Jeepster's price came to $4,659.56.

When speaking about performance of four-wheel-drive vehicles, you must discard the normal comparisons of quarter-mile times, cornering forces, and stopping distances. These are measured on paved surfaces, something which is a second priority in off-road cars. Instead, you have to compare climbing ability, maneuverability through rocks, and the car's capacity to withstand punishment. Beyond drive trains you must consider tire size, spring rates, wheelbases, widths, and ground clearance.

Weighing these elements and after driving the three vehicles over some mighty rough country, we have to conclude that the Blazer is the real per-

protection of skid plates and there are not many obstacles capable of stopping the vehicle. Maneuverability, despite the car's size, 104-inch wheelbase and 177.5-inch overall length, was good due to the power steering and disc brakes. And punishment, the Blazer endured it all. Occasionally, when driving quickly over rough ground, we would lose our rhythm while avoiding boulders and hit one. The car would just power right over the rock, crash down, giving occupants a thorough jolt, and then continue totally unphased by the experience. In fact, the Blazer was so well adapted to its purpose that we spent most of the time in two-wheel high with an occasional stint into four-wheel high and a very short period while descending a rather precipitous trail when we shifted to four-wheel low for safety. It was a most impressive experience.

But, as great as the Blazer is, it does have its drawbacks and these concern the car's dimensions. The wheelbase

26

The Great RV Binge

strikes us as being on the upper limits of what you'd want for serious off-roading. While the length is nice for traveling over ruts, tending to smooth out the ride, it can get you in trouble when encountering steep rock climbs. The front wheels will make it up with no problem but the frame can get hung up since the rear wheels are so far back. On the other hand, a short wheelbase, like the Bronco's 92 inches, will simply bounce over the rocks without getting stuck.

Width is also a consideration and the Blazer had 13.8 inches on the Jeepster

and was 10.1 inches wider than the Bronco. This naturally restricts maneuverability in tight quarters, but then you could say that if the quarters are that tight you shouldn't be there in the first place. And, we sort of agree with this philosophy.

Next in performance was the Bronco, not set up as nicely as the Blazer but its power, 205 hp at 4000 rpm, was enough to pull it through without too much trouble. It was equipped with the standard suspension composed of front coil springs with a capacity of 800 pounds (rated at the pad) and longitudinally-mounted rear leafs with a pad rating of 930 pounds. Combined with the 6.50 x

16 tires, this was good for a ground clearance of 8.22 inches, enough to get over most obstacles. Because of its softer springing, as compared to the Blazer, the Bronco had a good deal of body roll, a most uncomfortable feeling while driving over rocks; yet its ride, particularly on rutted roads, was much harsher. This is due to the short wheelbase, which tends to transmit all road shocks to the passenger. If you don't let discretion be the better part of speed, the jolts can pound you to a pulp. However, this same factor made the car very maneuverable, and we like to ponder how good this machine would be with an automatic

CONTINUED ON PAGE 91

SPECIFICATIONS FORD BRONCO

Engine	V8 ohv
Bore & stroke — ins.	4.0 x 3.0
Displacement — cu. in.	302
HP @ RPM	205 @ 4,600
Torque: lbs.-ft. @ RPM	300 @ 2,600
Compression Ratio/Fuel	8.6:1/regular
Carburetion	2 bbl
Transmission	3-spd. manual
Final Drive Ratio	3.50:1
Steering type	Worm & roller
Tire size	6.50 x 16
Brakes	Drum/Drum
Front Suspension	Coil springs, shocks, stabilizer bar
Rear Suspension	Progressive leaf springs, telescopic shocks
Body/Frame Construction	Box section
Wheelbase — ins.	92
Overall length — ins.	152.1
Width — ins.	68.8
Height — ins.	68.6
Front Track — ins.	57.4
Rear Track — ins.	57.4
Curb Weight — lbs.	3,100
Fuel Capacity — gals.	12.7
Gas Mileage range	
On road	10.1-10.9 mpg
Off road	6.7-7.1 mpg

SPECIFICATIONS CHEVROLET BLAZER

Engine	V8 ohv
Bore & stroke — ins.	4.0 x 3.48
Displacement — cu. in.	350
HP @ RPM	245 @ 4,800
Torque: lbs.-ft. @ RPM	350 @ 2,800
Compression Ratio/Fuel	8.5:1/regular
Carburetion	2 bbl
Transmission	Automatic
Final Drive Ratio	3.73:1
Steering type	Recirculating ball
Tire size	10.00 x 16.5
Brakes	Disc/Drum
Front Suspension	Longitudinally mounted leaf springs, heavy duty shocks
Rear Suspension	2-stage tapered leaf springs, heavy duty shocks
Body/Frame Construction	Perimeter
Wheelbase — ins.	104
Overall length — ins.	177.5
Width — ins.	79.0
Height — ins.	68.7
Front Track — ins.	60.4
Rear Track — ins.	60.4
Curb Weight — lbs.	3,807
Fuel Capacity — gals.	21.0
Gas Mileage range	
On road	9.1-11.0 mpg
Off road	6.1-6.6 mpg

SPECIFICATIONS JEEPSTER COMMANDO

Engine	V6 ohv
Bore & stroke — ins.	3.75 x 3.4
Displacement — cu. in.	225
HP @ RPM	160 @ 4,200
Torque: lbs.-ft. @ RPM	235 @ 2,400
Compression Ratio/Fuel	7.4:1/regular
Carburetion	2 bbl
Transmission	Automatic
Final Drive Ratio	3.31:1
Steering type	Recirculating ball
Tire size	8.55 x 15
Brakes	Drum/Drum
Front Suspension	Multi-leaf springs, telescopic shocks, stabilizer bar
Rear Suspension	Leaf springs mounted off-center, telescopic shocks
Body/Frame Construction	Box section
Wheelbase — ins.	101
Overall length — ins.	168.4
Width — ins.	65.2
Height — ins.	62.4
Front Track — ins.	50.0
Rear Track — ins.	50.0
Curb Weight — lbs.	2,966
Fuel Capacity — gals.	15.0
Gas Mileage range	
On road	13.1-13.9 mpg
Off road	9.1-9.8 mpg

FORD BRONCO

Base price $3,466.54
Price as tested 4,125.28

Good Points
- Short wheelbase
- V8 engine
- Ground clearance
- Free running hubs
- Width
- Skid plates
- Auxiliary fuel tank

Need Improvement
- Manual steering
- Manual transmission
- Passenger comfort
- Cargo space too limited
- Bad transfer case shift movement

CHEVROLET BLAZER

Base price $3,355.00
Price as tested 5,560.10

Good Points
- Passenger comfort
- Suspension
- Cargo area
- Tires
- Ground clearance
- Free running hubs
- Disc brakes
- Automatic transmission
- Power steering
- V8 engine
- Skid plates

Need Improvement
- Better tire storage
- Body too wide
- Wheelbase almost too long

JEEPSTER COMMANDO

Base price $3,207.82
Price as tested 4,659.56

Good Points
- Power steering
- Power brakes
- Automatic transmission
- Cargo area
- Passenger comfort
- Narrow width
- Fuel economy

Need Improvement
- Insufficient ground clearance
- Automatic hubs
- No skid plates
- Needs a little more power
- Suspension too soft
- Tires should be 6 ply

CHEVROLET BLAZER

4WD OWNER SURVEY REPORT

THE CHEVROLET BLAZER (and its 4-eyed twin, the GMC Jimmy) are the newest entries in the 4wd recreation vehicle field, having made their debut in 1969. The Blazer is a shortened version of the Chevrolet/GMC 4wd pickup, which has been tailored to the recreation vehicle field by the addition of a full-length fiberglass top and an option list that will let the price vary from a basic $3250 for the bare-bones 6-cylinder version to over $6000 for the fully equipped, power-everything V-8. In overall total sales, the Blazer has trailed Ford's Bronco in the past, but the two are racing neck-and-neck for sales leadership in 1971.

We received a total of 184 completed questionnaires from Blazer and Jimmy owners and have lumped the two together because they are mechan-

in their selection of transmissions as 55% had the 3-speed automatic, 35% the 4-speed heavy-duty manual and only 10% the standard 3-speed manual.

Our owners had also chosen other standard manufacturer options, again no surprises here. Virtually 100% chose free-running front hubs, 74% power steering, and 56% chose a limited slip differential. Radios were found on 95% of the Blazers and air

conditioning on over a third (37%). We don't have an exact figure on the price paid by the average Blazer owner for his vehicle but from the equipment found on them we would estimate it to be over $5000.

Eighty-five percent of the Blazers had been bought new and over 90% of them are used for daily transportation as well as for recreation. Just about half the owners report having an interest in competition, and of this

ically identical. We had 120 "acceptable" questionnaires after discarding those which applied to vehicles that had covered less than 5000 miles. Most of the vehicles in the survey were 1970 models (63%) and the balance was evenly divided between '69s and '71s.

It was obvious from the equipment on the Blazers in our survey that the owners of these vehicles aren't going for the low-priced version. Blazer buffs showed an overwhelming preference for the V-8 engine (the 307 V-8 in '69, the 350 in '71) and less than 4% chose the standard 6-cylinder engine.

The same trend was also apparent

SUMMARY: CHEVROLET BLAZER

Most Popular Mfgr/Dealer Options
V-8 engine
Free-running hubs
Automatic transmission
Radio
Power steering
Limited slip
Air conditioning

Most Popular Accessories Added by 10% or More of Owners
Trailer hitch
Auxiliary fuel tank
Spare tire mount
Skid plates
Winch
CB radio

Added by 5-10% of Owners
Steering stabilizer
Tape player
Driving lights
Dual exhausts

Troubles Reported by 5-10% of Owners
Alternator
Front axle
Distributor
Hubs
Shift linkage
Transfer case (linkage)
Transmission (manual)
Wheel bearings
Steering
Clutch

Reported by 10-20% of Owners
None

Reported by Over 20% of Owners
None

Five Best Features
Comfort/size
Power
Maneuverability
Versatility
Brakes ('71s only)

Five Worst Features
Water leaks
Too wide
Fuel consumption
Top & tailgate rattles
Highway wander

Wheels/Tires
Owners using larger-than-standard tires 48%

How Owners Feel About Blazer Dealers
Rated "good" 53%
Rated "fair" 28%
Rated "poor" 19%

New or Used?
Bought new 84%
Bought used 16%

Buy Another?
Will buy another 4wd 80%
Will buy another Blazer 71%

number 67% claim they are spectators while 30% say they are participants. The two favorite types of participation are given as races and rallies.

In the owners' opinions about their dealer's service, the Blazer dealers came out in the middle compared to other 4wds we have surveyed. Overall, 53% of the Blazer owners rated their dealers as "good," 28% regarded them as "fair" and 19% considered their dealers as "poor." By comparison, Blazer dealers rated better than Bronco and Toyota dealers but not as good as Jeep and International dealers.

The most common complaint about dealer service was lack of knowledge about 4wd vehicles on the part of service personnel (10% said this), with poor workmanship ranking just behind (at 9%). As a group, Blazer owners don't do much of their own service—only 5% reported that they do this themselves.

In examining the list of extras that had been added by owners after buying their Blazers, it was obvious that they had spent considerable money on accessories. The most common single item was a trailer hitch (15%) but over 10% of the owners had also added a rollbar or rollcage, auxiliary fuel tank or tanks, outside spare tire mount, skid plates, winch and citizens band radio. In addition, 5-10% had installed a steering stabilizer, tape deck, driving lights and dual exhausts.

Almost half (48%) of the Blazer owners are now using larger-than-standard tires on their vehicles. By brand, the most popular make of replacement tire was the L78-15 Armstrong Norseman with the Gates XT Commando 10-15 and Goodyear 10-16.5 next in order of preference. A few owners (just over 3%) had fitted Michelin or Sears 225-15 steel-belted radial tires to their vehicles and, while this total was too small to allow any conclusions to be made, no one reported any troubles with these tires and a few owners noted that the radials had improved both ride and handling.

Just about half of the owners also purchased wider-than-stock wheels. The 15-inch wheel with 8-inch rims was the most common replacement, 60% of the owners who had bought different wheels having chosen that width. Ten-inch rims were next in popularity, 14% of the wheel buyers having chosen the latter.

As we would expect, many owners expressed dissatisfaction with the original-equipment tires on their Blazers, complaining of rapid tread wear, poor ride, noise and poor balance. It is difficult to pinpoint the number of miles that the original tires might be expected to last, but our owners reported an average of 15,000 miles, which seems about right. No owner reported having found the perfect tire, but one who was using Goodyear 10-16.5s estimated that he was going to get over 30,000 miles before they would require replacement.

Normal replacement life for shock absorbers was reported to be 13,000 miles and for every owner that asked, "What can be done to control front-end bounce?" there was another who reported, "Double shocks keep front end under control." The only rear suspension crutch that received significant mention was that Monroe Load Levelers helped the highway sway problem, four owners having reported that this worked for them.

Plug life, 10,000 miles, seems to be about average on Blazers. Although owners of '71s may have been getting slightly less plug mileage than this, new-car pride may have accounted for the earlier replacement of sparkplugs on late-models. It's difficult to say.

In tabulating the troubles that Blazer owners have experienced with their vehicles, we found several very interesting things. There were a number of minor problems but no major problems. In our summary box, you will see that there are several components reported in the 5-10% category but none in either the 10-20% or over 20% categories.

In total numbers, the Blazer was found to have ten problem areas reported by 5-10% of the owners. These were: Alternator, front axle, distributor, hubs, shift linkage, steering, transfer case, transmission, wheel bearings and clutch (on manual-transmission models). Comparing the Blazer with its primary competitor, the Ford Bronco, the Bronco had five problem areas in the 5-10% group (front axle, shift linkage, starter, steering, transmission), two in the 10-20% category (clutch and differential) and one in the over-20% category (U-joints). Based on this, it is probably accurate to say that the Blazer owner should expect to have more little troubles than the Bronco owner, but fewer big ones.

Miscellaneous comments made by Blazer owners that may be of interest included the following: "Bad flat spot in carburetion on steep uphill climbs," "Used a rear bench seat from a wrecked van at half the Blazer price," "Highway wander cured with radial tires," "Would like limited slip in front as well as rear," "Fixed leak over door with small aluminum awning," "Needs sliding side windows for rear-seat ventilation,". "Transmission cooler solved tendency of overheating when towing trailer," "A winch is your best friend," "3.07 rear end gears too tall for off-road work," and "Limited slip treacherous on slick roads."

Blazer owners had many things they liked about their vehicles, the comfortable and spacious interior being mentioned most often. Also ranking high with the owners was the Blazer's power with the V-8 engine, its handling (usually specified as off-road handling) and its versatility. Earning additional praise were the power steering, automatic transmission, the disc brakes of the 1971 model and the fact that there was room to sleep inside when the rear seat was removed.

Among the features owners liked least about their Blazers, the biggest gripe of all by far was about water leaks. Almost a third of the Blazer owners complained about this. Also listed as "worst" features were the width of the vehicle ("too wide for mountain trails" was a common comment), rattles emanating from the top and tailgate, fuel consumption and the propensity the Blazer seems to have for wandering from side-to-side when going down the highway. The drum brakes of the pre-'71 models were also cited as a "worst" by owners of vehicles built in those years.

As for the future, 80% of the owners said that they would be buying another 4wd vehicle in the future and of these, 71% said they would buy another Blazer. This is a high degree of model loyalty and well reflects the impression that Blazers have made on the people that own them. 🚗

The 1973 fulltime 4-wheel drive Blazer cresting a hill in style and comfort. This undulating terrain is ideal Blazer land.

The Blazer shows its new metal configuration and up-dated look; glass area has been increased to provide better visibility.

BLAZER
W/FULLTIME 4WD

DESCRIPTION AND ANALYSIS OF THE CHANGES IN THE 1973 BLAZER

The Blazer on Test Hill No. 3 storming its way to the top at Saddleback Park, California. Hill climbing in luxury.

Interior of the Blazer with the tilt-steering wheel at lowest position. Instruments are first class, professional type.

THOS. L. BRYANT PHOTOS

THE CHEVROLET BLAZER is perhaps too well known to require a complete description at this point in its history but there have been some important changes with the 1973 model that make it worth taking a look at the whole machine.

To put the Blazer in perspective it is necessary to understand that it is something of a compromise in design. When Chevrolet decided that their entry in the hybrid/utility 4wd class was going to share the basic components of the pickup truck line, the mold for the Blazer was created. As a result, the Blazer is actually a short-wheelbase version of the K10 4wd pickup but also available with a full-length roof. The Blazer and the K10 share the same sheet metal all the way back to the doors, they have the same basic running gear and suspension, they have the same powertrains and even the same trim options.

Because it shares these components with the pickups, the Blazer is consequently considerably larger than its direct competitors in the hybrid/utility class. It's almost a foot wider than the Bronco, for instance, and more than two feet longer. Therefore it won't go through so narrow a place and can't be described as being as agile or maneuverable as the smaller machines in its class. Whether or not this is a disadvantage depends on your point of view. With most buyers it is undoubtedly true that the greater bulk of the Blazer is welcomed because it means that there is more room for people and things inside.

Being a regular member of the light truck family does give the Blazer a number of advantages that the other utility/hybrids don't enjoy. Ford's Bronco, International's Scout II and Jeep's Commando are all distinctly different than the regular line of pickups built by these companies. The advantage comes to the Blazer in that it can automatically share the updating changes made in the pickups while the relatively low-volume Bronco, Scout II and Commando are less likely to get updated

with the same frequency. The Bronco, for instance, was introduced in 1966 and while there have been two re-designs of Ford pickups since that time, the Bronco is still little changed from '66. Only with the 1973 model has Ford been able to introduce an automatic transmission for the Bronco while the Ford pickups have had it for years and it has been a regular option for the Blazer since it made its debut in 1969. The same with power steering. And the Bronco doesn't yet have factory air, power brakes, or even a clean-up of the body to correct some of the original shortcomings. The tendency that American buyers have for selecting just about all the luxury they can get with their 4wd vehicles has resulted in the Blazer being the best-seller in the hybrid/utility class and makes you wonder if Ford ever wonders whether they should have built the Bronco in the pickup truck mold rather than making it a separate vehicle in their production line-up.

DIMENSIONS

The only dimensional change of note with the '73 model results from the front wheels having been moved 2.5 inches to give better access to the pan. So the wheelbase is now 106.5 instead of 104.0. The length, width and height have not changed appreciably though they are slightly different than last year's "official" numbers.

It remains, of course, the largest of the hybrid/utility class 4wd vehicles and in this regard perhaps the following comparison chart will be of interest:

	Wheel base	Length	Height	Width
Chevrolet Blazer	106.5	184.5	69.5	79.0
Ford Bronco	92.0	152.1	70.7	68.8
Int'l Scout II	100.0	165.7	66.4	70.0
Jeep Commando	104.0	174.5	62.4	65.2
Toyota L. Cruiser	90.0	152.4	76.0	65.6

STYLING, BODY, INTERIOR

The 1973 Blazer continues the Blazer look of previous years and no one who has seen one before is going to be in any doubt what this one is. Yet there are a number of differences.

The Blazer continues to be offered in two configurations, the no-top roadster pickup and the full-top wagon. There are four choices so far as trim is concerned, everything from the painted-bumper Custom to the super-fancy Cheyenne Super.

The most noticeable difference in the '73 is that it has rectangular-shaped wheel cutouts where previous models were more or less round. There is still clearance for tires as large as 10-16.5 and these are included on the option list, as well as most everything else down to the standard G78-15s.

All the exterior sheetmetal ahead of the doors is different from '72—new grille, new fenders, new hood. There is also curved glass in both the doors of the cab and the quarter windows at the rear. Sliding glass quarter windows are available as an option and at the rear there's now a crank-up rear window instead of the liftgate/dropgate arrangement previously used. There's more glass area with the '73, all the openings having become larger.

The top is also of a new design which has increased the thickness of the fiberglass on the sides and made it lighter across the roof. Stiffening ribs have been molded into the roof area to provide additional rigidity.

Inside the driving compartment there was a change in the seat to give just a bit more space to the driver, getting his chest about an inch further from the steering wheel. The dashboard and instrument panel have been restyled and some of the controls relocated for greater convenience. The air conditioning has been revised for better flow and the interior ventilation system has been improved.

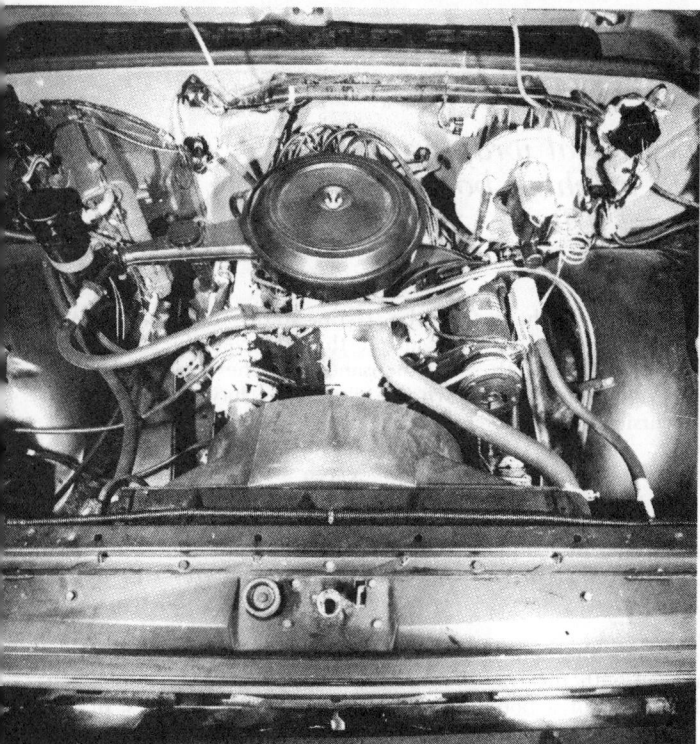

Overall view of 350 V-8 in 1973 Blazer. The area is full of gear but is no worse to work on than any other modern car.

The 1973 Blazer with fulltime 4wd makes a nice package with modern appearance and updated lines as it heads for the hill.

CHASSIS & SUSPENSION

The Blazer is built on a ladder-type frame with a separate steel body. The same suspension system of live axles on leaf springs at both ends has been retained but there have been some changes made with the new model. At the front, where the wheelbase was increased for better access to the oil pan, the springs are now a bit longer and wider to give a slightly softer ride. A front stabilizer bar has been added as well. At the rear the springs have been canted downward. Chevrolet describes these suspension changes as being made to improve roll stability and while they do have this effect it seems to us from our examination (and our experience in driving a pilot line model) that it also increases understeer—and more understeer isn't really needed in the Blazer, or any other 4wd vehicle.

As before, the Blazer comes with power-assisted disc brakes as part of the standard equipment at the front and it is still the only 4wd in this country to offer discs. Shame on everybody else.

ENGINE & POWER TRAIN

There are three engines available for the '73 Blazer, the same ones offered with the '72s except that the horsepower is slightly less as a result of the 1973 smog requirements. The engines are the 250-cu-in. inline 6, 307 V-8 and 350 V-8. By far the most popular of these has been the 350 and we expect that this will continue even though the latest emission control equipment is going to further reduce the fuel economy.

In the transmission department the 3-speed manual continues as the standard gearbox while the 4-speed manual and 3-speed automatic are the options.

The only change in the powertrain is that fulltime 4wd is now available as an option with the Blazer equipped with the 350 V-8 and automatic transmission. The fulltime system is discussed at some length in our article on that subject in this issue in case you want more details.

OPTIONS & ACCESSORIES

As it has from the beginning, the Blazer offers just about every possible option and accessory. These include integral air conditioning, power steering, automatic transmission, AM-FM as well as AM radio, tilt steering wheel, tinted glass, skid plate, tow hooks, extra instruments and so on. About the only option not to be found on the list is automatic cruise control but we feel confident that Chevrolet will correct this oversight within the near future.

DRIVING IMPRESSIONS

We considered ourselves fortunate to be able to get our hands on the first fulltime 4wd Blazer to arrive on the west coast. We were looking forward to putting it through its paces for a full road/off-road test but this was a pilot-line model and on driving it we found so many incomprehensible quirks that we decided we should wait for a regular production model before making any judgments about it. We aren't going to enumerate these peculiarities because we don't know which are typical of the 1973 model and which are a result of its being non-production. So except for saying that the driving position has been improved by the new seat location, that the increased height of the hood has further reduced forward visibility, we're going to have to ask you to wait until we get our hands on a genuine production model before telling you the nitty-gritty about its performance. ●

The Blazer Story

Under '73's all-new sheetmetal wrapping Chevy's on- or off-road machine boasts full-time 4-wheel drive.

BY JOHN LAWLOR

When Chevrolet's 4-wheel-drive Blazer first appeared in 1969, it had a couple of enormous advantages over its competitors in the on-and-off-highway vehicle field. First, it was bigger and roomier than anything of its type ever offered before. Second, it was a Chevrolet.

Other so-called "bobtailed" 4x4's, such as the International Scout, Ford Bronco, and Jeep CJ and Commando, were all influenced by the compact military Jeep of World War II. They were short and narrow vehicles, engineered entirely separately from International's, Ford's, and Jeep's standard light truck lines.

Not so the Blazer. It was created by shortening the standard Chevrolet 4-wheel-drive truck. In other words, it was *literally* bobtailed. But it wasn't cut down to as compact a length as the Scout, Bronco, or the two little Jeeps. And it retained the full width of the truck. That gave it enough interior room for four people *plus* their camp-

ing gear. Its competitors might have space for four or capacity for a generous load, but they couldn't carry both at the same time. For anything more than an overnight excursion, they became strictly 2-seaters.

The Blazer was ideal for family travel. Previously, the man who wanted a 4-wheel-drive vehicle big enough for his whole brood had to accept a full-size, 4-door wagon, like International's Travelall, Jeep's Wagoneer, or Chevrolet's own Suburban.

The new Chevy 4x4 gave the family man the room he needed with the traditional utility configuration of a bobtailed design.. The Blazer's bodywork, like that of the Scout, Bronco, and the smaller Jeeps, was essentially an open, 2-door "tub." With an optional fiberglass top, it could be transformed into a functional 2-door wagon.

The Blazer was also a Chevrolet. That meant it was available with such popular and time-tested components as the small-block Chevy V-8 engine and

Turbo Hydra-Matic transmission. And it meant that the vehicle had appeal to thousands of Chevrolet enthusiasts who might never have considered a 4x4 produced by International, Jeep, or, least of all, Ford.

The design was later shared with another General Motors division, GMC, which marketed the same basic vehicle as the Jimmy. But with that one exception, the Blazer still has no rivals in its category for sheer spaciousness. Its roominess, combined with the magic of its Chevrolet nameplate, have made the Blazer one of the most popular of all 4-wheel-drive vehicles. In fact, it now outsells every one of its immediate competitors.

'73 BLAZER

Chevrolet hasn't been content with that achievement. For 1973, the Blazer was restyled with the same new sheetmetal as Chevrolet's full-size light trucks. And beneath its glittering new appearance, the new Blazer featured

1. *The sign is Spanish for "End of Pavement," but what it really means to the driver of a Chevy Blazer is "Beginning of Adventure." Chevy's rugged four-by-four has become one of America's most popular vehicles for back country exploration.*

2. *The Blazer is a bobtail in a very literal sense. It was created by cutting down a four-wheel drive Chevrolet pickup. The body is basically a two-door "tub." The fiberglass roof, which converts it into a wagon, is a factory option.*

3. *With its origins in a full-size truck, the Blazer is the biggest and roomiest four-by-four of its type. Unlike most competitive vehicles, it has enough space for four passengers and a full load of camping gear for fairly long trips.*

4. *For 1973, the Blazer features the same new styling as Chevrolet's standard-size light trucks. It also boasts a significant engineering innovation in the form of a full-time four-wheel drive system, improving highway stability.*

2

3

4

the most significant innovation in on-and-off-highway vehicles since the birth of the original military Jeep more than 30 years ago. It offered, as an option, a *full-time* 4-wheel-drive system. Jeep also introduced a full-time system for 1973, but restricted its availability to the Wagoneer and full-size pickups. The Blazer and its corporate twin, the Jimmy, were the first bobtailed 4x4's to be built in this country with such a feature.

Traditionally, 4-wheel drive has been intended for off-highway use only. In fact, most manufacturers have warned *against* engaging it on paved roads. Yet the new full-time system doesn't really affect off-highway capabilities at all. It's designed expressly to improve high-speed stability on pavement! It's a wholly new concept in 4-wheel drive, related more closely to some of the fastest racing cars in history than to

previous on-and-off-highway vehicles. To understand what it's all about, it's necessary to consider the limitations of conventional 4-wheel drive and how the full-time system overcomes them to provide unique advantages of its own.

When any vehicle—2-wheel or 4-wheel drive—is traveling in anything but a straight line, its wheels are all rotating at different speeds. The tracks left during a tight turn on soft dirt provide clear evidence of this. Each wheel leaves its own track, because each is following its own path around the turn. The rear wheel on the inside on the turn will follow the tightest circle, while the front wheel on the outside will follow the widest. All four wheels are actually going different distances and therefore are trying to go different speeds.

A driving axle, of course, has differential gearing to allow the wheel on

the outside of a turn to go slightly faster than the one on the inside. But previously, 4-wheel-drive systems haven't provided any differentiation between the front and rear. The individual differentials on the front and rear axles have been rigidly connected through the transfer case and were forced to turn at the same overall speed, even when the front and rear wheels and, with them, the axles were trying to force the differentials to turn at slightly different speeds.

In the dirt, this hasn't mattered. Any loose surface allows enough wheel slippage to prevent any strain on the drivetrain components. Pavement is another question. On a hard surface, the tires are biting more firmly and the tendency of the front and rear wheels to turn at different speeds causes excessive tire wear and creates binds on the axle shafts, differential

The Blazer Story

gears and driveshafts that may result in one or another of them breaking.

That's why conventional 4-wheel drive shouldn't be used on the highway. If it is, some form of failure or breakage is likely to occur eventually. What makes the full-time system possible is a *third* differential between the front and rear axles. This additional, inter-axle unit allows the front and rear differentials to seek their own separate speeds without imposing any strain on the drivetrain. Thus the binds that develop with conventional 4-wheel drive are prevented.

FERGUSON FORMULA

The development of modern full-time four-wheel drive began with a system introduced in the early 1960's by Harry Ferguson Research, Ltd. over in England.

The Ferguson Formula, as it was called, involved considerably more than just a third differential. To minimize the understeer characteristic of 4-wheel drive, the Ferguson transfer case normally delivered 37% of the engine output—or, more correctly, the transmission output—to the front wheels and 63% to the rear wheels. However, the third differential was a limited-slip unit. If the wheels at one end of the car lost traction, those at the other end would get added power. It also incorporated an anti-lock braking system and all in all was a highly sophisticated arrangement that provided exceptional stability and control at high speeds.

The most dramatic applications of the Ferguson Formula were in a series of cars entered in the Indianapolis 500 by STP's Andy Granatelli. These began with a vehicle combining the famous Novi V-8 engine with a chassis built by Ferguson and later culminated in the controversial STP turbine cars. Many feel that the spectacular performances achieved by the latter were due as much to their 4-wheel drive as to their turbine powerplants.

THE MINI BOOT

Among designers of on-and-off-highway vehicles, one of the earliest advocates of full-time 4-wheel drive was Vic Hickey, a former General Motors engineer who had contributed to the development of the original Blazer. In early 1969, Hickey's own firm, Hickey Enterprises, displayed a prototype called the Mini Boot. This was a compact vehicle with a rear-mounted Chevy II 4-cylinder engine, independent suspension and full-time drive to all four wheels. The Mini Boot had a

chain-driven transfer case, using the same type of silent chain as the front-drive systems of the Cadillac Eldorado and Oldsmobile Toronado. Unlike the Ferguson Formula, the Mini Boot normally provided a 50/50 split of power between the front and rear wheels. To counteract the resulting understeer, Hickey engineered a deliberate oversteer into the geometry of the independent rear suspension. His intent was to

build something more than just another on-and-off-highway vehicle. At the time he first revealed the Mini Boot, he also showed sketches of proposed bodywork for it. The emphasis was on sports and GT styles, rather than utility designs. Like Ferguson, he meant to take advantage of full-time 4-wheel drive for high-performance use.

Unfortunately, the staggering costs of manufacturing a motor vehicle to-

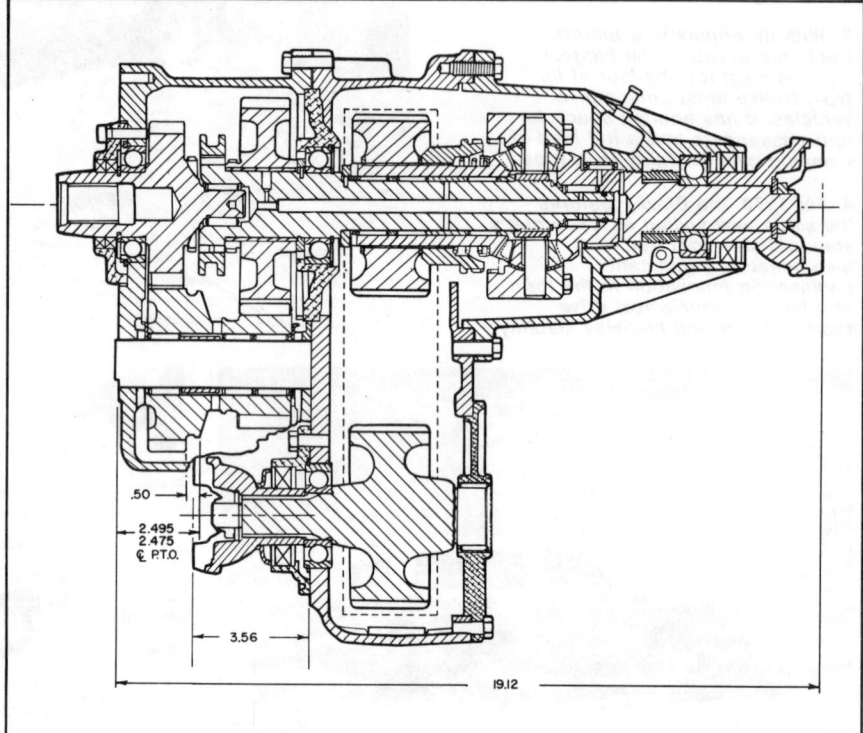

day, combined with increasing government safety regulations affecting design details, prevented the Mini Boot from ever being seen on an assembly line. But with it Vic Hickey had provided a preview of things to come. The first production on-and-off-highway vehicle with full-time 4-wheel drive was England's Range Rover, introduced in late 1970. This was produced by the same manufacturer as the Land Rover, but was a completely new and different machine.

The third differential in the Range Rover's transfer case also provided a 50/50 division of power. For rough, off-highway conditions, a floor lever actuated a lock on the third differential that, in effect, reverted the system to conventional, non-differentiated, 4-wheel drive.

Chevrolet's new system has combined a silent chain drive, similar to that of the Mini Boot, with a manually-controlled lock for the differential, like that of the Range Rover. The power split is, again, 50/50. However, it's accomplished in an unusual manner. The transfer case is immediately behind the transmission, and

3

4

5

1. Heart of the new drive system is a two-speed transfer case which uses a silent chain to drive the front drive shaft and a special, inter-axle differential which allows the front and rear axles to vary in speed in relation to each other.

2. The front drive shaft is offset to the right to clear the bottom of the engine. The chain drive is of the same silent type which has been used so successfully on the front drive systems of the Cadillac Eldorado and Oldsmobile Toronado.

3. The inter-axle differential is between the transfer case and the forward end of the rear drive shaft. Interestingly, the new drive system was developed not by General Motors but by New Process Gear, a division of Chrysler Corporation!

4. The free-wheeling front hubs used on most four-by-fours to disengage the front wheels from the drive system are not necessary with the Blazer's full-time drive. The front wheels are under power at all times, on road as well as off.

5. Generous ground clearance adds to the Blazer's off-road capability. Although the front and rear differentials are both only seven inches from the ground, the transfer case is 10½ inches and the engine oil pan is a whole 15 inches.

6. The 350-cubic-inch version of Chevrolet's small block V-8 is mandatory with full-time drive, as is a Turbo Hydra-Matic transmission. Engines available with conventional drive include a 307-cubic-inch V-8 and a 250-cubic-inch six.

6

The Blazer Story

from it the chain drive delivers power to a shaft running forward to the front axle. The chain isn't involved in the application of power to the rear axle. This is claimed as an advantage, because the chain itself is normally subjected to no more than half the power output.

The third differential is behind the transfer case and affects the rear axle only. The front axle always turns at the same speed as the transmission's output shaft and the transfer case. The rear axle, on the other hand, varies in speed relative to the transmission, transfer case, and front axle. Thus differentiation is accomplished when the front and rear wheels want to travel at their own speeds, and binds within the drivetrain are avoided.

Unlike the Ferguson Formula, the Blazer's full-time 4-wheel drive system doesn't incorporate limited slip in its third differential. When one wheel loses traction, it may spin and absorb the entire power output. Without power at any of the other wheels, the vehicle will become immobilized. On paved surfaces, such a thing isn't likely to happen. But, on dirt and especially in sand or mud, it could be a serious problem. That's the reason for the lock which, in effect, deactivates the third differential to establish a direct connection between the front and rear axles—in other words, conventional 4-wheel drive.

That's also true of Rover's full-time system, though not of Jeep's. The latter does have a limited-slip third differential. Jeep provides a lock for the system, but it doesn't have to be used except under the most extreme circumstances. The Blazer's transfer case has two speeds, a direct-drive high range and a 2:1 low range. The third differential can be locked or unlocked in either range. The system is controlled with a floor lever that can be placed in five different positions.

Pulled all the way to the rear, the lever engages high range with the differential locked. One notch forward, it provides high range with the differential operating. This is the position used for normal highway driving. In the center, the lever puts the transfer case into neutral for a stationary power take-off. Just ahead of neutral, the lever engages low range with the differential operating and, all the way forward, it provides low range with the differential locked.

Interestingly, the Blazer's full-time 4-wheel drive was developed not by Chevrolet and not even by General Motors, but by New Process Gear, a

division of Chrysler Corporation! That's not really as unusual as it might seem. Most of the major auto and truck manufacturers sell components to each other. For 1973, Chevrolet has offered full-time 4-wheel drive only in the Blazer and only in combination with a 350-cu.-in. V-8 engine and Turbo Hydra-Matic transmission. There's nothing about the system that demands that particular powertrain configuration. Rover, for example, engineered its full-time drive with a 4-speed manual gearbox.

The problem has simply been one of supply. As New Process Gear increases production of the necessary components, its full-time 4-wheel drive will become available in other applications. In 1974, Chevrolet intends to offer it not just in the Blazer, but in the full-size pickup and Suburban wagon as well.

For the moment, though, the full-time system adds to the edge the Blazer has already had over its bobtailed competitors, with its generous size and, of course, with its Chevrolet nameplate.

1. *With a wheelbase of 106½ inches, the Blazer measures 184½ inches in overall length and 79 inches in width. With the optional wagon top, overall height is 71½ inches.*

2. *The sheer size of the vehicle, while it does provide exceptional interior roominess, can be a hazard on narrow mountain trails. Here, a new Blazer has gotten stuck right at the edge of a soft dirt road, with the left rear wheel starting to slide down the hill. Yes, it was later driven out safely!*

3. *Weight, too, is a consequence of the Blazer's size. Fully equipped, the Chevy four-by-four can weigh more than 5,000 pounds. This kind of bulk can bog down in soft terrain, such as beach sand.*

4. *Driven sensibly, the Blazer can conquer most back country conditions. The 350-cubic-inch V-8 used with the full-time drive system delivers 155 net horsepower. The 307 V-8 produces 115 hp and the 250 six 110 hp, also net figures.*

5. *Chevrolet designers have managed to give the boxy shape of the Blazer a crisp, stylish look. First introduced in 1969, the Chevy four-by-four now outsells all of its immediate bobtailed competitors. With full-time four-wheel drive, the vehicle can be expected to make still further gains in popularity.*

6. *A friendly Jeep driver comes to the rescue this time, pulling the stuck Blazer out of its predicament with a winch and cable. Applying a very light throttle, the driver of the Blazer has begun to regain traction and move under his own power.*

FULLTIME VS. PARTTIME 4WD:
BLAZER VS. BLAZER
THE DIFFERENCE IS SO SUBTLE THAT YOU MAY NEVER KNOW IT'S THERE

THE FIRST Blazer we drove with fulltime 4-wheel drive was a pilot-line model and behaved so strangely that we couldn't believe it was typical of the product that was going to be offered to the public. We've now gotten our hands on a regular production model and are happy to report that we were right. The production line version is better in every way.

But let's go back a minute. As you undoubtedly know, Chevrolet introduced fulltime 4wd on the top-of-the-line Blazer this year. What makes it "fulltime" is the incorporation of an open differential in the transfer case between the front and rear driveshafts. This enables power to be delivered to all four wheels all the time without the drivetrain wind-up that occurs in the conventional part-time 4wd system where the front and rear driveshafts are locked together. For 1973, when you order the 350 V-8 and automatic transmission, you get the fulltime model whether or not that was what you had in mind. If you specify a stick

shift, either the standard 3-speed or heavy-duty 4-speed, you don't get fulltime but the conventional part-time 4wd system where you run in 2-wheel drive most of the time, only engaging the front axle when you need additional traction.

In order to do a side-by-side test of a fulltime vs. part-time Blazer, we asked Chevrolet for one of each. We picked them up at Chevrolet's Mesa, Arizona, Proving Grounds and drove them back to Southern California. The two vehicles were considerably different. The fulltime model was the all-out luxury version with the 350 V-8 engine, automatic transmission, air conditioning, power steering, fanciest trim, chrome bumpers, extra instrumentation, and so on. The part-time Blazer had the 307 V-8, heavy duty 4-speed transmission, plainer trim and painted bumpers but it also had power steering. Both were equipped with belted-bias L78-15 Uni-Royal Fastrak tires with normal highway tread. Prices and the

The editor at work getting Blazer back on its wheels after rain-softened side-hill collapsed during off-road tests.

Blazer with conventional 4wd system had lots of understeer in cornering.

other pertinent details will be found in the accompanying data.

The drive back to Southern California let us check out the highway characteristics of the two models. First of all, let us state that the highway handling of the '73 models is far better than in the past. Previous Blazers have been notorious for their lack of directional stability when running down a straight smooth road. Neither the fulltime nor the part-time models showed any tendencies in this direction and it was a pleasure to cruise along at 70-75 without strain. The part-time model with the 307 engine tended to run out of breath earlier on long grades, as would be expected, but the lesser power of the smaller engine was not otherwise much of a hindrance.

During a rainy week that came after this we also noted with interest that neither Blazer leaked a drop. Water leaks have always been a source of annoyance to Blazer owners in the past and it's good to see that the factory has been paying attention.

As part of our overall test program for the Blazers, we took them to Baja California for a week at the time of the Mexican 1000. Laden with two people and camping gear they got us down the highway to the end of the pavement in good style. The ride was comfortable, the highway behavior was good and with the back seat removed there was plenty of room for all the miscellaneous gear. On the rear bumper of the fulltime model we attached a bike rack for the Editor's 125-cc Honda and are sorry to say that the bumper wasn't up to the strain of the attaching clamps and developed a couple unsightly bulges.

When the end of the pavement came, we very quickly learned that the fulltime 4wd Blazer, as delivered to the customer, didn't handle the bumps very satisfactorily. There is an abundance of wheel travel and relatively soft springing, which should make for a good off-pavement ride, but the shock absorbers weren't up to the job. The result was a ride that was so bouncy as to make anything but the very slowest travel impossibly uncomfortable. To keep up with the Publisher's Wagoneer and the Editorial Associate in the Vic Hickey LUV, both of which were traveling at what was for them a very comfortable pace, the Blazer was leaping and bounding in such a fashion as to keep the occupants and the camping gear in the air most of the time.

The only mechanical difficulty revealed by Baja's trails was that the steering box had not been cinched down properly. Examination revealed that the box was held on by only three bolts where there were four holes and that these three would work loose periodically. While underneath, we also discovered several other bolts that were not tight and spent a half hour completing the assembly job. This sort of thing is not unheard of on early production models where the man whose job this is has not yet worked up sufficient speed to get everything done before the assembly line moves on. This difficulty was on the fulltime Blazer. The part-time model did not have any mechanical problems at all during its Baja excursion.

After our combination of good-road and bad-road driving, we came to the conclusion that the fulltime 4wd Blazer with standard suspension had been tuned to highway travel rather than off-pavement running. Where we are ordinarily accustomed to an ill-handling, poor-riding highway machine that only begins to show its stuff on rough surfaces, the Blazer behaves just the opposite. It's very good on smooth pavement, then loses its aplomb when turned loose on a bad road. Better rebound control would make a world of difference to the standard Blazer, we concluded, and we'd suggest that bigger, heavier shocks are almost mandatory if you want to travel at anything but a crawl off the highway.

On returning to the office we set up our nitty-gritty testing program to see if we could discover any differences between the conventional Blazer running in 2-wheel drive and the other with its fulltime 4-wheel drive. Up to this point, whether on-pavement or off-pavement, we hadn't been able to detect any differences at all. If you didn't know which was which, there was absolutely nothing in the two vehicles' behavior that would give you any clue.

Not to keep you in suspense any longer, we'll tell you now that we never found a difference that the driver could feel. On the 200-ft skid pad at Orange County International Raceway we were able to *measure* a difference, though. In 2-wheel drive, the average lap time around the pad was 13.03 seconds. In the fulltime model, using the same kind of tires and the same tire pressures, we were able to lap at 12.90 seconds. This is an improvement of very small dimensions, of course, but at >

least we could at last say we'd found some difference. To see what else we could learn we also ran the two vehicles in locked-up 4wd and found that we could average 12.73 seconds per lap. We concluded from these tests that fulltime 4wd gave better cornering power than 2wd but not as good as locked-up 4wd. This, of course, was not unexpected.

It is also worth noting that these tests were done in optimum conditions on a clean, dry surface and that the spread between the three modes would increase dramatically in conditions of rain, snow, ice or mud. It is in those conditions of reduced traction that 4-wheel drive will be of maximum benefit, of course.

We then took the two machines to Saddleback Park to see what might be learned on our calibrated test hills. We discovered nothing that was either conclusive or surprising. With the part-time Blazer in 2wd and the other in normal fulltime 4wd, both would climb our Hill No. 2 (70 percent grade) but neither would climb No. 3 (84 percent). By locking the fulltime Blazer (so the center differential does not work) and shifting the part-time one into 4wd, it was possible to make it all the way to the top of No. 3 and to the top of No. 4 (88 percent) about half the time. On the unsuccessful attempts in the fulltime Blazer which, as you'll remember, has an automatic transmission, we were again reminded that backing down a steep slope with an automatic transmission can be tricky. Because there's little engine braking with the automatic, the front wheels tend to lock and send that end of the machine sideways. The proper procedure, of course, is to use the parking brake since it works only on the rear wheels and makes the descent much easier.

Our conclusion after our Baja and our Saddleback Park experiences was that we were unable to detect any off-road behavior where the Blazer's fulltime 4wd worked better than 2wd.

Overall, we're sorry to say that the fulltime 4wd Blazer was a disappointment to us. It showed no marked superiority in anything we tried with it, and we tried sufficiently hard that it ended up resting on its side at one point when the Editor lost his balance on a dreaded sidehill. We know there is a theoretical advantage with fulltime 4wd, even the open-differential type used in the Blazer, and we are aware that there will be some special conditions where fulltime 4wd will have better traction than 2wd. But as for being able to tell the advantages from the driver's seat, we have to say we sincerely doubt that there's going to be a time that the driver will ever be aware of the difference.

To wrap it all up, test results plus theory, our overall conclusions regarding the fulltime 4wd Blazer are these:

1. The fulltime 4wd Blazer is a good-driving highway machine that quickly loses its poise on rough surfaces.

2. Off the pavement, fulltime 4wd is unlikely to take you any place you can't go in 2wd and won't take you as many places as you can go in locked-up 4wd.

3. The Blazer's fulltime 4wd has marginally better traction than 2wd but is less effective than locked-up 4wd.

4. The advantages of the Blazer's fulltime 4wd are going to be apparent only where the surface is equally poor under all wheels, such as ice, snow or mud, and that even here you'll be more likely to maintain on-going mobility with conventional locked-up 4wd than with the new unlocked fulltime 4wd. ●

BLAZER VS. BLAZER

VEHICLES

Fulltime 4wd Model: 350 V-8, automatic transmission, air conditioning, Cheyenne trim package, top, AM/FM ratio, extra instruments, power steering, rear seat, L78-15 Uniroyal Fastrak tires with street tread. West coast list price, $5715.

Part-time 4wd Model: 307 V-8, 4-speed manual transmission, AM radio, rear seat, top, free-running front hubs, L78-15 Uniroyal Fastrak tires with street tread. West coast list price, $4575.

GENERAL DATA

307 V-8 Engine:
Bore x stroke, in. . . . . 3.88 x 3.25
Compression ratio 8.0:1
Net horsepower rating 115

350 V-8 Engine:
Bore x stroke, in. . . . . 4.00 x 3.48
Compression ratio 8.5:1
Net horsepower rating 155

Ground Clearances:
Front differential, in 7.0
Rear differential 7.0
Oil pan 15.0
Transfer case 10.5

Accommodation:
Standard seat(s) . . . . driver only
Headroom (driver), in 41.0
Pedal to seatback 37.0
Seat to ground 36.5

DIMENSIONS

Wheelbase, in 106.5
Track, front/rear 65.8/62.7
Overall length 184.5
Height 71.5
Width 79.0
Fuel capacity, gal. 24.0
Brakes: power-assisted discs front, drums rear
Brake swept area, sq in 363

PERFORMANCE

Acceleration, time to speed, sec:

	307	350
0-30 mph	5.0	4.8
0-45 mph	9.5	7.5
0-60 mph	17.0	12.1
0-70 mph	27.5	19.3
Standing 1/4-mile	21.6	19.5
Speed at end, mph	65	71

Braking tests:
Pedal pressure required for 1/2-g deceleration rate from 60 mph, lb . . 30
Stopping distance from 60 mph, ft . 154
Brake fade in 6 stops from 60, % 60
Overall brake rating . . . . good

CORNERING (100 FT RADIUS)

	Speed	%g
2-wheel-drive	32.9	0.721
Fulltime 4wd	33.2	0.739
Locked-up 4wd	33.6	0.756

INTERIOR NOISE AT 70 MPH

307 V-8 (with basic trim), dBA 79
350 V-8 (Cheyenne trim) 75

CLIMBING ABILITY

Gradient in %	70%	84%	88%
2wd	yes	no	no
Fulltime 4wd	yes	no	no
Locked-up 4wd	yes	yes	1/2

Note: Locked-up 4wd would climb 88% gradient once out of two tries.

PERFORMANCE
with a price tag!

CHEVY BLAZER
V
FORD BRONCO

IF anyone asked us why we chose the Bronco and Blazer as our first ever four-wheel-drive comparison, we'd have to be honest and say "because they've created more interest and conversation amongst off-roaders than any single item since the first Sunraysia Desert Rally."

Let's face it, we didn't select them because they're easy-to-get, cheap, or widely available. In fact, from what we've heard (despite denials by at least one of the importers) there won't be any more imported for some time to come. It seems our ever-tightening ADRs make all but Holdens, Falcons and Valiants illegal on Australian road.

But let's dispense with the hum-drum and sort out a little of the nitty-gritty. Both vehicles sell in the same price range — the Chevy Blazer varying between $11,500 and $12,500 depending on where you buy it and who does the left/right conversion, and the Ford Bronco sells at $11,500 inclusive of the conversion.

Both are equipped with V8 engines. In the Blazer's case its the low compression 350 CID Chevrolet unit all hung up with anti-smog and emission control devices (although there are less of these fitted if your Chev was purchased in Alabama, and not

California), and in the case of the Bronco it's the Cleveland 302 CID powerplant, suitabley toned-down with emission controls, an inefficient exhaust system and a small-throat two-barrell carburettor. Both also have power steering and four-wheel-drive, but here the similarities end.

The Chevrolet Blazer is big, brutish, powerful, good-looking and extremely well equipped with creative comforts. The Bronco (and here I know I'm asking for trouble) on the other hand is not much more than a short, small, stubby, ugly (though lovable) pre-war Jeep with a V8 stuffed under the bonnet and a horn paint job.

The Bronco dash is a flat metal sheet, housing a speedo and a few switches; the seats are too small, too flat and too thin; and the back seat is nothing more than a "jump seat" for a couple of kids or a third adult should an emergency present itself. The whole vehicle presents an image of total utilitarianism. That may well be a good point — but for $11,500?

On the other hand, the interior of the Blazer positively exudes "luxury" and comfort, although no-one can convince me either vehicle is really worth the capital outlay demanded to own one in Australia. The dash in the

Blazer is fully padded and full instrumentation is housed in a "wrap-around" cockpit right in front of the driver. On the Cheyenne package Blazers imported to Australia air-conditioning and radio are standard. The front bucket seats are big and comfortable, providing plenty of cushioning, support and holding power even in the roughest off-road situations. The seats are separated by a "parcel bin" big enough to house a small refrigerator, and the steering column has a tilt adjustment to suit even the most unusually-shaped driver. In the rear of the wagon, the back seat provides comfortable accommodation for two, and would probably not be uncomfortable even for three or four people at a pinch.

Our test unit was privately-owned and one of the first Blazers to arrive in Australia. It came equipped with factory-standard options such as the 16.5 x 9.00 wheels and 16.5 x 10.00 tyres, and a rubber encased roll bar just behind the front seats. The Blazer is carpeted throughout — something which is of doubtful value to an off-roader and of course has the full-time four-wheel-drive.

The Bronco however is a "no nonsense" bit of gear. The interior is functional, although again the interior is carpeted. The seating is color-coded to the exterior paintwork, and all sheet-metal inside the cab is a straight continuationof the exterior paint job. However it is lacking in easy-to-read instrumentation, something which is most important in a proper off-road situation.

Both vehicles have three-speed column selector automatic gearboxes and in the case of the Bronco the four-wheel-drive/high/low range selection is a separate operation. It's sometimes a difficult one also, with the changes from low to high range and from four-wheel-drive to two-wheel-drive being very stiff and hard to find. Normally I'd put this down to the newness of the car — but I've since noticed that several American magazines picked this same point when the first of the 1973 models were released last year.

On the Chev the operation is simplified somewhat by the constant four wheel-drive system. Selection of high/low range is an easy crash type change using the floor-mounted Hurst shifter and can be carried out at almost any speed. Lo-loc and hi-loc (the extra positions, on the selector quadrant) allow the driver to lock the limited slip diffs to allow all four wheels to turn at

exactly the same speed in really tough going.

Once off the road and in four-wheel-drive however, the Bronco begins to shape up very well. In both cases the automatic gearbox shows its value immediately you hit hard going. Gear changes are faultless, ensuring the vehicles are kept moving without loosing revs or momentum normally lost with a gear change. The Bronco also has a tremendous weight advantage over the Blazer which checks in at a staggering 44cwt and obviously with little improvement would outperform the Blazer with very little trouble. However a "modified Bronco" test will come later.

Speaking of modifications though, it's interesting to note some of the changes made to the Blazer — and the effects they've had. First up the Blazer returned a hungry 8mpg, a good indication that something had to go. The first things to go were some of the anti-pollution fittings not required in Australia. The standard carburettor and manifold were also replaced — and a 725 Holley carbie and a Torquer manifold fitted. This lifted fuel consumption to 12mpg. The latest change has been the fitting of a 2in. Phillips twin exhaust system, which has increased consumption to around

THE Bronco interior is just the opposite. The flat metal dash is painted the same color as the rest of the bodywork. There's no padding no ornamentation . . . just two plain round instrument panels. One is the speedo, the other houses the ancilliary gauges. The seats are too flat and lack proper lateral support.

THE interior of the Chevrolet Blazer reeks of opulence with its deep carpets, air-conditioning, radio, wrap-around dash console with full instrumentation, and leather finish padding. The huge "bits bin" between the two front bucket seats is almost big enough to house a small refrigerator.

15mpg. The changes have also had staggering effects on performance.

John Warren has promised a rework of the Bronco (four-barrell carbie, hi-riser manifold, twin straight-throughs etc.) so it will be interesting to compare notes again in a future issue.

The Blazer's constant four-wheel-drive eliminates another small but significant "creature problem"...that of lunging in and out of the cab to lock the free-wheeling front hubs (as on the Bronco) for four-wheel-driving.

Both vehicles perform well off the road, although the standard road-rubber on the Bronco precluded us from any serious four-wheel-driving. But the potential is there and we plan to explore it fully at a later date. However our comparison drives at least emphasised the need for proper rubber, even in the easiest of off-road situations. The Blazer on the other hand made good use of its ten inch wide feet and clawed its way up sand dunes, through swamp water and mud, over rocks and up clay gullies...all without a falter.

Visibility from both the Blazer and the Bronco rates an all-round good on the flat in most situations. However the width and height of the Blazer can become awesome in many off-road situations. In fact the wide, flat bonnet

can cut off visibility completely as you approach the crest of an uphill run, making it impossible for the driver to see over the ridge until you're almost on the way down. By that time it's too late — and believe me it can frighten hell out of you!

The sensible driver of course knows this and will stop and ease over the edge. In situations like this the big 350-cube engine and automatic transmission really show their worth. You can stop and move off again without digging in, stalling or rolling backwards.

The visibility problem of course doesn't affect the Bronco which is much more compact and nowhere near as bulky as the Blazer.

On the highway both the Bronco and the Blazer were hard to separate in the ride categories. Both were relatively smooth and certainly free of the fore and aft chop which is so characteristic of four-wheel-drives. Comfortwise the Blazer edges slightly ahead — mainly because of its more luxurious interior trim. Sound levels in the Bronco again are higher, and again this fact is attributable purely to the fact that it is virtually an unlined shell.

In the handling department the Blazer is a long way ahead, but to those who are familiar with full time

SPECIFICATIONS — CHEVROLET BLAZER v FORD BRONCO

	Chevrolet	Ford
Make:	Chevrolet	Ford
Model:	Blazer Cheyenne two-door wagon.	Bronco Ranger, two-door wagon.
Supplier:	Arthur Greig, North East Crescent, Lillipilli NSW	Peter Warren Ford P/L, Hume Highway, Liverpool, NSW.
Price:	$12,500 (incl. right-hand drive conversion).	$11,500 (incl. right-hand drive conversion.)

ENGINE

Cylinders:	V8	V8
Displacement:	350CID	302CID
Bore x Stroke:	4.00in x 3.50in	4.00in x 3.00in
Compression ratio:	8.5 to 1	9.4 to 1
Maximum power:	160bhp @ 3800rpm	230bhp @ 5000rpm
Maximum torque:	250lb.ft @ 2400rpm	300lb.ft @ 2600rpm
Carburettor:	four-barrel	two-barrel
Fuel pump:	mechanical	mechanical

TRANSMISSION

Type:	Three-speed turbo-hydramatic, column selector. Constant four-wheel-drive. Floor-mounted Muncie range selector. Lockable differentials.	Three-speed auto, column selector, console mounted two/four-wheel-drive selector and transfer case lever. Constant-mesh, two-speed transfer case.

SUSPENSION

Front:	Hypoid drive axle with tapered leaf spring.	Mono-beam with coils and radius rods, free-wheeling hubs.
Rear:	Semi-floating axles with progressive multi-leaf springs.	Semi-floating axle with progressive multi-leaf springs.
Shock Absorbers:	Double-acting hydraulic.	Double-acting hydraulic.

STEERING

System:	Recirculating ball with variable ratios, power assisted.	Ross worm and roller with linkage shock absorber and power assistance.

BRAKES

	Power-assisted, dual-circuit, hydraulic discs front, drums rear. Self-adjusting.	Power-assisted, dual-circuit, hydraulic. Drums all round. Self adjusting.

DIMENSIONS

Wheelbase:	106.5in.	92.0in.
Overall length:	184.5in.	152.2in.
Overall width:	79.5in.	69.1in.
Overall height:	71.5in.	70.6in.
Front track:	65.76in.	57.4in.
Rear track:	71.25in.	57.4in.
Front overhang:	33.5in.	26.9in.
Rear overhang:	44.5in.	33.2in.
Ground clearance:	7.0in. (min)	6.4in. (min)

WHEELS AND TYRES

	Pressed steel disc 10.00 x 16.50 wheels with Uniroyal off road dual-purpose tyres.	Pressed steel disc, 5.5K rims with E78 x 15 Conventional cross-plys.

CAPACITIES

Fuel tank:	Not available	12.2 gal.
Transmission:	16 pints	Not available
Transfer case:	6.75 pints	Not available
Engine:	9.5 pints (incl. filter)	8 pint (incl. filter)
Cooling system:	27 pints	Not available

ELECTRICAL

Alternator:		55 amp
Battery:	12 volt, 66 plate 70 amp/hr	12 volt, 66 plate 70 amp/hr
Headlights:	Twin, 7.25in diameter	Twin, 7.25in diameter

four-wheel-drive (Jensen, Range Rover and several very advanced prototype Formula One racers) this will come as no surprise. Cornering, even at high speed is flat and comfortable with absolutely no hint of body roll or front-end kneel. The Blazer in fact handles like a sports car. The Bronco however is a little prone to kneeling in corners with a shade of understeer which becomes quite piggish and heavy to handle (even with power steering) when approaching the apex of a corner at a rapid rate of knots. On the standard wheels and tyres the Bronco also feels a little top-heavy, although never really unstable.

The power steering on both vehicles is very easy to get used to, with the variable ratios balancing out the extremes at either end of the lock-to-lock swing. Turning circles put the Bronco ahead with its shorter wheelbase on 33.6ft (maximum clearance, bumper to bumper) with the bulkier Chev coming in at 40.3ft.

By comparison with some of our more common sedans, the turning circles, even on the Chev, are not to be laughed at. The Bronco of course is even well inside the turning circles of some of the smaller sedans available on the Australian market.

Manouvreability in the bush is good on both vehicles, again a point which is attributable to the power steering. The Yanks have been the first to realise and admit that you don't really need hairy arms and giant biceps to be an off-roader.

Both steering systems are light, fast and responsive even in heavy sand or mud, and with the variable ratios there is no fear of over-correction in emergency situation. The value shows up even more so when crawling over tricky terrain — a situation which normally demands the strength of a Sumo wrestler to control, or hold the steering steady.

The automatic transmissions can of course be locked in first or second, and do afford excellent low-speed crawling capabilities. However the automatic doesn't give as much braking effect when used as an engine brake on steep downhill runs. In this situation the manual version would probably shape up a lot more successfully.

Both vehicles have definate potential and until such time as we are able to spend a week or so with each, both properly set up for off-roading (the Chev already qualifies in this category) and really put them through their paces off road, there's little more to be said.

But keep heart, we'll get them sooner or later and see how they really stack up against the more conventional and cheaper models available.

1974 CHEVROLET BLAZER

THE 1974 VERSION OF AMERICA'S LARGEST SELLING SPORTS UTILITY 4WD

CHEVROLET INTRODUCED THE Blazer in early 1969 and since then it has garnered the lion's share of the 4-wheel drive sports utility market. Blazers are the largest and bulkiest in the utility vehicle class and, as such, have a lot of appeal for those buyers who want to carry around lots of gear and people. Those, on the other hand, who want to go out and explore canyons and narrow ravines look on the Blazer as a behemoth. Since it has been the largest selling 4wd utility vehicle for several years now, there must be a reason.

The early Blazers were fairly bare-bones type vehicles with very little in the way of fancy extras. However, the options that you could buy included such items as the fiberglass top, a right hand passenger's seat in front and so on; many items that we normally think of as standard equipment. This is still true, but, in addition, you can order your Blazer from the Chevrolet factory with just about everything in the way of accessories for creature and driving

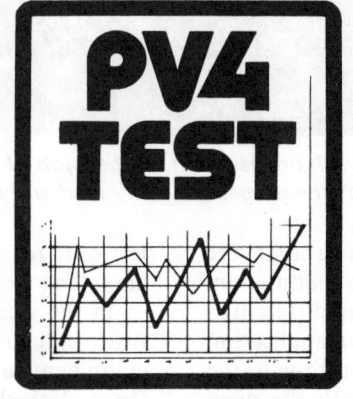

comfort and many people seem to do that.

In the field of the power train, Chevrolet offers two engines: The 250-cu-in. inline 6 and the 350-cu-in. V-8. The 307 V-8 has been dropped from the 4wd vehicle lineup for '74. For transmissions you can opt for the 3-speed Turbo Hydra-Matic automatic or a heavy-duty 4-speed manual in addition to the standard 3-speed manual.

For the '73 models, Chevrolet introduced fulltime 4-wheel drive on the Blazer. This is available only with the 350 V-8 and has been expanded for '74 into the pickup and Suburban as well. Chevrolet uses the New Process fulltime 4wd transfer case which attaches to the rear of the gear box and uses a duplex chain to drive the transfer case. There is a differential in the transfer case which splits and delivers torque to the front and rear driveshafts just as the traditional differential in the axle divides it from wheel to wheel. An important distinction between this New Process unit and the Warner Gear.

The '74 Blazer is little changed. It's still one of the best looking 4wds.

Chevrolet does about the best job of anyone in the dashboard arrangement. All of the gauges are easily read and the controls are within easy reach.

fulltime system used in various Jeep models is that the differential used by Chevy is an "open" one while that used by Jeep is of the "limited-slip" type. The limited-slip differential is more effective than the open variety in such an application since it is torque-sensitive and able to deliver the torque to the driveshaft that will take it without slipping. With the open center differential, the loss of traction at one wheel results in no power being delivered to any other wheel.

In 1973 the Blazer with fulltime 4wd didn't have a limited-slip differential available for the rear axle. This meant that the loss of traction at any wheel meant that no power would be delivered to any other wheel. For '74 a limited-slip rear axle differential is offered as an option and this is important since it means you can lose traction on one rear wheel and still maintain on-going mobility. Loss of traction on a front wheel, where no limited-slip is available, still means that the center differential will spin and no power will be delivered to either end. There is, of course, a "locked" position for the transfer case which means that the front and rear driveshafts are locked together, just as in the conventional 4wd system, so power is sent to both front and rear in equal amounts.

The list of optional equipment has been expanded in two important areas on the Blazer for '74: A factory-installed padded roll bar can be ordered, something that every off-road driver should consider mandatory; and the second is a swing-away spare tire carrier which frees some precious cargo space within the vehicle.

The Blazer is the largest in overall dimensions of the 4wd sports utility vehicles, although the 106.5-in. wheelbase is second now to the 109-in. wheelbase of the Jeep Cherokee. However, the overall length of the Blazer is 184.5 inches, which is just a hair longer than the Cherokee (183.7) and considerably longer than the Ford Bronco (152.1) and the International Scout II (165.8). The Blazer also has everyone else beat in overall width and height.

The bulk of the changes on the '74 Blazer versus the '73 are very minor and fall in the area of refinements rather than exciting engineering improvements. At this point it appears that Detroit engineers are having to spend so much time on emissions controls and engine development that very little is

left over for tooling up large modifications in the vehicles that are selling well now.

In the area of brakes, Chevrolet has set the pace in the light truck industry by offering disc brakes on the front as standard equipment on all models. This year, those vehicles with a Gross Vehicle Weight Rating (GVWR) in excess of 5600 pounds are outfitted with larger brakes on the rear than previously and larger than the lighter-duty models. The smaller vehicles have 11 x 2-in. drums at the rear while the heavier trucks have 11.15 x 2¾-in. drums. This is true of the Blazer as well.

TEST & IMPRESSIONS

Our test model Blazer was the Cheyenne edition, which is the top of the line. The other designation is the Custom, which is the base model vehicle. It was delivered to us with the 350 V-8, automatic transmission, fulltime 4-wheel drive, air conditioning, power steering and brakes, AM/FM radio, tinted glass, fiberglass top, passenger's seat, center console, rear seat, tilt steering wheel, oversize outside mirrors and B. F. Goodrich

A padded roll bar is a new factory-installed option for '74. It should be ordered by every purchaser from now on.

1974 CHEVROLET BLAZER

PRICES

Basic list, FOB Detroit
K-5 6-cyl	$3297
K-5 8-cyl	$3513

Standard equipment: 250-cu-in. ohv 6-cyl. engine, 3-spd manual transmission, 2-spd electric wipers/washers, heater/defroster, drivers seat only, LH sunvisor, painted bumpers, backup lights, E78 x 15B tires, power brakes (disc front, drums rear)

ENGINES

Standard	250-cu-in. inline ohv 6
Bore x stroke, in	3.87 x 3.53
Compression ratio	8.5:1
Net horsepower @ rpm	100 @ 3600
Net torque @ rpm, lb-ft	175 @ 1800
Type fuel required	91 octane

Standard	350-cu-in. V-8 2-bbl
Bore x stroke, in	4.00 x 3.48
Compression ratio	8.5:1
Net horsepower @ rpm	145 @ 3800
Net torque @ rpm, lb-ft	250 @ 2200
Type fuel required	91 octane

DRIVE TRAIN

Standard transmission	3-spd manual
Clutch dia., in	10.0 (6-cyl); 11.0 (8-cyl)
Transmission ratios: 3rd	1.00:1
2nd	1.68:1
1st	2.85:1
Synchromesh	all forward gears

Optional 4-spd manual	$108
Transmission ratios: 4th	1.00:1
3rd	1.70:1
2nd	3.58:1
1st	6.55:1
Synchromesh	on top 3

Optional 3-spd automatic	$236
Transmission ratios: 3rd	1.00:1
2nd	1.52:1
1st	2.52:1

Rear axle type	semi-floating hypoid
Final drive ratios	3.07, 3.73, 4.11
Overdrive	none

Free-running front hubs	$75
Limited slip differential	$128
Transfer case: Dana 20, New Process 205 (conventional), New Process 203 (full time)	
Transfer case ratios: 2.03, 2.00, 1.96 & 1.00:1	

CHASSIS & BODY

Body/frame: ladder-type frame with separate steel body

Brakes (std): front, 11.86-in. dia. disc; rear, 11 x 2-in. drums (11.15 x 2.75 with max. GVW)	
Brake swept area, sq in	376 (432)
Swept area/ton (max load)	121 (139)
Power brakes	std

Steering type (std)	recirculating ball
Steering ratio	24:1
Turns, lock to lock	3.4
Power steering	$144
Power steering ratio	20/16.4:1
Turning circle, ft	37.6

Wheel size (std)	15 x 6.0
Optional wheel sizes: 16 x 5.0, 16 x 5.5, 15 x 8.0	
Tire size (std)	E78 x 15B
Optional tire sizes: G78 x 15B, 6.50 x 16C, 7.00 x 15C, 7.00 x 16C, H78 x 15B, L78 x 15B, LR78 x 15C, 10.00 x 15B	

SUSPENSION

Front suspension: live axle on leaf springs, front stabilizer bar and tube shocks	
Front axle capacity, lb	3400
Optional	none

Rear suspension: 2-stage leaf springs on live axle and tube shocks	
Rear axle capacity, lb	3750
Optional	none

ACCOMMODATION

Standard seats	front drivers seat
Optional seats: front passenger seat, $78; rear bench seat, $121	

Headroom, in	38.8
Pedal to seatback, max	44.2
Steering wheel to seatback, max	18.3
Seat to ground	35.0
Floor to ground	20.2

Heater & defroster	std
Tinted glass: $18 (without top) $30 (with top)	
Air conditioning	$410

Unobstructed load space (length x width x height) in.	
With seats in place	33 x 50 x 41.6
Rear folded or removed	76.5 x 50 x 41.6
Tailgate (width x height)	66.8 x 22

INSTRUMENTATION

Instruments: 0-100-mph speedometer, 99,999.9-mi. odometer, fuel gauge
Warning lights: alternator, oil pressure, water temp, brake system warning, hazard warning, turn signals
Optional: ammeter, water temp and oil pressure, $12; tachometer, $56

GENERAL

Curb weight, lb (test model)	4935
GVW (max. laden weight)	6200
Optional GVWs	4900, 5350, 5800

Wheelbase, in	106.5
Track, front/rear	65.8/62.7
Overall length	184.5
Overall height: 71.5 (with top), 69.5 (without top)	
Overall width	79.5
Overhang, front/rear	30.5/41

Approach angle, degrees	31
Departure angle	24

Ground clearances (test model):	
Front axle	7.7
Rear axle	8.0
Oil pan	15.5
Transfer case	10.0
Fuel tank	14.3
Exhaust system (lowest point)	12.2

Fuel tank capacity (U.S. gal)	24
Auxiliary 30 gal. replacement tank	$19

PERFORMANCE DATA

TEST MODEL

K-5 with auxiliary top, 350-cu-in. V-8, automatic transmission, full time 4wd, engine oil cooler, HD battery, poly wrap air cleaner, Cheyenne option, AM/FM radio, air conditioning, power steering, power brakes, tilt steering wheel, L78 x 15 tires, wood grained exterior trim, rear bench seat, front passenger seat, 30-gal fuel tank, padded roll bar, wheelhouse carpeting, 3.07 rear axle ratio.
West Coast list price $6313

ACCELERATION

Time to speed, sec:
0-30 mph	5.4
0-45 mph	8.3
0-60 mph	16.4
0-70 mph	22.3

Standing start, 1/4-mile, sec	21.2
Speed at end, mph	66.5

SPEED IN GEARS

High range, 3rd (3000 rpm)	79
2nd (4000 rpm)	75
1st (4000 rpm)	45
Low range, 3rd (4000 rpm)	53
2nd (4000 rpm)	37.5
1st (4000 rpm)	22.5

BRAKE TESTS

Pedal pressure required for 1/2-g deceleration rate from 60 mph, lb	55
Stopping distance from 60 mph, ft	173
Fade: Percent increase in pedal pressure for 6 stops from 60 mph	64
Overall brake rating	good

INTERIOR NOISE

Idle in neutral, dBA	55

Maximum during acceleration	71
At steady 70-mph cruising speed	70

OFF PAVEMENT

Hillclimbing ability	good
Maneuverability	very good
Turnaround capability	very good
Handling	good
Ride	good

GENERAL

Heater rating	very good
Defroster effectiveness	very good
Wiper coverage	good

FUEL CONSUMPTION

Normal driving, mpg	8.4
Off pavement	6.3
Range, normal driving, miles	202
Range, off pavement	151

Our test model Blazer came equipped with the 350-cu-in. V-8 engine. This is now the only V-8 offered by Chevy in 4wd vehicles as the 307 has been dropped.

Good looks account for much of the Blazer's success in sales.

L78-15 Silvertown Belted tubeless tires. Steel-belted radial tires are now being offered as an optional item, but we did not get them.

We drove the test Blazer for slightly more than 1500 miles, the bulk of it on the pavement on a long distance run to Phoenix, Arizona and back. Blazers drive in a style all their own, with outstanding highway cruising comfort. The '74 model seems to have less of the steering sloppiness and wander which we experienced in last year's test model which admittedly was a pilot vehicle and not out of the regular production line. We were able to drive the Blazer on a 20-hour trip without any great discomfort or getting overly tired, which speaks well of the seats, driving position and overall handling of the vehicle.

The visibility is quite good for on-pavement travel and not so good for off-pavement. The sheer bulk of the Blazer and the high profile make it difficult to see over the hood on rough off-pavement areas and especially when cresting inclines. This, of course, is why there are companies in the off-road accessory business who are marketing low-profile hoods for the Blazer.

The ride off the road is in the "good" class with one rather serious reservation. The suspension, which is the standard leaf springs and tube shocks, is really not beefy enough for the weight of the vehicle. Any serious hard driving quickly results in fore and aft pitching and tossing which can get bad enough to hamper forward progress. Driving briskly along a rough off-road surface frequently results in non-strapped down pieces of camping gear or whatever crashing from floor to ceiling in the back with alarming regularity. That is why there are also people in the accessory business who make kits to beef up the suspension and add more damping effect on rebound.

For such a large vehicle, the Blazer displays a surprising amount of good maneuverability and nimbleness. While you may not be able to charge up into the narrow rocky canyons with the smaller Jeeps and Land Cruisers, the Blazer will give a good account of itself in the vast majority of off-road conditions encountered. We have been able to go just about anyplace in a Blazer that we wanted to, without much fear of getting hung up or stuck.

In our off-road testing at Saddleback Park, the Blazer performed well on our test hills, losing out to the steepest ones only due to the traction problem in loose silt. The power was there and with a good set of off-road tires rather than street treads, we would have done much better.

At Orange County International Raceway, where we measure acceleration and braking ability, we were somewhat disappointed with the Blazer's results in acceleration. Our test model had the 3.07:1 rear axle ratio, which is simply too high for a vehicle of the weight of the Blazer. However, the next choice is the 3.73 which is somewhat on the low side. At any rate, the Blazer managed to thunder from 0-60 mph in 16.4 seconds, which does not compare too favorably with the '73 Blazer with similar equipment which accomplished this feat in 12.1 seconds. The standing-start quarter-mile run took 21.2 seconds with a speed of 66.5 mph. For '73 the figures were 19.5 seconds at 71 mph. The 1974 emissions controls have obviously taken their toll in straight-line acceleration.

In the braking tests, the big Chevy 4wd used up 172.6 feet of track to come to a complete stop from 60 mph, which is quite good for the size and weight involved. However, the brakes did have a tendency to fade, going from 45 pounds of foot pressure for the first ½-g stop from 60 mph to 85 pounds by the sixth stop. The brakes also showed a tendency to overheat and began smoking rather badly during the six stops from 60 test. This has not been common in our experience with Chevrolet brakes in the past.

As we have been talking about the bulk of the Blazer, it would seem appropriate to point out that it weighed 4935 pounds. This compares with 4450 for the Jeep Cherokee, 3750 for the Bronco and 4280 for the Scout II.

With regard to fuel consumption, the '74 Blazer is not thrifty. We averaged 8.4 miles per gallon during the term of our test, which is not good. Admittedly, however, there are not too many other V-8s which are doing a great deal better. Nevertheless, the '74 Cherokee tested in this issue with a 401-cu-in. V-8 did manage in the neighborhood of 12 mpg.

The Chevrolet Blazer is a good vehicle. It has a good number of features to recommend it and there are obviously a lot of off-roaders who like them. For carrying gear and passengers they rank right at the top. The highway ride and drivability are excellent. It appears likely that the Blazer will continue to dominate the market in '74.

SAFARI BLAZER
DO-IT-YOURSELF SUSPENSION IMPROVEMENTS

UNIQUE AND INEXPENSIVE ACCESSORIES YOU CAN INSTALL YOURSELF

BY RAY R. KAWAL

This article presents a number of projects designed especially for owners of 4wd Chevy Blazers and pickups who want more of a vehicle than they originally purchased—*at a reasonable cost*. Many readers of PV4 have undoubtedly seen and admired the hundreds of products available to the off-road enthusiast but they are dismayed when they see the asking price. If you're at all handy with a few tools, some or all of these projects will interest you.

*HEAVY-DUTY
AUXILIARY FRONT SHOCKS*

Most Blazer and Chevy 4WD pickup owners agree the front suspension is a little too soft for off-road use. If you

have access to an arc welder, a complete installation for heavy-duty dual shocks will cost less than $17; otherwise add about a half hour of a welder's time.

The materials needed are an additional pair of HD shocks (No. 87-8238 available with a lifetime guarantee from J.C. Whitney & Co. for $13 plus postage), two 6-in. and two 5-in. long Grade 5 (three marks on the head) 1/2-in. NC bolts, two 3/4-in. spacers (1/2-in. I.D.), and a 7 x 14-in. piece of 3/16-in. thick steel plate. Cut two brackets for each side with a torch or saber saw using the illustration as a guide. Bend the lower brackets slightly where indicated to fit on the axle housing (remember to bend each bracket in opposite directions for left and right).

Remove the existing bolts securing the original shocks and install both pairs of shocks and brackets using the new bolts and spacers. Remove the brackets and trim as necessary to provide a close fit to the frame (upper bracket) and the axle housing (lower bracket). With the shocks completely assembled, weld the upper bracket to the frame with 1-in. long beads top and bottom. Weld the bottom brackets to the axle housing being careful not to apply too much heat to damage the axle bearing seals; apply the welds in 1/4-in. to 1/2-in. increments using a water soaked rag to cool; 1-in. welds at the top and bottom are adequate.

Add a little black paint and you have a new suspension system. You should

The new dual shock mounts are welded to the axle between spring mount and brakes.

The anchor plate for stabilizer bar comes drilled and tapped for 3/4-in. bolt for easy installation of this suspension helper.

The completed dual shock absorber installation. The upper bracket is welded to the frame while lower bracket is on the axle.

have at least 3/4-in. clearance with the wheels completely turned if your tires are no larger than 11 x 15 Armstrong Tru-Tracs mounted on 8-in. rims.

HEAVY-DUTY FRONT STABILIZER FOR PRE-'73 4WD CHEVY

Don't let your 4wd's high center of gravity sway both you and your cargo on every curve. Install a heavy-duty factory type stabilizer bar like mine for less than $20. You'll be amazed at the increased control and firm stability. Although you'll find the Chevy parts book doesn't list one for 1972 and earlier 4wds, a HD bar from a '73 works great.

Start by ordering the following parts from your friendly Chevrolet dealer:

Qty	Part
1	Heavy Duty Bar
1	Right hand anchor plate
2	U-clamps
2	Rubber bushings
1	Left frame mounting bracket
1	Right frame mounting bracket
2	3/4-in. bolts
4	3/4-in. washers
4	1-in. long 3/8-in. bolts, lock-washers, nuts

Install the bar by first replacing your right hand anchor plate (the spring is clamped to the axle between this and the U-bolts) with the one you purchased. Notice that the new plate is drilled and tapped for the 3/4-in. bolts to secure the right rear end of the stabilizer bar.

The left anchor plate can now be removed and modified. (If you don't have access to a drill press and a 3/4-in. NF tap, you can eliminate this modification and purchase a left anchor plate for a '73 Chevy P.N. 326425 for a few extra dollars.) Your pre-'73 plate has a large boss towards the inside of the vehicle that can be drilled and tapped to accept the 3/4-in. bolts that secure the left rear of the stabilizer bar. File or grind the boss flat to smooth the rough edges, then drill and tap similar to the right anchor plate you purchased. Note that the right end of the bar is secured to the right plate towards the outside of the vehicle while the left end is bolted to the inside of the left plate. Now reinstall your modified left anchor plate.

Using one 3/4-in. bolt and two washers at each end, install the bar with the front about 1-1/2-in. from the frame crossmember (in front of the engine). If you tighten the 3/4-in. bolts the bar will stay in place, or you may want to hang the front in position with a piece of wire. You'll now complete the installation using the U-clamps, bushings, frame brackets, and 3/8-in. bolts.

Being particular that your vehicle is on *very level* ground, mount the left and right frame brackets to the frame and crossmember so the U-clamps and bushings can secure the front of the bar. This is not as easy as it sounds, since the pre-'73 frame crossmember is in a slightly different position than on the late model 4wds. I found it necessary to cut and fit the left bracket and use it on the right side and vice versa. This step is much easier if you have a cutting torch to fit the brackets to the frame, then weld the brackets in place. You may decide to drill and bolt these brackets to the frame, but this will require some clever fitting. Or you may even want to make your own frame mounting brackets instead of purchasing the ones listed. In any case, the position of the two front bushings and U-clamps on the bar is not critical, but they should be kept a reasonable distance apart for maximum stability. The modified Chevy brackets will provide a very professional installation, especially if they are reinforced as shown in the accompanying photo.

Once the frame brackets are in place, you can easily secure the front of the bar using the U-clamps, bushings, and 3/8-in. bolts. Completely installed, you'll be pleased at the difference in roadability of your Chevy. Since the stabilizer bar is working only when your vehicle and the front axle are not parallel (as in traveling around a curve), the installation will not detract from ride comfort on the highway. Now you can sell your Porsche and race your Blazer.

REAR LEVELING BLOCKS

Take a look at your Blazer, and you'll probably notice the rear dragging its tail. Why pay over $30 for the parts to level your vehicle when you can make your own for about $2? If your

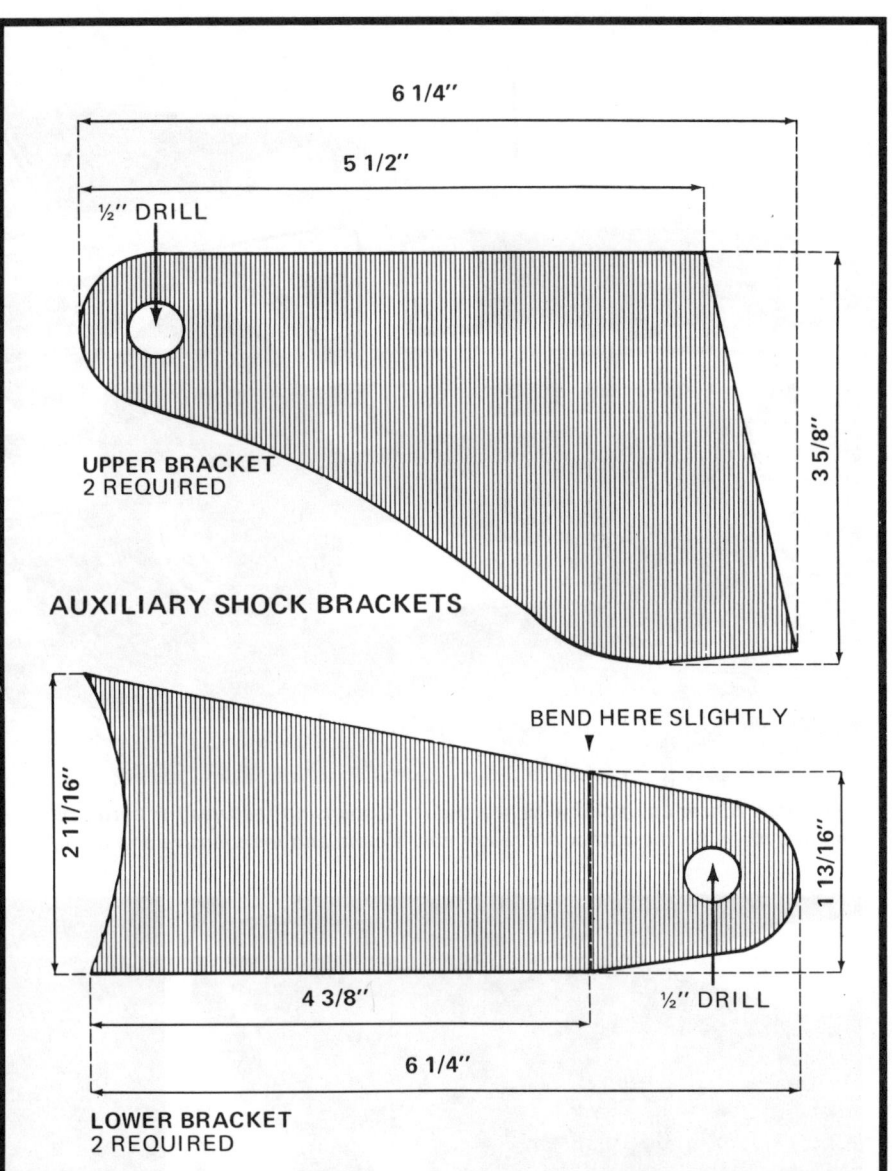

AUXILIARY SHOCK BRACKETS

UPPER BRACKET
2 REQUIRED

½" DRILL

6 1/4"

5 1/2"

3 5/8"

LOWER BRACKET
2 REQUIRED

BEND HERE SLIGHTLY

2 11/16"

4 3/8"

6 1/4"

1 13/16"

½" DRILL

When installing the stabilizer bar and brackets, be sure vehicle is on level ground and axle is parallel with front bumper.

The Safari Blazer equipped with heavy-duty suspension features for better performance in the rough going. The additions and changes made by the author are reasonably simple and inexpensive and do add a lot to improve the vehicle.

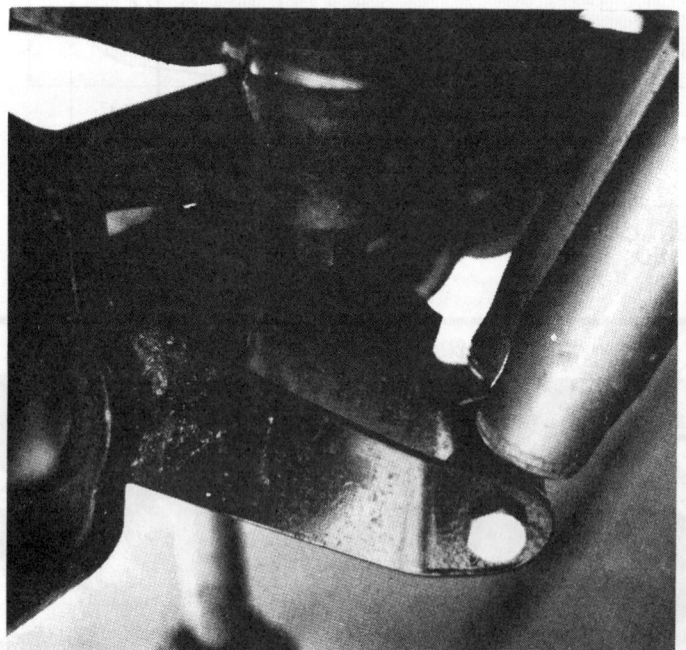 

These detail shots of the lower shock assembly for the duals on the front show the use of the factory bracket and the spacer between the shocks. Water-soaked rag is used in welding bracket to axle to avoid damaging seals or weakening the axle itself.

spring-to-axle U-bolts have at least 1-in. of threads protruding below the nuts (as most do), you can reuse them with at least 1-in. thick spacers, usually sufficient for a Blazer. The thickness of the spacers is limited only by the length of thread available on the U-bolts, but remember the very thick spacer will decrease rear shock absorber travel and increase U-joint angle. By installing these spacers you'll not only raise the rear of the vehicle but also increase ground clearance (which we all love) by using up the protruding threads.

The parts needed are two 5-in. lengths of 2-1/2 x 1-in. thick steel bar-stock and two 1-in. long pins of 9/16-in. diameter steel rod. Drill a 9/16-in. hole in the middle of each spacer and the rest is simple. Remove the U-bolt nuts (one side at a time) and jack up the vehicle so the spacer and pin can be inserted between the spring and the spring pad. Lower your Blazer, then install and tighten the nuts to 120 ft-lbs. Your rear bumper should now miss a few more of those off-road potholes. ●

Some facts to consider about 4-wheel-drive economy and value.

Introducing the 1975 Blazer.

Blazer for '75 combines the fun of a 4-wheeler with the serious business of economy and value.

With a new High Energy Ignition system that delivers up to 35,000 volts to each plug, for improved ignition performance and quick starting. A new 250 Six that delivers more usable horsepower and torque than the engine it replaces. And lets you travel further between recommended lubes, oil changes and filter changes.

Full-time 4-wheel drive available.

No need to get in and out of Blazer to lock or unlock front hubs when you move on or off road. With Chevy's system (available with V8 engine), you're in 4-wheel drive all the time. And all controls are readily available from inside the vehicle.

You get the traction you need for off-road going plus good stability and handling under varying road conditions. Conventional 4-wheel drive available on 6-cylinder models.

Blazer is also big at the supermarket.

Blazer has more usable space inside than you'd expect in a 4-wheeler. Without the available rear seat, Blazer's wagon-type tailgate gives you access to 31 square feet of floor space for stowing your packages.

Chevrolet

LASTING CHEVY VALUE

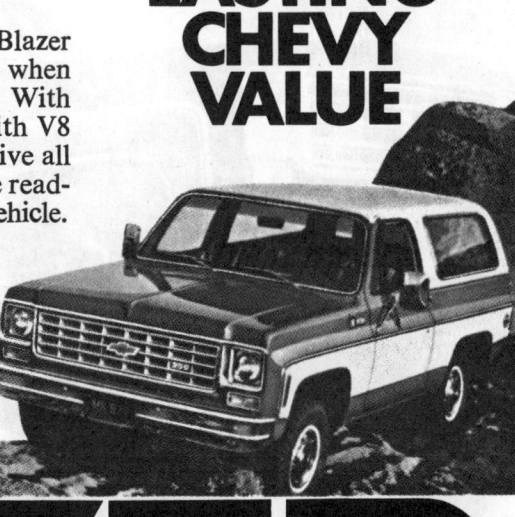

'75 CHEVY BLAZER

55

Big-Bore Off-Road Chevy:

400 BLAZER

THE TEST CREWMAN assigned primary responsibility for the road test report on the 1976 Chevrolet Blazer is a desert rat, hence he very nearly didn't return to *Pickup, Van & 4WD*'s editorial office to put down on paper his views concerning this vehicle. He went off somewhere, deep into California's "low desert," taking a pristine '76 Blazer. At length, he returned, dusty and sweaty, grinning widely, in a dirty, slightly dinged Blazer and said, "That, friends, is some kind of dyn-o-mite!"

Piecing his happily incoherent report together, what follows is the best that could be made of his impressions. He had much to say of the "look" and the "feel" of the new Blazer.

The Blazer looks right in mid-desert, strong, aggressive, square, invulnerable. It has the look of a machine that can handle anything anyplace where roads are sketchy at best, and where there are no roads at all. Sitting still, the Blazer looks to be taking on the terrain. Moving, it seems to be attacking. The Blazer, strangely, looks better dirty, because dust and grime are marks of its outstanding off-road accomplishment.

The '76 Blazer feels as right as it looks. Bucket seat, seat belt, tilt steering wheel, control knobs, shift levers, all are within reach of the driver. Consequently, the driver has the feeling of being thoroughly in control of this massive piece of machinery, the feeling he can make the Blazer tiptoe lightly over water-washed creek boulders, or charge a dune to the top, or fly, roostertailing dust, along the loose, silty bottom of a dry wash. The initial feel is not dispelled by the vehicle's subsequent performance. It does all these things, and more, does what the driver commands, whether in the desert situation, or on rain-slick city streets, or caught up in rush hour expressway traffic, or tracking a muddy road covered by 4 in. of new, wet slush.

Chevrolet's design and styling people are largely responsible for the look. The Chevy engineering department should be credited with the feel.

The 1976 test vehicle was supplied to *Pickup, Van & 4WD* with Cheyenne trim, meaning use of wood-grain paneling with maroon expanded vinyl upholstery and cut pile carpeting inside, with maroon paint, wood-grained beltline panel, black molded fiberglass hard top, styled steel "Rally" wheels and aggressive 10 x 15 off-road tires outside. The vehicle had the look of an outdoorsman ready to set out on a hunting trip, a rockhounding expedition, a mountain camp-out, or simply a hard trek through some rough country. The "look" contributes much to the "feel."

The test Blazer was mechanically equipped in such a way that the vehicle clearly had the capability to carry out the off-pavement adventures it appeared on the surface to be able to perform. Chief among these performance options was Chevrolet's big, easy-breathing →

PV4 TEST

The desert rat says it's very strong and surefooted, but a shade too wide...

400 BLAZER

400-cu-in. V-8 engine, a moderately economical and unfailing deliverer of acceleration and driving torque in virtually every driving situation. The engine was coupled through a 3-speed Turbo Hydra-matic transmission to the New Process full-time 4wd system, with a locking rear differential fitted with a 3.07:1 gearset. In high range, out of lock, the Blazer had the more or less neutral feel of a hefty station wagon. In high range, with the 4wd system in the lock mode, the distribution of torque where needed for tractive effort made for precise and positive control in the washboard, pothole, crossgrain running off pavement. Simply put, when one wheel breaks loose, or lifts on rebound from impact, the engine's motive force is directed to the axle that's in contact with the ground. Combined with the added security blanket effect of that locking rear differential, the driver is given a feeling of being in control of the situation, at speed, in the rough stuff. It's a pleasant feeling.

The test Blazer was equipped with heavy-duty front springs and heavy-duty shock absorbers that both provided sufficient wheel travel in fast travel over rugged terrain and presented a ride of more comfort than had been anticipated in view of some of the ride characteristics evidenced by test Blazers in years past.

Two additional contributors of the being-in-control feel of the vehicle were its power steering and power brakes, with discs up front. The steering offered the quickness necessary for that kind of rapid "aiming" required in fast off-pavement travel, and the brakes were always adequate, with well modulated response, when it became necessary, in prudence, to back off a bit, slow down a bit, to negotiate a tight one or a narrow one, or to avoid one of those suspension benders that occasionally leap up from nowhere. Let it be said that the Blazer's brakes respond well to a little fear.

FREE OF FALLING BOLTS

After running on about look and feel, the desert rat test crewman finally was questioned about likes and dislikes. "Anything you especially liked about the vehicle?" he was asked.

The desert rat, and other test crewmen who drove the vehicle, agreed that the new-for-1976 full forward cab, with fully framed doors, marks a very major improvement in Blazer design. The full cab obviously strengthens to a great degree the vehicle's structural integrity. In terms of benefit for an owner, this means fewer squeaks, rattles and around-the-windows-and-windwings rumbles, a plague with earlier Blazers. And, the fiberglass top now bolts to the arched member at the rear of the cab, not, as previously, with metal flanges to the windshield header. The result is absence of top securing bolts vibrating loose and falling out after just a few miles in a new vehicle. Succinctly, the Blazer's top is now secure, and free of that nagging, falling-bolt syndrome.

Perhaps the best part of the new cab design is that the arch at the rear of the cab smoothly encloses a tubular steel roll bar. As well as providing protection, the roll bar, well hidden, does not intrude into the passenger compartment as a head knocker for those entering and exiting the rear seat.

The fully framed doors now close securely. There are now no winter wind leaks around poorly sealed roll-up windows. And the well sealed windows offer theft protection in that they obviously would prove more difficult for a joyrider or car-clouter to jimmy.

One thing the new cab does is obviate the vehicle's capability for open air travel. Those who wish to ride outdoors entirely must opt for Jeep, Scout or Toyota—or buy a cutting torch. The fiberglass top is removable, but its removal leaves sort of a short bed pickup looking vehicle without a rear panel in its cab. Running in dust or dry silt with the fiberglass section removed might result in a layered accumulation inside the vehicle that would be more than adequate for a small spring planting.

The desert rat, who avoids dust baths (sometimes baths of any kind) and

New forward cab section features an arch that encloses a tubular steel roll bar, and to which the fiberglass top section is bolted. Bolts remain securely in place nowadays.

PRICES
Basic list, FOB Detroit
- K-5 Blazer Six with top $5132
- K-5 Blazer V-8 with top $5327

Standard Equipment: 250-cu-in. in-line Six, 3-spd manual transmission, 2-spd conventional transfer case, heater/defroster, 2-spd electric wiper/washers, driver bucket seat, painted front and rear bumpers, removable fiberglass top, integral roll bar, power disc brakes, H78 x 15B tires

GENERAL
Curb weight, lb (test model)	5040
GVWR (test model)	6200
Optional GVWRs	none
Wheelbase, in.	106.5
Track, front/rear	65.8/62.7
Overall length	184.4
Overall height	71.1
Overall width	78.5
Overhang, front/rear	33.4/44.5
Approach angle, degrees	33
Departure angle, degrees	22

Ground clearances (test model):
Front axle	8.8
Rear axle	8.5
Oil pan	17.1
Transfer case	11.5
Fuel tank	13.8
Exhaust system (lowest point) ...	11.0
Fuel tank capacity (U.S. gal.)	25
Auxiliary 31-gal. replacement tank	$22

ACCOMMODATION
Standard seats	driver bucket seat
Optional seats front passenger bucket seat, $91; full-width rear bench seat, $170	
Headroom, in.	37.0
Accelerator pedal to seatback, max	45.2
Steering wheel to seatback, max ...	18.4
Seat to ground	36.2
Floor to ground	21.7

Unobstructed load space (length x width x height)
With seats in place ..	38.8 x 50.0 x 42.3
Rear folded or removed	76.0 x 50.0 x 42.3
Tailgate (width x height) ...	66.8 x 22.7

INSTRUMENTATION
Instruments: speedometer, odometer, fuel gauge
Warning lights: oil pressure, alternator, water temp, brake system warning, hazard warning
Optional: voltmeter, water temp and oil pressure gauge, $20; tachometer, $73

hence didn't remove the top for off-pavement operations, said the new cab was, "Really great!"

Pressed about dislikes with respect to the Blazer, he came up with only a few.

The Blazer's wide, squared-off forward body section, he admitted, simply puts too much metal in the way of the need for a clear view of the terrain, particularly in slow rock crawling operations, or in very narrow canyons, or when cresting a sharp rise, such as the top of a sand dune. The square corner of the front fender inhibits that all-important look at the left front wheel area when attempting to creep up the side of a round boulder. And, when topping a dune, the broad hood blanks out the sky—and any opportunity to see what's downslope on the other side.

The tapered hoods and fenders of Jeep and Toyota offer a clearer look at what's ahead. On occasion, the desert rat crewman said, he halted, hopped out of the Blazer, and walked ahead in order to determine what obstacles might lie in the vehicle's path, impedimentia he feared he might not be able to see from the Blazer's driving position. It seems some full visibility must be sacrificed for some of that distinctive Blazer *macho* look.

Another point of concern finally elicited from the desert rat driver was that the Blazer is a wee bit wide—a shade wider than the Jeep CJ-7, for example.

He made this determination while playing "catch-me-kiss-me" with a CJ-7, chasing the Jeep up a narrow erosion channel cut by a cloudburst through a section of tumbled desert badlands. "I saw it coming," desert rat said, "a narrow place, and the Jeep just scooted on through, without touching the banks on either side of the cut. I took a sight line along the left side and just kept my foot in it. The noise the wall on the right side made let me know that the Blazer is wider than the CJ-7." The scrape was minor, but it was evidence that sheer width can sometimes be an inhibiting factor in desert fun and games. The test crewman also revealed some trouble with tree limbs in running up a creek bed, but was forced to admit that the Blazer's width, with optional rear seat and spare wheel and tire removed, was pleasantly adequate for sleeping out of the nighttime chill.

Optional accessories with which the 1976 test Blazer was equipped were

ENGINES

Standard	250-cu.-in. in-line Six
Bore x stroke, in.	3.87 x 3.53
Compression ratio	8.25:1
Net horsepower @ rpm	100 @ 3600
Net torque @ rpm, lb-ft	175 @ 1800
Type fuel required	leaded or unleaded
Standard V-8	350-cu.-in. V-8
Bore x stroke, in.	4.00 x 3.48
Compression ratio	8.5:1
Net horsepower @ rpm	165 @ 3800
Net torque @ rpm, lb-ft	255 @ 2800
Type fuel required	leaded or unleaded
Optional 400-cu.-in. V-8	$144
Bore x stroke, in.	4.125 x 3.75
Compression ratio	8.5:1
Net horsepower @ rpm	175 @ 3600
Net torque @ rpm, lb-ft	290 @ 2800
Type fuel required	leaded or unleaded

DRIVE TRAIN

Standard transmission: 3-spd manual*
Clutch dia., in. 12.0
Transmission ratios: 3rd 1.00:1
2nd 1.68:1
1st 2.85:1
Synchromesh all forward gears
*Not available with full-time 4wd

Optional 4-spd manual $135*
Transmission ratios: 4th 1.00:1
3rd 1.70:1
2nd 3.58:1
1st 6.55:1
Synchromesh 2nd, 3rd & 4th gear
*Not available with full-time 4wd

Optional 3-spd automatic $300*
Transmission ratios: 3rd 1.00:1
2nd 1.52:1
1st 2.52:1
*Not available with conventional 4wd

Rear axle type semi-floating hypoid
Final drive ratios: 3.07:1, 3.73:1, 4.11:1
Overdrive none

Free-running front hubs std with conventional 4wd
Limited slip differential $152
Transfer case New Process 205 2-spd (conventional 4wd), New Process 203 2-spd (full-time 4wd)
Transfer case ratios 1.96:1 & 1.00:1 (NP205)*, 2.00:1 & 1.00:1 (NP203)**
*Available only with manual transmission
**Available only with automatic transmission

CHASSIS & BODY

Body/frame: ladder-type frame with separate steel body

Brakes (std): front, 11.86-in. dia. disc; rear 11.15 x 2.75-in. drum
Brake swept area, sq in. 432
Swept area/ton (max load) 139
Power brakes std
Steering type (std) recirculating ball
Steering ratio 24:1
Power steering $179
Power steering ratio variable 16/13:1
Turning circle, ft 37.6
Wheel size (std) 15 x 6JJ
Optional wheel sizes: 15 x 7JJ Rally, 15 x 8JJ, 15 x 8JJ Rally, 16 x 5K
Tire size (std) H78 x 15B
Optional tire sizes: L78 x 15B, LR78 x 15C, 6.50 x 16C, 7.00 x 15C, 7.00 x 16C, 10 x 15B

SUSPENSION

Front suspension: leaf springs on live axle with tube shocks
Front axle capacity, lb 3600
Optional none
Rear suspension: leaf springs on live axle with tube shocks
Rear axle capacity, lb 3750
Optional none

Additional suspension options: HD front and rear shocks, $19; HD front springs, $38

400 BLAZER

cruise control, air conditioning, tinted glass, sliding side windows in the removable top, and an AM/FM radio receiver, all of which seemed of the creature-comfort variety, and which won the approval of citified test crewman. The options appreciated most by the desert rat, however, were the 31-gal. fuel tank, which offers a bit more than 350 miles range at 55 mph, and perhaps more than 250 miles in off-road travel, and the steel underside shield for the big tank that assures the fuel will stay with the vehicle even after a minor ground clearance miscalculation. The optional tachometer proved helpful with the vehicle in low/lock mode, in which it is not difficult to over-rev an engine. The tach indicated the shift points to keep the 400 engine operating at peak torque in the correct gear to match vehicle to terrain.

One factor the wiley desert rat noted with respect to the Blazer's aggressive tires was that they were a bit too aggressive for abrupt starts in deep, soft sand. The Blazer, he said, was of neces-

sity stopped on the steep side of a dune because a Ford Courier had become stuck. When the Courier was set moving again, the crewman eased the Blazer into "Drive" in high gear, unlocked, and all four of those big tires immediately started to dig in. Experience, and wisdom gained through the medium of a shovel handle, caused the test crewman to let the Blazer roll free, rearward down the dune and, at the bottom, on firmer footing, engage the transfer case in low/lock and the Hydra-matic in low range. Taking his foot off the brake pedal, he allowed the 400-cu-in. V-8 to idle the Blazer gently to the top of the shifty dune, without the four rugged treads burying themselves in the sand.

Out of the desert environment, the Blazer performed equally as well. On the dragstrip, the 400 V-8 projected the vehicle through the standing-start quarter-mile in 18.2 sec, with a terminal speed of 73 mph. The vehicle achieved 0-60 mph in a brisk 11.9 sec. In braking tests, the Blazer came to a controllable halt in 176 ft, ballpark for this kind of vehicle. In six stops from 60 mph, road testers recorded 65 percent fade as heat built up, mainly

in the rear drums, which seemed to lose their full effectiveness.

In fuel mileage testing with electronic equipment, the big engine delivered 11.5 mpg in the city/freeway test cycle, and 8 mpg in off-road running. This is equal to many vehicles powered by engines of 50 cu in. less piston displacement. The advantage is more torque per gallon of fuel. The secret is a low cruise figure of 2050 rpm at 55 mph. The big engine delivers a bundle of torque at a modest number of revolutions per minute, hence can be said to economize on gasoline.

Though off-pavement and dragstrip chores were completed, the Blazer was kept around for a time as the desert rat's favorite vehicle of the moment. Ultimately, however, the Chevrolet people called for return of their property. The desert rat was seen to run his hand along that squared front fender, then stand back for a last long look. Then he said he would like to drive it to the drop-off point, just for one last feel of the 1976 Blazer. When a test crewman actually volunteers for this kind of assignment, "That, friends is some kind of dyn-o-mite." ●

TEST MODEL

K-5 Blazer, Cheyenne trim, 400-cu-in. V-8, automatic transmission, full-time 4wd, Calif. emission cert., chrome bumpers front and rear, wheelhouse carpeting, gauges, tachometer, tinted glass, air conditioning, sliding side windows, below eyeline mirrors, body side molding, fuel tank shield, AM/FM radio, front passenger seat, rear bench seat, HD shocks, cruise control, HD front springs, power steering and brakes, tilt steering wheel, 31-gal. fuel tank, Rally wheels, 10 x 15B tires, 3.07:1 axle ratio with locking rear differential

West Coast list price (includes $472 freight) $9300

ACCELERATION

Time to speed, sec:
0-30 mph 4.1
0-45 mph 7.4
0-60 mph 11.9
0-70 mph 16.8
Standing start, ¼-mile, sec 18.2
Speed at end, mph 73

SPEED IN GEARS

High range
3rd (3500 rpm) 94
2nd (4000 rpm) 76
1st (4000 rpm) 46
Low range
3rd (4000 rpm) 54
2nd (4000 rpm) 38

1st (4000 rpm) 23
Engine rpm @ 55 mph 2050

BRAKE TESTS

Pedal pressure required for ½-g deceleration rate from 60 mph, lb 45
Stopping distance from 60 mph, ft . 176
Fade: Percent increase in pedal pressure for 6 stops from 60 mph 65
Overall brake rating .... very good

INTERIOR NOISE

Idle in neutral, dbA 56.5
Maximum during acceleration 74.0
At steady 60 mph cruising speed ... 74.5

OFF PAVEMENT

Hillclimbing ability .... excellent
Maneuverability .... very good
Turnaround capability ...... very good
Driver visibility .... fair
Handling .... very good
Ride .... very good

ON PAVEMENT

Handling .... very good
Ride .... good
Driver comfort .... very good
Engine response .... excellent

FUEL CONSUMPTION

City/freeway driving, mpg 11.5
Off pavement 8.0
Range, city/freeway driving, miles .. 287
Range, off pavement 200

CHEVROLET BLAZER CHALET

Chevy's solid off-roader totes its own house along.

BACKGROUND/When Chevrolet introduced the Blazer (and its four-eyed twin, the Jimmy, came from GMC) in 1969, a whole new dimension was added to the four-wheel-drive field. The Blazer was drastically different in size—falling between traditional "bobtail" 4X4 rigs (Jeep or Bronco, for example) and four-wheel-drive pickup trucks. Moreover, it was not a designed-from-scratch vehicle; clever Chevy engineers simply took their ½-ton pickup truck, chopped chunks out of the body and drivetrain, and presto! A new concept was born. Chevy Blazers are available in four-wheel or two-wheel drive, but we are dealing only with the K-5—the four-wheel-drive version.

What's more, the Blazer K-5 gave the four-wheel-drive movement a healthy shot in the arm. It was obviously an idea whose time had come. Strangely, Jeep and other pioneer manufacturers of four-wheel-drive vehicles didn't suffer any loss of sales when the new kid on the block made its debut. Their sales either held up or increased. Blazers just expanded the market and attracted new buyers who wanted to go four-wheeling with more room, comfort and conveniences than previous 4X4 vehicles had offered.

Due to many different reasons—labor strikes, deadline restrictions, transportation difficulties, etc.—we were forced to test a couple of '76 models rather than 1977 vehicles exclusively. The Blazer Chalet we tested was one of the '76 units. This should create no real problems with prospective customers; the '77 light trucks from Chevy are identical to the '76's except for a redesigned grille insert.

The first Blazers had a wheelbase of 104 ins., which was 23 ins. longer than CJ-5 Jeeps at the time. For 1973, when full-time four-wheel drive was introduced, the Blazer's wheelbase was stretched to 106.5 ins., where it remains for 1977 models.

GENERAL/The Blazer's size and ancestry have had both good and bad results. From a positive standpoint, its extra width and length make it roomier than earlier 4X4 vehicles. Since it is a descendant of Chevy pickups, it is available with the same extensive list of options that they offer—power steering and brakes, air conditioning and many others. On the other hand, the Blazer's size—especially its width—has proven to be a handicap at times in the real four-wheeler world. Four-wheel-drive purists continue to prefer smaller Jeeps, Scouts and Broncos for serious off-pavement driving. Market research figures indicate that, on the whole, newcomers to 4X4 vehicles have been more important to the Blazer's success than former owners of smaller four-wheel-drive rigs.

Perhaps these market research figures induced Chevy designers to produce the Chalet option, which was introduced as an interim model in April of '76. Produced for the weekend camper who doesn't need a unit capable of extended camping, the Chalet fills the bill admirably.

The 350-cu.-in. 4-bbl. V-8 has been the standard 8-cyl. engine from the beginning, and it still is. Outside California, a 250-cu.-in. 6-cyl. has been the base powerplant and is carried over for 1977. Also added for '77 (again, outside California) is an optional 2-bbl., 305-cu.-in. V-8, while the 2-bbl. 350 is no longer available.

The three smaller engines (250, 305 and 350) are available with any of the three optional transmissions: 3-speed manual, 4-speed manual or 3-speed automatic. The three engines are also options in either 2- or 4-wheel-drive Blazers, while the 4-bbl. 400 V-8 is available only in the K-series Blazer, and then only when coupled to the automatic trans. California customers can choose only between two 4-bbl. V-8's: the 350 or 400.

CHASSIS/Drop-center, ladder-type frames are still being used for '77 to keep the overall height of the standard Blazer (without the Chalet option) as low as possible; side rails are of deep-section channel construction. Rear shock absorbers are staggered—one leaning forward, the other aft—to reduce rear wheel-hop.

The Blazer front suspension was redesigned somewhat for 1975, but the basic configuration remains the same: solid hypoid axle, multi-leaf springs and tubular shocks. Plastic liners separate all spring leaves to reduce noise and friction. Front stabilizer bars are standard, and heavy-duty units are used on V-8 Blazers.

Power brakes are standard, with discs up front and drums in the rear for all models. Brake sizes are tailored to GVWR, a Chevy practice for several years. To handle the boost in maximum GVWR to 6700 lbs., rear brake drum size was increased in 1975 from 11 ins. in diameter by 2 ins. wide to 11.15 ins. in diameter by 2.75 ins. wide for top-rated models. Front disc rotor diameter remained at 11.86 ins.

DRIVELINE/Standard transmission is a 3-speed manual unit with a 2.85:1 ratio in 1st gear and 1.68:1 in 2nd. All three forward gears have synchromesh rings for easier shifting. A 4-speed manual box, with a non-synchro 1st gear that has a real "granny" ratio of 6.55:1, is optional. The clutch used behind V-8's has a 12-in. diameter, while the 250-cu.-in. 6-cyl. uses an 11-in.-diameter clutch disc. The optional automatic is the popular Turbo Hydra-Matic 3-speed transmission, with ratios of 2.52:1, 1.52:1 and 1:1.

All Blazers, whether equipped with manual or automatic transmissions, use New Process 2-speed transfer cases. Auto-equipped rigs use the NP #203 full-time four-wheel-drive unit with a nominal 2:1 low range and 1:1 high range. Manual transmissions (3- or 4-speed) transmit power through an NP #205 standard transfer case.

BODY/As mentioned, the Blazer's body is basically derived from that of Chevrolet pickups, with the back of the cab sliced off. Blazers can be ordered in three different body styles: convertible, hardtop or Chalet.

Either of the tops covers the bed area, and any '76 or later Blazer can use either top. Both tops come in black or white, and the hardtop can be obtained with sliding side windows for better air circulation. Two additional folding top colors, blue and tan, are available for 1977.

The 'glass hardtop bolts into place, but this doesn't make the Blazer an instant convertible. It's a time-consuming chore (and a two-person job) to remove or replace the top. However, it is easier than on pre-'76 models. From experience, we recommend checking the top bolts regularly for tightness.

All Blazers also come with a bucket seat as standard equipment on the driver's side; a right-side passenger's bucket seat is optional, and there is an optional rear bench seat (but not with the Chalet). The front bench seat is no longer offered. Front buckets feature a

BLAZER CHALET

counterbalancing setup; they can be tilted forward easily and don't crash heavily to the floor when pushed back to the upright position. Optional rear bench seats were positioned some 7 ins. further forward in 1975. This increased cargo area behind the rear seat by 12 cu. ft., bringing the total cargo area with a rear seat in place to 44 cu. ft.—but also reducing rear legroom.

As can be seen in the accompanying photographs, the Chalet option is a small camper bolted directly to the Blazer's body. It uses the same holes as the hardtop. There are four versions in which the Chalet can be ordered. The first level is very basic and includes only the reinforced plastic camper shell with steel cage and pop-up roof, convertible seat/bunks with sleeping accommodations for two people, a sink, two-burner LPG stove (no oven), icebox, demountable dinette table and color-coordinated curtains and drapes. All four levels of the Chalet offer walk-through access to the cab.

Each of the remaining three levels includes those items already listed, plus additional conveniences. The second level adds a 5000-BTU heater, and the third level adds a 3-way refrigerator along with an extra battery and AC/DC power hookup kit. The fourth version only adds overhead bunks to sleep two more adults.

TEST VEHICLE/The Blazer Chalet we tested had the deluxe Cheyenne package and almost every option known to Chevy engineers, including a 400-cu.-in., 4-bbl. V-8. The camper was the fourth-level version, with every available option.

Among the extras were power steering, adjustable steering wheel, Turbo Hydra-Matic transmission, air conditioning, AM/FM radio, front bucket seats, deluxe chromed front and rear bumpers, front-mounted spare tire carrier and cruise control.

The Chalet camper option adds 30.5 ins. to the Blazer's overall length, which then totals 18 ft., 5 ins. This measurement includes the front-mounted spare tire and the rear step.

OBSERVATIONS/Chassis dyno tests were quite disappointing on all the '77 test vehicles from a power standpoint. Nearly every vehicle had trouble reaching 3500 rpm, which was our maximum test rpm with the previous book. Therefore, we lowered rpm requirements to 2000, 2500 and 3000 for all tests. However, the Chalet was the first vehicle on the dyno and we were unaware that we would have problems with the vehicles to be tested on a later date, so we took rear wheel horsepower readings at the rpm level closest to our last edition's test levels. We were forced to reduce rpm readings (with the Chalet at 3300 rpm the speedometer on the dyno was competely off the scale) on late-model trucks for two reasons: increased smog controls and higher rear end ratios. The engines cannot be twisted in the higher rpm ranges, and even if they could, the rear end ratios are so tall that speeds become ridiculous.

Although gas mileage figures with the 400-cu.-in. engine were better than the 350 by 50%, the horsepower readings were almost identical, with the 400 losing a few horses in the higher rpm test. The 400 didn't come through the sniff test quite as clean as the '75 350 either. Both engines emitted 20 HC parts per million, but the 400 gave off 2.1% carbon monoxide compared to .25% for the earlier 350-cu.-in. V-8.

During the entire testing procedure we watched the Chalet's body molding, both external and internal, for stress points or cracking. None appeared. Mounting bolts remained tight throughout the test, and the camper did not shift around at all, even during violent off-road maneuvers.

ON-PAVEMENT/The Blazer Chalet has one of the best rides on-pavement of any four-wheel-drive vehicle we tested; the longer wheelbase smoothed out the jointed concrete surfaces which give bobtail drivers fits, and the camper box's added weight supplied additional stability over the longer wheelbase models. The front springs soaked up road shocks before they could be transmitted to the frame.

Even at the top legal speed of 55 mph, the Chalet showed no tendency to wander about the traffic lane such as we experienced with earlier Blazer models. Possibly the streamlined design of the Chalet contributed to this tracking stability. Most side winds failed to cause enough wandering to be of any concern, unless they were either high or gusting. Passing (or being passed by) semi-tractor/trailer combinations required minor corrections to overcome a slight swaying.

The high seating position provided by the bucket seats affords excellent visibility for on-pavement driving, and there is plenty of leg room, even for those who top 6 ft. The optional tilt steering wheel makes it easy for drivers of all sizes to slip in and out of the vehicle.

OFF-PAVEMENT/Here is where the added weight of the Chalet caused problems to appear. The negative arch of the front springs allows only 1½ ins. between the rubber snubbers and the Dana 44 front axle housing, and this means bottoming on any but the most minor obstacle. Without the added weight of the Chalet this may not be critical, but with the Chalet bolted into place, any speed above a walk causes severe front end thumping.

In addition, the increased overhang at both ends greatly reduces entrance and exit angles. During testing we continually dug up dirt with both the spare tire and camper step. An aftermarket spare tire carrier would carry the tire higher and more securely than the factory front-mounted carrier. The size of the factory tires precluded any severe climbing tests; they were too narrow and the tread pattern too non-aggressive to overcome the increased weight of the Blazer Chalet when the climb angle became steep. Chalet's high center of gravity also precluded any thoughts of banzai charges over hills to try to overcome the street tires' shortcomings.

Removing the Chalet camper unit would greatly increase the agility of the Blazer by lowering the center of gravity and reducing the extreme additional rear overhang. Admittedly a time-consuming and difficult job, unbolting and dropping off the Chalet

---

BOX SCORE

Each of the following factors was rated on a scale of 1 to 10, as: Poor, 1 to 2. Fair, 3 to 4. Good, 5 to 7. Excellent, 8 to 10. An 8-point award, for example, was given if the category warranted better than a GOOD rating, but not the highest of EXCELLENT. Each book staff member compiled his own Box Score, then averages were drawn accordingly. Here's how the Chevy Blazer Chalet stacked up.

On-pavement handling/performance	8
Off-pavement handling/performance	5
Maneuverability	7.1
Stability	6
Acceleration	5
Gearing	7.3
Braking	8.5
Hillclimbing ability	6.5
Prolonged travel comfort	8.9
City travel comfort	8.7
Interior access (front seat)	8.2
Rear seat access (if applicable)	6
Load space access	8
Engine access	8.2
Engine splash shielding	5.6
Instrument/controls layout and access	7.6
Visibility	5.8

would also leave the Blazer with no rear cab wall, no rear seat and no tailgate. Still, the combination would really make a helluva hunting wagon.

Driven slowly and sensibly, a K-5 Blazer, with or without the Chalet, can be taken into all but the most far-out, straight-up-and-down, narrow trails and forest paths. Regardless of whether the Chalet is in place or not, an important problem to those who habitually drive in hilly country is the lack of forward visibility when you top a ridge in a Blazer. The hood is so high, broad and flat and extends forward so far that you can see nothing but sky as you reach the crest of a hill.

TRAILER AND RV USE/Chevrolet rates Blazers as capable of towing trailers with a gross weight of up to 6000 lbs. and a tongue weight of up to 750 lbs. That's with V-8 engine, 4.11:1 axle ratios (or 3.73:1 with 400 V-8) and equalizing hitch, plus heavy-duty cooling and electrical systems options. With 3.73:1 axle ratios (excluding the 400 V-8), a maximum trailer weight of 4000 lbs. and a tongue weight of 500 lbs. is the recommended limit.

Chevy began offering a weight-distributing hitch platform as a factory-installed option for Blazers (also pickups and Suburbans) several years ago. This option is offered again for '77 and is a worthwhile and safe one for anyone planning to buy a Blazer as a tow vehicle for a trailer grossing more than 2000 lbs. It can also be dealer-installed for those who already own Blazers. The option number is RPO VR4. The advantage of this unit is that it has been specifically engineered to fit and is designed to place the stress of heavy loads at the frame points best able to cope with them. Any current load-equalizing hitch with ball head will plug right into the platform receiver. Dealers can also install extra-light (trailers up to 1000 lbs. gross) and light-duty (up to 2000 lbs. gross) hitches on Blazers.

When the Chalet is in place, its subframe just about precludes towing a trailer with any tongue weight at all. The frame extension is not strong enough to support tongue weight or gross towing weight of any but the most light-duty trailer. A special hitch platform would have to be fabricated in order to tow a boat or utility trailer.

SUMMATION/The Blazer Chalet isn't a "pure" four-wheel-drive vehicle in the sense that, say, the CJ-5 Jeep or a few of the other smaller bobtail 4X4 rigs are. The littler machines undoubtedly will go places where the Chevy might fear to tread. However, it will fulfill the four-wheeling needs of most families, plus those of commercial users who want a work/play vehicle and don't need a whole lot of cargo-carrying capacity. 🔱

CHEVROLET BLAZER CHALET—GENERAL

Curb weight (lbs.)	5840
Payload (lbs.)	860
Track (ins.) front/rear	67.5/64.0
Overall length (ins.)	221
Overall height (ins.—when traveling)	93.5
Overall width (ins.)	94.0
Overhang (ins.) front/rear	50.5/67.25
Ground clearance (ins.):	
Mid-wheelbase	10.2
At lowest differential	8.25
At lowest chassis point/component	10.2/transfer case
Approach angle (degrees)	18
Departure angle (degrees)	17
Floor height (ins.) front door	22
Floor height (ins.) rear door	30.5
Tailgate width (ins.)	N/A
Tailgate height (ins.)	N/A
Cargo length (ins.) w/rear seat	N/A
Cargo length (ins.) camper floor	96
Cargo width (ins.) extreme	N/A
Cargo width (ins.) between wheelwells	N/A
Cargo height (ins.)	N/A
Steering (turns lock-to-lock)	3.33

ENGINES

	Displacement (cu. ins.)	Bore (ins.)	Stroke (ins.)	Compression ratio	Net hp @ rpm	Net torque @ rpm
Standard	250 6-cyl. (1-bbl.)	3.875	3.53	8.2:1	100 @ 3600	175 @ 1800
Optional	305 V-8 (2-bbl.)	3.74	3.48	8.5:1	140 @ 3800	235 @ 2000
Optional	350 V-8 (4-bbl.)	4.00	3.48	8.5:1	165 @ 3800	255 @ 2800
Optional	**400 V-8 (4-bbl.)**	**4.126**	**3.75**	**8.5:1**	**175 @ 3600**	**290 @ 2800**

DRIVETRAIN COMBINATIONS

Engine	Transmission	Transfer case	Axle ratios
250 6-cyl. (1-bbl.)	3-speed manual 4-speed manual	Conventional NPG 205	4.11 3.73/4.11
	Turbo-Hydro	Full-time NPG 203	
305 V-8 (2-bbl.)	3-speed manual 4-speed manual	Conventional NPG 205	3.73/4.11 3.07/3.73/4.11
	Turbo-Hydro	Full-time NPG 203	
350 V-8 (4-bbl.)	3-speed manual 4-speed manual	Conventional NPG 205	
	Turbo-Hydro	Full-time NPG 203	
400 V-8 (4-bbl.)	**Turbo-Hydro**	**Full-time NPG 203**	**3.07**/3.73

CHASSIS

Model	Wheelbase (ins.)	GVW's (lbs.) Stand.	Opt.	Turning circle (ft.)
K-5	106.5	6200	6700	40.7 R; 42.4 L

Brakes Stand.	Opt.	Tires sizes Stand.	Opt.	Steering Stand.	Opt.	Fuel capacity (gals.) Stand.	Opt.
Disc/drum (power)	N/A	E78X15	G78X15 to 10X15	Conventional	**Power**	24	30

BASE PRICE
(FOB factory. Manufacturer's suggested retail.)

Model	Price
K-5	$5483.35
Chalet	$9443.85

TEST VEHICLE PERFORMANCE

Fuel consumption (mpg)—on-pavement	14.98
Fuel consumption (mpg)—off-pavement	6.19
On-pavement acceleration: 0-30 mph (secs.)	6.2
On-pavement acceleration: 0-55 mph (secs.)	13.5
Rear wheel horsepower @ 2500 rpm	70
Rear wheel horsepower @ 3000 rpm	80
Rear wheel horsepower @ 3300 rpm	72

Emissions at idle: **20** HC parts per million; **2.1%** carbon monoxide.

● Certain equipment, option combinations may not be available in some areas. See your dealer.

CHEVY BLAZER

A BIG AND GUTSY BARREL OF FUN

If you make a careful study of the Blazer, you'll find your ratings depend heavily on where and how the truck is used. We've been driving Blazers since they were first introduced in 1969 and have kept abreast of the new models, as well as all the latest options. Our relationship with this vehicle has been mostly one of love, with the occasional argument. For example, deep in the most primitive and rural Baja California, we found good reasons for both emotions with the 1977 model test vehicle. We hated it when both mirrors were folded back and the Blazer's sides scratched on a narrow sandwash track. Admittedly, we were going rather fast, but preferred not to slow down so we could keep up momentum and avoid getting bogged down to the axles. A narrower vehi-

cle would have slithered its way through unscathed.

On the same trip, however, we were driving along a country lane with darkness and rain approaching. We had two passengers in our Blazer with the rear seat removed, and a load of miscellaneous gear in the back. Suddenly we happened upon a stranded motorcyclist friend whose bike had terminal holes in the pistons. Although loaded with food and drink, we offered to pick up the rider and his bike too, for it would surely have disappeared if left abandoned along the trail. Impossible to squeeze a full-size trail bike into a Blazer? We thought so, too, but by rearranging the cargo, collapsing the motorcycle's front forks, rotating the handlebars down, and rolling the bike forward so that the front tire nuzzled

the driver's right shoulder, we did it.

The remainder of the trip up a remote mountain, along a slippery road in fog and drizzling rain to a guest rancho, was made in relative ease, bearing in mind we had three people in front on a pair of bucket seats. Comfortable? No, but it would have been impossible in a smaller vehicle.

That same Blazer, with scratches and damage from plowing through some scrub brush at 40 mph repaired, served us admirably in everyday city commuting. And, with the dealer-installed 11x15 Armstrong Tru-Trac tires, it was ready for the driver's command to push into snow, mud, sand or wherever the weekend adventurer might choose.

There are some people who would like their Blazer to be prestigious enough to park in the executive ga-

Never let it be said that the Chevy Blazer can't take it. These two action shots prove differently. However, we don't recommend you make this your normal practice. At rest the vehicle shows the styling that makes it fit right in—even at that exclusive country club.

age too. Well, why not? We know at east one case where an owner dumped his new Cad in favor of a Blazer—and loves it. Of course, to be really in, you may have to dress up the Blazer. Custom wheels and large tires, winch, roof rack, external spare, auxiliary gas cans and driving lights are favorites to start off with. These items add to the rugged outdoor image and are certain to be noticed in the city, but they won't rate a second glance out in the boonies because everyone else in sight will have the same ones.

Frankly, we've always had a haunting suspicion that some of the best equipped and shiniest Blazers (including other 4x4s) seen on the city streets rarely get used off-road. It's just that the macho symbolism of controlling such a device gives the

driver a special trip, and he need not venture off-road to realize the benefits of driving a rugged vehicle.

Let's expand on the test vehicle. It was capable of doing everything we asked it to do, and after a 3000-mile mix of ordinary driving coupled with about 500 really serious miles the only mechanical complaint was that the standard shock absorbers were used up. That is not uncommon, and explains why there is a thriving after-market business in specialty shocks for those drivers who are serious about bouncing over the outback.

A Blazer can be ordered in dress from a neat fabric top to a removable hardtop, the latter being more popular. The removable part of the hardtop is mostly for show—we've never seen a late model with the top off. Actually it would be easy enough; the

front seats would be covered and the built-in rollcage would be intact. But where does one store a top of this size and weight?

Most customers order a Blazer with top, a $5483 basic package. Depending upon preferences for comfort and convenience options, not to mention financial considerations, one may choose from engines beginning with a 250-cubic-inch six at 100 hp, a 305-inch V8 (140 hp), a 350 V8 at 165 horses, and our choice, a 400-inch V8 which delivers 175 hp. If you opt for the two-wheel-drive Blazer, not considered here, the engine cutoff is at 350 inches. There are limited choices in axle ratios, and ours had the optional 3.73:1 (3.07 is standard). While it emphasized off-the-line performance, it also emphasized marginal fuel economy.

CHEVY BLAZER

The fact that the Blazer is intended to be at home in sophisticated surroundings should be evident by the other options available. We selected a test unit with most of what Chevy offers and here are the most significant features: rear seat, tinted glass, air conditioning, locking rear differential, cruise control, Hydra-matic transmission, 31-gallon fuel tank, fuel-tank shield plate, tilt steering wheel, power steering, clock, AM/FM radio, and such niceties as chromed grille and bumper guards, special two-tone paint and Cheyenne equipment. At Chevrolet, Cheyenne isn't in Wyoming, it's in the parts department, and includes a lot of attractive chrome trim, body insulation, wood-grain instrument trim with extra instruments, a cigar lighter, dual horns and extra interior rugs/trim. The package also includes special hub caps, a meaningless gesture if you happen to scrap the stock wheels and tires as we did. The package listed at $735, and is probably worth the cost. A skeptical Blazer customer might spend a day or so juggling option combinations in an effort to beat the Cheyenne package price, but it is doubtful that he would save more than a couple of bucks.

Although they are not on the option list, we added a set of Trail Scout white spoke wheels ($29.95 each) and Armstrong Tru-Trac 11x15s (retail $59.95 per tire). The wheel/tire combo came from Rancho Chevrolet's Off-Road Center in Reseda, California, but prices may vary depending on the retailer.

We wanted the biggest set of tires that could be stuffed into the wheel openings, and Chevy's max size is 10x15. It wasn't so much that the extra inch would help, but we've learned that the oversize Armstrongs are at least as quiet as factory optional tires, and most certainly do an equal or better job when the going gets tough.

Total price of our test Blazer, including $464 destination to Los Angeles, was $9354; certainly not a low-bucks vehicle, but one which must be considered good value, especially compared with other four-wheel-drive machines.

Whenever you punch a big hole in $10,000, the product had better perform—and performance is what we set out to test. As a general statement we can say that the Blazer will go anywhere other 4x4s will go, and in most cases do the job more com-

Our test vehicle was fitted with accessory rims and tires that made climbing the rough, rutted road shown here a simple task. Dropping down into the main rut provided some anxious moments, but the full-time four-wheel drive pulled us out with no problem.

fortably. We climbed a rocky trail, step by tortuous step, plowed through sandy river bottoms, slipped along wet clay roads, splashed through a step ahead of a desert flash flood (a foolish stunt, but had we waited or turned back we would have missed dinner), and zipped along paved highways, which is where most of an off-road vehicle's mileage is spent.

After a searching analysis we had to answer the performance question, and our answer was that with a little faith the Blazer will carry you through. Acceleration, although not measured, was more than adequate for any traffic situation, while top speed was near impossible to measure. Because of the combination of tires and gearing the Blazer simply could not reach what we believed was a realistic terminal speed in distances available to us. With today's 55-mph limit the question is academic, but in Mexico where there are still a few open stretches, we were able to exceed 90 mph without difficulty.

The only complaint we could muster, other than inadequate shocks,

was fuel economy. We thought that the large tires might cancel out the degrading effect of the 3.73 gears, but it was not so. After correcting for an odometer which was 11 percent slow (we did not change the speedo drive gear when the tires were changed), the overall gas mileage at legal highway cruise ran consistently at 8.9 mpg. We did use the air conditioning, which might account for a mile or so off the total. In other words, a featherfoot who likes open windows might squeeze 10 mpg from our Blazer. In off-road conditions we were unable to measure gas mileage with any accuracy except to report that the gauge seemed to drop by the minute. To be safe, a figure of five or six mpg should be used for strenuous off-roading—and that's why you see most 4x4s with auxiliary gas cans racked at the rear.

A brief comment on handling is in order—it's greatly improved. Early Blazers seemed to wander along the highway with a special flair for doing it their way. It wasn't dangerous, just annoying. At least one aftermarket accessory maker managed to im-

Even with the large tire and rear seat in place, luggage space is ample for a family of four. Take the rear seat out and you're basically looking at a short-bed pickup truck.

Chevy uses leaf springs both front and rear. Our test vehicle was equipped with the 400-c.i.d. engine, the top of the line for the 4x4 Blazer. The largest 2WD model engine is a 350-c.i.d.

If you didn't know better, you'd think the interior was that of a luxury car. The seats are extremely comfortable; door trim and carpeting are well appointed.

The 400-c.i.d. engine is hidden underneath the components for the power equipment. The engine has massive amounts of torque, and with the Turbo-Hydro it will take you anywhere.

prove on the wander problem—which Chevrolet engineers never really acknowledged was real. Our '77 test Blazer did not wander. In fact, it handled pretty well considering the fat all-terrain rubber placed on the road.

Off the road no one could object to how a Blazer picks its way through difficult terrain. Under certain conditions, the faster one drives the better, because the vehicle "floats" from bump to bump. The hazard here, of course, is the deep rut lurking out of phase with the others. Strike one too fast and the suspension could suffer. In normal off-roading all the driver needs is enough sense to select high or low range, and from either point move the transfer case lever into Lock position as required on very soft surface conditions. In the past, incidentally, it has been difficult to recognize Lock because the relationship of the transfer case shifter to its position marking plate was purely accidental. This year a light on the panel notes Lock, which makes positive lock engagement a reality without fishing through a difficult-to-feel shift se-

quence. Top to bottom, it shifts Lo Lock-Lo-Neutral-Hi-Hi Lock—quite simple, and now much easier with the indicator light.

As just about everyone knows, the Blazer features "full-time" four-wheel drive. What this really means is that power is split between front and rear wheels through an interaxle differential. In fact, all four wheels do not drive simultaneously with equal power. Some differential action is required on the front wheels. Without it, assuming a limited-slip front axle, steering would be difficult on pavement and there would be excessive wear on the front driving axle gears.

Our Blazer had a limited-slip rear. We selected the worst possible condition (a very steep hill with an inconsistent surface, soft to hard), selected Lo Lock for maximum traction and got stuck. Three wheels dug in while one front remained motionless. How come? By selecting Lock we had locked out the interaxle differential, thereby throwing equal power fore and aft. The limited-slip rear caused both rear wheels to work, but a conventional differential on the

front permitted the front wheel on the hardest surface to do nothing. The result was zero travel. And we had done exactly what is recommended under the circumstances.

It is entirely possible that if the guilty wheel had traction as soft as the other three, we might have buried all four and been just as stuck as before. On the other hand, we might have powered to the top of the hill. This means that four-wheel drive has limitations, and that even the best can get stuck so that hand labor or a winch will be the only way home.

Assuming we don't get stuck, there are some subtleties to roughing it in a Blazer which is equipped with all the comfort options currently extant. Dust, for example, can be reduced by turning on the air conditioning and pressurizing the interior slightly so that dust entrance is inhibited. Adjust temperature to suit and note that it works best when the system is recirculating interior air rather than drawing in fresh air from outside.

Other items, including tilt wheel and cruise control, speak for themselves. Cruise is nice on the high-

CHEVY BLAZER

way, and most handy when towing a trailer. Power brakes are standard, and we wouldn't be without power steering unless our aim was to develop biceps à la C. Atlas. The Blazer's front buckets were reasonably comfortable, while the center console is deep enough for someone to develop a mini-refrigerator for storing beverages. As long as we're going all the way, why not include power windows and door locks? Both items are available on '77 Chevy pickups, and the Blazer is born from the same engineering embryo.

In summary, the Blazer shaped up as a great combination off-road and family utility vehicle, with very few compromises. Granted, its interior is not as quiet on the highway as a new Caprice, but put 11x15 tires and four-wheel drive on a Caprice and it wouldn't be so quiet either. We'd like to see headrests at least on the front bucket seats, and as long as we're wishing, why not a reclining device for the passenger seat?

The bottom line, really, is whether or not the Blazer is a good buy. In the beginning we said that rating a Blazer depends on how it is to be used, and we'll stick with that. If it fits logically into a family's scheme of motoring then it is a good buy, and one need not load it with every option to make it palatable. Although we used all the options, we enjoyed the basic vehicle just as much. ●

During our time with the Blazer we found that it could withstand a great deal. Waterproofing the engine is a good idea; we ran the car in water up to the center of the axle and it never missed a beat. Even though we did bottom the suspension once or twice, we were asking more of the vehicle than we should have.

HOT ROD 4-WHEEL & OFF-ROAD ROAD TEST SPECIFICATIONS
Chevrolet Blazer

GENERAL:
Base List Price $5483
Options .. 3-passenger rear seat, locking rear differential, 400-c.i.d. V8, tinted glass, air conditioning, external mirrors, 3.73 axle, cruise control, Turbo Hydra-matic, 31-gallon gas tank, fuel tank shield plate, tilt steering wheel, power steering, 4000-watt battery, electric clock, AM/FM radio, auxiliary speaker, chrome grille & bumper guards, California emissions, special 2-tone paint, Cheyenne equipment, custom bucket seats
Price As Tested $9354

ENGINE:
Type V8
Displacement .... 400 cubic inches
Bore & Stroke .... 4.125x3.75 inches
Compression Ratio 8.5:1
Net Power .... 175 hp @ 3600 rpm
Net Torque .... 290 ft/lbs @ 2800 rpm
Carburetion .... 2V Rochester Quadrajet
Recommended Fuel .... Regular or low-lead
Emissions Control .... Positive crankcase vent, exhaust gas recirculation

DRIVETRAIN:
Transmission .... Turbo Hydra-matic
Transfer Case .... Full-time NPG-203
Reduction Ratio 2.0:1
Gear Ratios .. Third: 1.00:1; Second: 1.48:1; First: 2.48:1; Reverse: 2.10:1; Final Drive Ratio: 3.73:1

CHASSIS:
Body/Frame .... Steel body on ladder-type frame

Suspension .... Front: Leaf springs; Rear: 2-stage leaf springs
Steering .... 3.5 turns lock to lock
Brake System .... Front: Disc; Rear: Drum
Wheels .... 15x6 inches
Tires .... Armstrong Tru-Trac 11x15
Gross Vehicle Weight Rating .... 6200 lbs

DIMENSIONS:
Wheelbase .... 106.5 inches
Ground Clearance At Lowest Point .... 8.25 inches
Track .... 66.7 inches front; 63.7 inches rear
Length .... 184.4 inches
Width .... 79.6 inches
Height .... 72 inches
Overhang .... 50.5 inches front; 45 inches rear
Fuel Capacity ...... 25 gallons stock, 31 with optional tank
Cargo Area ...... Length: 76.6 inches with rear seat removed; Width: 50 inches; Height: 47 inches
Curb Weight .... 4614 lbs

FUEL ECONOMY:
Mileage On 114-Mile Test Loop .... 14.9 mpg

OVERALL COMMENTS:
(On a scale of 1-10, 5 is average.)
Exterior Finish Quality 8
Interior Finish Quality 8
Handling 7
Brakes 9
Driver Comfort 8
Dashboard Readability/Accessibility 7
Acceleration In Traffic 8

This vehicle test on a '77 Chevy Blazer establishes a couple of "firsts" for **PICKUP, VAN & 4WD.**

The first "first" is that the Blazer is fitted with a 4-speed manual transmission. All Blazers previously tested by this publication's staff were equipped with automatic transmissions. This isn't surprising in consideration of the fact that approximately 83 percent of all Blazers are built with automatic gearboxes.

The second "first" is the new 305 cu-in. V-8. The Blazer offered the first opportunity for test crewmen to evaluate this small V-8 in a light-duty truck.

Other "firsts" could actually be added as well. The Blazer was fitted with a 4-speed manual transmission, and the vehicle had conventional four-wheel drive with free-running front hubs. Blazers tested to this time all had full-time 4wd. Chevy introduced a con-vertible top Blazer near the end of the '76 model year, too late to be included in this publication's evaluations of '76 model trucks. The '77 was fitted with a white vinyl top, the fourth "first."

Needless to say, test crewmen were anxious to take delivery of this very different Blazer. Arrangement was made to obtain the Blazer from Chevrolet Engineering in Warren, Mich. The Michigan delivery point was selected for several reasons, not the least of which was the opportunity to drive the▷

A Couple of "Firsts":
SOFT-TOP BLAZER
Conventional 4WD, 305 V-8, downpours and dust storms in a safari-style Chevy...

PHOTOS BY DON E. BROWN AND GLENN HAMAGUCHI

SOFT-TOP

vehicle across the U.S. for on- and off-pavement evaluation. As a result of more stringent emission control laws, the 305 V-8 cannot be sold in the state of California, thus the Michigan delivery point. Also, a stopover in Akron, Ohio, was scheduled to meet with Goodyear tire people. Before reporting on the vehicle test program and the cross-country run, here's a close look at the '77 Blazer and what's available.

The Blazer can be ordered either as a hardtop or convertible. Both tops are completely removable. However, most people who have purchased hardtop Blazers rarely, if ever, remove the tops. The convertible top can be rolled up on the sides and rear, safari style. With either top removed, the rear section, behind the driver's seat, is completely open. The driver/passenger compartment remains covered with a partial steel roof which contains a roll bar-type support.

Base price of the convertible is $100 less than the hardtop—$5383 vs $5483, FOB, Detroit.

Standard accommodation includes a driver's bucket seat only. A fold-up passenger bucket seat and 3-passenger rear bench seat are options. Two levels of trim are offered—Custom Deluxe (standard) and Cheyenne.

The Cheyenne package includes chrome front and rear bumpers, chrome hub caps, brush-finished applique panel on the tailgate, Cheyenne nameplates, upper and lower body side and tailgate moldings, plus wheelwell lip moldings. Interior items include cigar lighter, a console between bucket seats, passenger bucket seat, carpeting, front compartment headliner, instrument cluster to replace warning lamps, spare tire cover and color-keyed door trim panels, plus other finish and detail parts. The Cheyenne package lists for $735.

Chevy offers a Special two-tone paint scheme, or an Exterior Decor Package which includes the two-tone paint, plus the secondary paint color (invariably Frost white) on the hood with color-coordinated striping at either side of the hood panel, and also a bright spring-loaded, stand-up type hood emblem. The inboard hood stripe color matches the primary color, while the outboard stripe is of a contrasting color. The test Blazer was outfitted with the Exterior Decor Package trimmed in Mariner blue. Price of the package is $330 on the Custom Deluxe or $190 combined with the Cheyenne trim level.

Standard powertrain components for the Blazer include a 250-cu-in. in-line Six engine, 3-speed manual transmission, conventional 2-speed transfer case and 4.11:1 axle ratio. Other powerplant options are 305, 350 and 400 V-8s. Gearboxes in addition to the 3-speed manual are a 4-speed manual and 3-speed Turbo Hydra-matic. All

three transmissions are offered with 250 Six, 305 and 350 V-8s. However, the 400 V-8 can be specified only with the automatic. The 250 Six and 350 V-8 are not available with the Blazer in California.

As is Chevrolet policy, full-time 4wd is standard with the automatic transmission and conventional 4wd is available only with a manual transmission.

Axle ratios offered include a 3.07:1 and 3.73:1 in addition to 4.11:1 gearing. Perhaps the most effective all-around axle ratio offered by Chevy is the 3.40:1 ratio. Unfortunately, this ratio is restricted to two-wheel-drive pickups, vans and Suburbans. Evidentally, Dana/Spicer does not offer the 3.40 ratio with the Model 44 front drive axles that Chevy installs in Blazers. This is something of a manufacturer's mistake, as will be discussed later in this test report.

The 305 is an interesting addition to the Blazer engine lineup. This engine was supposed to be included as an option on '76 Chevy trucks. However, engine production was not sufficient to supply both passenger car and truck requirements during the '76 model run. In fact, at this writing, the 305 remains in short supply for truck installation.

Looking at the 305's specifications, there isn't all that much difference between this engine and the bigger-bore 350 V-8. Horsepower rating of the 305 is 140—25 hp less than the 350 at the same 3800 rpm for a difference of 18 percent. Torque output is much closer—235 vs 255, a difference of about 8 percent. However, the 305 achieves peak torque at 2000 rpm, 800 rpm lower than the 350. The 350 is equipped with a 4-barrel carburetor, whereas the 305 is fitted with a 2-barrel unit. The stroke of the two engines is identical at 3.48 in., but the bore of the 305 is smaller in diameter by 0.26 in.

Dual exhausts are optional with 305 and 350 V-8s, standard on the 400 V-8. Although Chevrolet does not release horsepower ratings to show the difference between single and dual exhausts, there can be no doubt the dual-equipped engines deliver greater horsepower. At an added cost of $33, the duals represent the best buy on the option list. Of course, the locking differential at $160 is a close second best buy for a 4wd Blazer, especially with full-time 4wd. Another wise purchase for the off-roader is the 31-gal. replacement fuel tank (standard tank is 25 gal.) at a cost of only $23.

The test Blazer was fitted with the dual exhaust system, locking rear differential with 3.07:1 ratio, 31-gal. fuel

Mich., after a flight from the West Coast editorial office of **PICKUP, VAN & 4WD.** The weather was bitterly cold in the Detroit area and did not improve with arrival in Akron, Ohio, to confer with some Goodyear engineers. Naturally, during the short meeting, the talk gravitated to off-pavement tires. Goodyear offers a comparatively new tire for off-road applications, the Wrangler R/T. Actually, the tire has been on the market for more than a year, but because of last year's lengthy rubber industry strike, the tire was not produced in quantity until recently. A set of the new Wranglers was mounted on Cragar Trail Master white spoke wheels to replace the Blazer's stock Suburbanites. The Wrangler R/T is an interesting tire. Of bias-belted construction, the Wrangler is fabricated with a polyester cord body with fiberglass cord belts. The four tires mounted on the Blazer were 31 x 11.50 x 15Bs and carried a maximum inflation pressure of 20 psi. A full report on the new Goodyears will be presented in a future issue of this publication.

The trip out of Akron was accom-

panied with a driving rainstorm and high winds. The Blazer handled extremely well on the rain-slick asphalt and met gusty sidewinds with very little road wander or drift. Of course, with conventional 4wd and free-running hubs, the Blazer was cruising in two-wheel drive.

It was feared that the high winds would cause the convertible top to slap against the sidebows to create a high noise level within the Blazer. Test crewmen regularly complain about noisy slap and buffeting in soft-top vehicles—hence the fears. The fears were unfounded. The vinyl top breathed in and out with shifting winds, but never flapped or buffeted. The sound level within the Blazer was higher than that recorded in hardtop Blazers, but this was because the vinyl top does not have the noise insulation that a hardtop offers. In other words, what noise was present within the Blazer came from outside the Blazer, not from the vinyl top itself. This fact was borne out in a later test with a precision sound meter. The '77 Blazer registered a sound level of 76.5 dBA (quiet as most hardtop vehicles), compared with 74.5 dBA recorded in a previous test of a '76 Blazer hardtop.

The interior of the vehicle remained dry even with the wind-driven rain pounding the Blazer on all sides.

In the vicinity of Columbus, Ohio, the Blazer seemed to be running out of horsepower. It became necessary to press the accelerator to the floor to maintain the legal limit of 55 mph. Doubt increased as to the wisdom of matching the new 305 V-8 with a 3.07 axle. Even on level stretches of pavement, the 305 did not display a reserve of abundant power for passing. Downshifting to third, however, would allow passing another vehicle in a minimum amount of time. It was not until the next day when a radio newscaster stated that winds in the Columbus area had▷

Cheyenne trim includes instruments instead of warning lamps, woodgrained panels and console, above. Right, cargo deck carpeting is part of the Cheyenne package; bench seat is optional.

tank, power steering and brakes—in addition to the 305 V-8 and 4-speed manual transmission. Other options included Cheyenne package, rear bench seat, wheelhouse carpeting, tinted glass, below eye-line mirrors, heavy-duty front springs with heavy-duty front and rear shock absorbers, fuel tank skidplate, tilt steering wheel, styled spoke wheels, tachometer, Exterior Decor Package, AM radio and L78 x 15B Goodyear Suburbanite tires. Total price of the test Blazer was $7941, not including freight.

As stated earlier, the test crewman took delivery of the Blazer in Warren,

SOFT-TOP

The 305-cu.-in. V-8 doesn't do much to fill the Blazer's capacious engine compartment. With 4-speed manual gearbox, the small engine was adequate for off-road work.

been blowing 40 to 50 mph with gusts to 70 that the realization came that perhaps, after all, the Blazer with a 305 V-8 isn't underpowered.

Heading into the flatlands of Oklahoma brought good weather, minimal wind and level turnpikes. The 305 performed more strongly here, but still lacked the power punch necessary to accelerate quickly in high gear at freeway cruise. The optional 3.73 axle would be a much more effective alternative, especially with the taller-than-stock Wrangler tires. The most useful ratio for performance and economy would be a 3.40, but as cited earlier, this ratio is not available on Chevy 4wd vehicles. A steady 55 mph is accomplished at only 2000 rpm, right at the 305's peak torque, but the Blazer, at over 4700 lb, is a tad heavy for the small-sized 305 with a tall axle.

Once onto the flatlands, it became evident the Blazer was subject to a recurring lean surge. This phenomenon was most noticeable between 60 and 70 mph. For some unexplainable reason, the surge would disappear and then return some miles later. It should be pointed out that if the Blazer had been equipped with an automatic transmission, chances are the lean surge would never have been noticed.

Arrival in New Mexico provided an opportunity to log some off-pavement time with the Blazer. A couple of years ago, (PV4, June '75) test crewmen drove a new '75 Ford Econoline van off-pavement from El Paso to the Pacific Ocean. A portion of this route was re-traced with the Blazer.

If the winds encountered in Ohio were severe, they were just a warmup for New Mexico. The high winds picked up topsoil from farmlands, resulting in almost zero visibility in clouds of dust. Some small communities could hardly

be seen through the swirling grit. Other than the obvious discomfort of driving in a dust storm, the Blazer performed beautifully. Heavy-duty suspension, combined with the low air pressure Goodyears, soaked up the rough terrain of the country roads. Handling was precise, with no side-hop even on washboard sections. A side trail took the Blazer up a rock-strewn creek bed. Engaging 4wd and locking the hubs allowed some slow rock crawling. The 6.55 low gear was sufficient for easing up and over obstacles without the necessity to engage low range, even with the tall 3.07 axles.

Back on the West Coast the Blazer was taken to Orange County International Raceway for performance testing. Considering the small V-8, the Blazer performed reasonably well in the acceleration runs. The standing-start quarter-mile was traversed in 19.8 sec with a terminal speed of 70 mph. The

---

New low pressure Goodyear Wrangler R/Ts provided firm grip on rain-slick pavement, precise handling off-road.

4-speed evidently helped here. The 305 pulls strongly as long as engine rpm is kept above 2500. Test crewmen observed that the 305 will spark knock (ping) badly if lugged in third or fourth gear at low engine rpm.

The cross-country run produced an average of 11 mpg. This, of course, was recorded while bucking strong headwinds for long portions of the trip, as well as maintaining a cruising speed somewhat in excess of 55 mph most of the time. It was thought that fuel economy would improve significantly when checked with electronic fuel flow test gear while maintaining a maximum speed of 55 mph. Unfortunately, the Blazer only recorded 12.8 mpg in the city/freeway driving cycle. One of the prime reasons to specify the 305 V-8 would be in the interest of economy. However, at 12.8 mpg, the 305 delivers only about 1 mpg better fuel mileage than several Chevy 4wd vehicles equipped with 350 and 400 V-8s tested during 1976.

It's possible that, fitted with the 3.73 axle instead of the 3.07, the Blazer's performance would improve without much, if any, sacrifice in fuel economy.

The '77 Blazer is a pleasure to drive. The convertible top offers a great deal of flexibility for various types of funtruckin'. Quality control in assembly was observed throughout the vehicle as all trim components and moldings fit properly. The bucket seats, combined with the variable positioning of the tilt steering wheel, put the driver in a comfortable position even for a 4000-mile cross-country jaunt. A Blazer isn't the most effective or efficient vehicle for hard-core off-roading, but it's difficult to beat this Chevy unit for an all-purpose vehicle that takes the wife to the supermarket, hauls the family's little league ballplayers to practice, takes dad to work and back, and allows the entire family to thrash the outback on weekends. The '77 version of the Blazer is no exception. ●

PRICES

Basic list, FOB Detroit
K-5 Six with convertible top $5383
K-5 Six with hardtop $5483

Standard Equipment ....250-cu.-in. in-line Six engine, 3-spd manual transmission, 2-spd conventional transfer case, heater/defroster, 2-spd electric wiper/washers, driver bucket seat, painted front and rear bumpers, removable fiberglass hardtop or vinyl convertible top, power front disc brakes, H78 x 15B tires.

GENERAL

Curb weight, lb (test model).....................4735
Weight distribution, %, front/rear 54/46
GVWR (test model).................................6200
Optional GVWRs ....none
Wheelbase, in..106.5
Track, front/rear 65.8/62.7
Overall length 184.4
Overall height 72.0
Overall width 79.6
Overhang, front/rear 33.4/44.5
Approach angle, degrees 34
Departure angle, degrees 23
Ground clearances (test model):
Front axle 8.9
Rear axle 8.6
Oil pan 17.3
Transfer case 11.5
Fuel tank 13.9
Exhaust system (lowest point)............11.3
Fuel tank capacity (U.S. gal.) 25
Auxiliary..................................31-gal. tank, $23

ACCOMMODATION

Standard seats ....driver bucket seat
Optional seats ....passenger bucket seat, $95; rear bench seat, $179
Headroom, in...38.1
Accelerator pedal to seatback, max 45.1
Steering wheel to seatback, max 18.2
Seat to ground 36.4
Floor to ground 21.9
Unobstructed load space (length x width x height).
With seats in place ....42.0 x 50.0 x 42.3
Rear folded or removed ...76.0 x 50.0 x 42.3
Tailgate (width x height)................66.8 x 22.7

INSTRUMENTATION

Instruments ....speedometer, odometer, fuel gauge
Warning lights.............oil pressure, alternator, water temp, brake system warning, hazard warning, seat belt warning
Optional ....voltmeter, water temp and oil pressure gauges, $21; tachometer, $76

ENGINES

Standard ....250-cu.-in. in-line Six*
Bore x stroke, in..............................3.87 x 3.53
Compression ratio 8.0:1
Net horsepower @ rpm ....100 @ 3600
Net torque @ rpm, lb-ft ....175 @ 1800
Type fuel required..............leaded or unleaded
*Not available in California
Optional 305-cu.-in. V-8, $120*
Bore x stroke, in..............................3.74 x 3.48
Compression ratio 8.5:1
Net horsepower @ rpm ....140 @ 3800
Net torque @ rpm, lb-ft ....235 @ 2000
Type fuel required..............leaded or unleaded
*Not available in California
Optional 350-cu.-in. V-8, $210
Bore x stroke, in..............................4.00 x 3.48
Compression ratio 8.5:1
Net horsepower @ rpm ....165 @ 3800
Net torque @ rpm, lb-ft ....255 @ 2800
Type fuel required..............leaded or unleaded
Optional 400-cu.-in. V-8, $369*
Bore x stroke, in............................4.125 x 3.75
Compression ratio 8.5:1
Net horsepower @ rpm ....175 @ 3600
Net torque @ rpm, lb-ft ....290 @ 2800
Type fuel required..............leaded or unleaded
*Available only with automatic transmission

DRIVETRAIN

Standard transmission ....3-spd manual*
Clutch dia., in.............11.0 (six), 12.0 (V-8)
Transmission ratios: 3rd 1.00:1
2nd 1.68:1**
1st 2.85:1**
Synchromesh ....all forward gears
*Not available with full-time 4wd or 400 V-8
**Gear ratios are 2.99:1 for first and 1.75:1 for second with 350 V-8
Optional ....4-spd manual, $142*
Transmission ratios: 4th 1.00:1
3rd 1.70:1
2nd 3.58:1
1st 6.55:1
Synchromesh ....2nd, 3rd and 4th gear
*Not available with full-time 4wd or 400 V-8
Optional ....3-spd automatic, $315*
Transmission ratios: 3rd 1.00:1
2nd 1.52:1
1st 2.52:1
*Not available with conventional 4wd
Rear axle type ....semi-floating hypoid
Final drive ratios 3.07:1, 3.73:1, 4.11:1
Overdrive ....none
Free-running front hubs.................std with conventional 4wd
Limited slip differential $160
Transfer case ....New Process 205 2-spd (conventional 4wd), New Process 203 2-spd (full-time 4wd)*
Transfer case ratios ....1.96:1 and 1.00:1 (NP 205), 2.00:1 and 1.00:1 (NP 203)
*New Process 205 available only with manual transmission. New Process 203 available only with automatic transmission

CHASSIS & BODY

Body/frame ....ladder-type frame with separate steel body
Brakes (std).............front, 11.86-in. dia. disc; rear, 11.15 x 2.75-in. drum
Brake swept area, sq in..............................432
Swept area/ton (max load)....................139
Power brakes ....std
Steering type (std) ....recirculating ball
Steering ratio 24:1
Power steering $188
Power steering ratio.............variable 16/13:1
Turning circle, ft.......................................37.0
Wheel size (std) ....15 x 6JJ
Optional wheel sizes ....15 x 7 Rally, 15 x 8 Rally, 15 x 7 styled spoke, 15 x 8 styled spoke, 16 x 5K
Tire size (std) ....H78 x 15B
Optional tire sizes ....L78 x 15B, LR78 x 15C, 10 x 15B, 6.50 x 16C, 7.00 x 15C, 7.00 x 16C

SUSPENSION

Front suspension ....leaf springs on live axle with tube shocks
Front axle capacity, lb 3600
Optional ....none
Rear suspension ....semi-elliptic leaf springs on live axle with tube shocks
Rear axle capacity, lb 3750
Optional ....none
Additional suspension options...........HD front springs (includes HD shocks), $60

TEST MODEL

K-5 Blazer with convertible top, Cheyenne trim level, 305 V-8, 4-spd manual transmission, dual exhausts, rear bench seat, tinted glass, wheelhouse carpeting, below eyeline mirrors, HD front springs and shocks, 31-gal. fuel tank, tilt steering wheel, power steering, styled wheels, tachometer, AM radio, two-tone paint, 3.07 locking rear axle, L78 x 15B tires (stock tires were replaced with Goodyear Wrangler 11.50 x 15)
Factory list price ....(does not include freight), $7941

ACCELERATION

Time to speed, sec:
0-30 mph 4.3
0-45 mph 8.5
0-60 mph 14.3
0-70 mph 19.8
Standing start, ¼-mile, sec.....................19.8
Speed at end, mph 70

SPEED IN GEARS

High range, 4th (3400 rpm) 92
3rd (4000 rpm)...65
2nd (4000 rpm)..30
1st (4000 rpm)...17
Low range, 4th (4000 rpm).........................55
3rd (4000 rpm)...33
2nd (4000 rpm)..15
1st (4000 rpm)...8
Engine rpm @ 55 mph 2000

BRAKE TESTS

Pedal pressure required for ½-g deceleration rate from 60 mph, lb 40
Stopping distance from 60 mph, ft 167
Fade: Percent increase in pedal pressure for 6 stops from 60 mph 77
Overall brake rating ....excellent

INTERIOR NOISE

Idle in neutral, dBA 60.5
Maximum during acceleration 76.5
At steady 60 mph cruising speed 76.5

OFF PAVEMENT

Hillclimbing ability ....excellent
Maneuverability ....very good
Turnaround capability ....excellent
Driver visibility ....fair
Handling ....very good
Ride ....very good

ON PAVEMENT

Handling ....very good
Ride ....good
Driver comfort.............................very good
Engine response ....good

FUEL CONSUMPTION

City/freeway driving, mpg 12.8
Off pavement 8.7
Range, city/freeway driving, miles 320
Range, off pavement...............................217

CHEVROLET BLAZER

**The heavyweight American approach to the 4WD workhorse.
Strong-looking with good performance, transmission and ventilation.
Primitive suspension results in poor ride.
Internal carrying capacity poor in relation to size and weight.
Expensive at over £9,000, the Blazer is nevertheless a good-looker**

FOUR-WHEEL DRIVE vehicles are enjoying something of a vogue at the moment. However packaged, the sale of freedom, in the guise of ''go anywhere'' vehicles, has become big business, but until recently the only American products to satisfy this market have been the somewhat basic Jeep and the Pioneer.

The Chevrolet Blazer K10 is what might be regarded as a typically American approach to the expanding market. There are at least 18 basic options in engine sizes and transmission types available in the US, but Lendrum and Hartnum have chosen to import only this one. The K10 is near the top of the range, and has a 350 cu in (5.7-litre) V8 engine with a four-barrel carburettor, automatic transmission (Turbo Hydramatic), and the Cheyanne cloth trim option. Chevrolet have used a very basic, permanently-engaged four-wheel-drive system. Drive is taken from the gearbox to a two speed transfer box beneath the front passenger seat, splitting the torque equally front to rear. It has a high and low range, the latter being a straight 2:1 reduction, and although the centre differential is lockable in both ratios, our Blazer was not fitted with the optional limited slip axle differentials. Normal Hooke jointed shafts take the drive to a leaf-sprung rear axle, and forward to a similar axle equipped with an offset differential, and a very basic fork welded onto each end into which the stub axles fit. The use of constant velocity joints has not been considered necessary, and Hooke joints positioned on the king pin axis suffice. Their shortcomings can only be felt through the steering when using a lot of power and lock at the same time.

Weighing in at over 2.3 tons unladen and costing just over £9,000, the K10 350 Blazer is one of the biggest and most expensive such vehicles available at the moment. It is also very comprehensively equipped. Built around a massive girder frame chassis, in the traditional manner, the vehicle has all the features considered necessary for traversing the American continent, including air conditioning, electric windows, tinted glass, engine oil cooler, transfer box and fuel tank shields, electronic ignition and power steering. The rear hardtop has sliding windows, and small quarter lights aft of the doors, that can be adjusted to direct air onto the occupants. The hardtop is removable, by undoing 12 bolts, but the lack of any replacement bulkhead makes this rather a draughty exercise.

Performance

Chevrolet claim a rather unimpressive-sounding 165 bhp (SAE) at 3,800 rpm, and 255 lb. ft. torque at 2,800 rpm on an 8.5 to 1 compression ratio for the 5.7-litre V8. However, it is enough when mated to the excellent three-speed automatic gearbox, to accelerate 2.35 tons from rest to 70 mph in just over 20 sec in high ratio, and 19.4 sec in low. Standing quarter times are almost identical to those for 70 mph, and it is a tribute to the excellent matching of engine torque to gearbox characteristics that we found it almost impossible to improve our acceleration times by holding individual gears.

Other road users tended to assume that a vehicle of this type and size would get in their way, but were visibly surprised by the excellent step-off from rest, and mid-range overtaking abilities, typified by a 30-50 mph acceleration time of 5.4 sec, bettering the equivalent Range Rover time by over a second. For normal road use the transfer box selector is positioned in high ratio, and left alone, and if one needs to "change down" so to speak, the procedure is to stop, or slow down to a near standstill, select neutral on the normal steering column selector, and then move the central transfer box selector into the mode required.

Geared at exactly 24 mph per 1,000 rpm in top and high ratio, motorway cruising is a quiet and relaxing business, although at 70 mph, fuel is being consumed at the rate of 11.3 miles to the gallon, from the 26 gallon tank. One is aware of the Blazer's size at high speed mainly because wind direction has such an effect on the amount of throttle one has to use. Our best one-way run at MIRA was 97 mph, but only 86 mph was achieved against a 10-12 mph headwind. The mean maximum of 90 mph corresponds almost exactly to maximum power at 3,800 rpm. To the prospective Blazer owner, these figures will not be of much concern. Held back only by physical size at high speed it has enough power to

the end of the day, what one is paying for in terms of fuel consumption. For a vehicle that is approximately 15 per cent larger overall than a Range Rover, it has if anything slightly less load-carrying space internally, and weighs at least seven cwt more. It follows, that to achieve a similar performance it has to use more fuel, the overall figure being 10.6 mpg.

Ride, Handling and Brakes

The product planning department at Chevrolet seem to have directed their energies towards styling rather than any attempt at producing a sophisticated suspension package. Like the CJ6 Jeep and Toyota Land Cruiser, the Blazer uses leaf springs all round but has a more sensible 50/50 weight distribution. Unladen it rides uncomfortably hard and harsh, and probably because of the

Above: A degree of athleticism is an asset when trying to work on the engine

Left: Negotiating the track shown below at 25 mph caused violent pitching, leading to intermittent total loss of steering control. The rear window has to be wound down with the centre lock/window winder, before opening the tailgate from the inside

Opposite page: With striking looks, the Blazer is at home on relatively smooth Forestry Commission land

climb anything that is likely to be encountered off the road, and it simply shot up the 1 in 3 test hill from a standing start. Any limitation is likely to come only from a lack of tyre adhesion.

Switching on the air conditioning has a noticeable effect on engine revs, and obviously absorbs a significant amount of power. Most of our test mileage was conducted while breathing unconditioned air, which suggests that consumption figures could well fall below 10 mpg for the enthusiastic driver who is also a clean air addict.

Economy

It would be unreasonable to expect such a large and heavy vehicle to be anything but thirsty by European standards, and one has to assess at

short wheelbase, violent pitching can be induced over rippled surfaces. The front suspension appeared to have an incompatible spring/damper combination, that allowed the unpleasant motion to start. Those who drove it usually commented unfavourably on the lightness of the steering, and with under three-and-a-half turns from lock to lock it is relatively direct, giving rise to criticisms of poor directional stability at high speed. However, when manoeuvring in the city, or trying to pick one's way through the rough, it really comes into its own, and takes all the sweat out of the operation. Given a smooth road, and such stiff suspension, corners can be taken very briskly indeed, but as soon as a bump intervenes, the Blazer protests with a judder and a sideways jump. The driver soon learns to ignore shortcomings in ride

and can press on regardless, for once "into it" the Blazer can be thrown around with amazing verve. Naturally enough one would expect a four-wheel drive vehicle to understeer with the power on, and the mere fact that one can talk in such terms about such a vehicle suggests that it cannot really be too bad. Lifting the throttle when really wound up halfway through a corner produces an incredibly gentle change to mild oversteer. Locking the centre differential for use on tarmac is not recommended in the interests of tyre wear, and it would be difficult to imagine conditions that would warrant doing it, though by treading hard on the accelerator while rounding a sharp corner in the wet a front wheel can be made to spin momentarily. It is only under these conditions that the effect of the Hooke jointed front drive shafts can

be felt. It is interesting to note that the average lock between kerbs of just over 40 ft does not seem to suffer unduly from their limitations. A hefty steering damper no doubt also plays a part in cushioning any geometry and suspension failings for the driver.

Quite why Chevrolet have chosen to equip the Blazer with such stiff springs is unclear, unless the American user usually carries heavy loads for most of the time. As mentioned before, negotiating badly rutted tracks at quite modest speeds usually results in the most violent pitching motion, which at its worst throws the driver from his seat at precisely the moment he experiences total loss of steering effect, due to the front wheels being in the air. The best technique for poor surfaces is to go as slowly as is comfortable; we could not discover a speed that the Blazer would "float" over the potholes and ruts. Although it looks greater, ground clearance is only 8½ in., just an inch more than the Range Rover, and half-an-inch more than the Jeep.

Prospective customers who are considering using the Blazer for towing, will be disappointed in the braking performance that we achieved. Throughout the wide variety of pressures (45-120 lb mean), required to achieve our 10 0.5g stops, the brakes behaved unpredictably, pulling left or right at random, especially towards the end. No actual fade was encountered, and on the dry braking strip from 30 mph, 100 lb pedal pressure produced a 1.0g stop, any further pressure simply locking the front wheels. This state of affairs would normally lead one to expect that the front brakes would lock even earlier on a wet road. In fact anything more than gentle braking in these conditions produced instant rear-wheel locking, which would quite likely be further aggravated by the attachment of a trailer. It seems that once the front disc brake pads are hot a reasonable state of brake balance exists, if erratic in direction; but on a vehicle of this type and (more important) weight, upon which the payload and towing capacity depend, a more effective braking system should be considered by the manufacturers. The parking brake had no trouble in holding the Blazer on a 1 in 3 slope.

Chevrolet Blazer

Behind the wheel

Sitting over three feet above the road gives one a distinct visibility advantage, which is just as well, for being left-hand drive and 10in. wider than the Range Rover, one has to measure the approach toward a vehicle of similar size with care, especially in a country lane. The door mirrors protrude at least another 8in. either side, which can further complicate matters; though fortunately they bend flat without damage when brushing against anything significant.

Our test car was fitted with most of the available instrumentation. On the left of the angled instrument panel are the water temperature, oil pressure, and battery voltage gauges, together with the clock. Directly underneath these are a rather strange little wiper switch, and straight push-pull lights switch. The speedometer and fuel gauge occupy the most dominant position, the latter taking the place of the clock when the rev counter is fitted. The steering wheel is adjustable for angle with a small lever mounted on the left-hand side of the column, behind that which operates the indicators and horn. Contrary to recent trends there is a foot-operated dip switch. Consisting of a foot pedal on the left of the foot well, the parking brake is released by a nearby toggle lever, which in turn is close to the bonnet release.

The brake release system could not have been better designed to cope with a smooth hill start, while towing a large load; just a light pull on the release lever, while opening the throttle, gives a perfect start every time.

One of the many air conditioning vents tops the third part of the instrument panel, below which are the air conditioning and heater controls, and the radio. Fuses are located on a panel on the firewall next to the steering column. Unfortunately the driving seat has neither back rest angle, nor enough rearward adjustment, nor did it tip to allow entry into the rear. The seat belts were of the reel type, thus allowing the belt to be adjusted loosely, without winding itself back, rather negating the value of belts in the first place.

Living with the Blazer

To the extent that one can have a conversation with a friendly bus driver at the lights and then win the ensuing grand prix; and have to use a stool to clean the ice off the screen if you are short, one lives *for* the Blazer. There is no fear that one's progress will go unnoticed. Having accepted the fact, attention must be directed toward other areas. the interior seems to be not quite sure at whom it is aimed. Carpeted throughout as it is, one could not imagine loading sheep into the back and going to market, much as they might enjoy breathing conditioned air from the many outlets throughout the interior; and anyway the spare wheel dominates the rear stowage space and reduces the maximum width at floor level to a mere 38in. There are some nice and practical touches — floor level lighting, and recesses for holding drinking vessels in the centre console, give one the impression that two-day camping trips across the local Californian desert are what Chevrolet had in mind with this particular variant. Access to the rear seats is only past the tipping front passenger seat, and when strapped in the occupants suffer no less from the uncompromising ride. The rear door/tailgate is opened by first unlocking the window winder from the outside, winding the window down (without removing the skin from fingers), and then releasing the main catch inside to drop the tailgate. This arrangement precludes the provision of a rear window wiper, which on this vehicle is an absolute essential, as all the road dirt seems to collect there, reducing vision to almost zero very quickly. One then has

Cheap looking but accurate instruments are flanked on the right by, from top to bottom, heater outlet, heater controls and radio. The ducting pipe to the door outlet can be clearly seen, as can one drinking vessel retainer in the centre console

Specification

ENGINE

	Front, four-wheel drive
Cylinders	V8
Main bearings	5
Cooling	Water
Fan	Viscous
Bore, mm (in.)	101.6mm 4in.
Stroke, mm (in.)	88.4mm 3.48in.
Capacity, cc (in³)	5,740 c.c. 350 cu. in.
Valve gear	ohv
Camshaft drive	Chain
Compression ratio	8.5-to-1
Octane rating	97 RM
Carburettor	Rochester four-barrel
Max power	165 bhp (SAE) at 3,800 rpm
Max torque	255 lb ft at 2,800 rpm

TRANSMISSION

Type		Turbo Hydramatic
Gear	Ratio	mph/1000rpm
Top	1.0	24.0
Assuming no converter slip		
Inter	1.48	16.0
Low	2.48	9.5
Final drive gear	Hypoid bevel	
Ratio	3.73 to 1	

SUSPENSION

Front—location	Live axle
springs	Leaf
dampers	Telescopic
anti-roll bar	Yes
Rear—location	Live axle
springs	Leaf
dampers	Telescopic
anti-roll bar	Yes

STEERING

Type	Recirculating ball
Power assistance	Standard
Wheel diameter	16in.

BRAKES

Front	11.6 in. dia. disc
Rear	11.15 in. dia. drum
Servo	Yes

WHEELS

Type	Pressed steel
Rim width	6J
Tyres — make	Goodyear
— type	All weather/wintertread
— size	LT 10-15 H78x15B (4PR)

EQUIPMENT

Battery	12 volt 55 Ah
Alternator	61 amp
Headlamps	Sealed beam
Reversing lamp	Standard
Hazard warning	Standard
Electric fuses	12 (on Firewall)
Screen wipers	2-speed and intermittent
Screen washer	Electric
Interior heater	Air blending
Interior trim	Cloth seats, pvc headlining
Floor covering	Carpet
Jack	Screw type, located under bonnet
Jacking points	4 under axles
Windscreen	Laminated
Underbody protection	Paint system

MAINTENANCE

Fuel tank	26 Imp. galls (118 litres)
Cooling system	26 pints (inc. heater)
Engine sump	9½ pints SAE 10/50W
Gearbox	18 pints SAE ATF220
Final drive	3½ pints SAE 90 (each)
Grease	12 points
Valve clearance	Inlet hydraulic Exhaust hydraulic
Ignition timing	8 deg BTDC (stroboscopic at 600 rpm)
Spark plug—type	AC
—gap	.030in.
Tyre pressures	F28; R28psi (normal driving)
Max payload	6,200 lb (2,815 kg)

Maximum Speeds

Gear	mph	kph	rpm
Top (mean)	90	144	3,750
(best)	97	155	4,050
Inter	80	128	5,000
Low	56	89	5,900

Acceleration

True mph	Time (sec)	Low	Speedo mph
30	**5.0**	(3.7)	30
40	**7.3**	(6.0)	40
50	**10.3**	(9.0)	49
60	**14.5**	(13.1)	58
70	**20.5**	(19.4)	69
80	**31.7**		78
90	**51.2**		89

Standing ¼-mile:
20 sec, 69 mph
19.4 sec in low, 70 mph
kilometre:
37 sec, 84 mph

mph	Inter	Low
10-30	—	3.4
20-40	—	4.2
30-50	—	5.4
40-60	7.6	—
50-70	10.6	—
60-80	18.4	—
70-90	—	—

Consumption

Fuel 97 RM four-star
Overall mpg: 10.6
(26.8 litres / 100km)
Calculated (DIN) mpg: 9.6
(29.6 litres / 100km)

Constant speed:

mph	mpg
30	17.1
40	16.8
50	15.3
60	13.6
70	11.3
80	9.2

Autocar formula
Hard driving, difficult conditions
9.0 mpg
Average driving, average conditions
12.2 mpg
Gentle driving, easy conditions
13.8 mpg
Grade of fuel: Premium, 4-star
(97 RM)
Mileage recorder: 1 per cent
under reading

Oil
Consumption (SAE 20/50)
1,000 miles / pint

Brakes

Fade (from 70 mph in neutral)
Pedal load for 0.5g stops in lb

	start/end		start/end
1	55/35	6	75/100
2	75/60	7	65/85
3	85/90	8	65/65
4	120/140	9	60/55
5	90/120	10	60/55

Response (from 30 mph in neutral)

Load (lb)	g	Distance (ft)
20	0.22	137
40	0.48	63
60	0.73	41
80	0.98	31
100	1.00	30
Handbrake	0.22	137

Max gradient 1 in 3

Clutch

Test Conditions

Wind	10 mph
Temperature	9 deg C (48 deg F)
Barometer	29.7 in. Hg
Humidity	70 per cent
Surface	wet asphalt and concrete
Test distance	887 miles

Figures taken at 801 miles by our own staff at the Motor Industry Research Association proving ground at Nuneaton.

All Autocar test results are subject to world copyright and may not be reproduced in whole or part without the Editor's written permission.

Regular Service

Interval (miles)

Change	3,000	6,000	12,000
Engine oil	Yes	Yes	Yes
Oil filter	Yes	Yes	Yes
Gearbox oil	No	Check	Yes
Spark plugs	No	No	Yes
Air cleaner	No	Yes	Yes

Total cost £17.75 £52.75 £100.82
(Assuming labour at £6.50/hour)

Parts Cost
(including VAT)

Brake pads (2 wheels) — front	£50.53
Brake shoes (2 wheels) — rear	£33.79
Complete twin exhaust system	£337.53
Tyre — each (typical advertised)	£75.62
Windscreen	£221.76
Headlamp unit	£37.49
Front wing	£152.46
Rear bumper	£120.65

Warranty Period
12 months / 12,000 miles

Weight

Kerb:
46 cwt / 5,152 lb / 2,339 kg
(Distribution F/R, 50/50)
As tested:
49.1 cwt / 5,499 lb / 2,496 kg

Turning circles:
Between kerbs:
L, 39ft 4in.; R, 41ft 1in.
Between walls:
L, 41ft 3in.; R, 42ft 8in.
Turns, lock to lock, 3.4

OVERALL LENGTH 15' 4.4"
23"
13" 60.5"
19"
65"
49"
50.5"
64.5"
64.5"
18"
OVERALL WIDTH 6' 7.6"
26.5"
37"
37"
42"
21-26"
30-33"
35"
9.5"
22"
58"
35-39"
15"
35-40"
18"
30"
OVERALL HEIGHT 6' 0"
GROUND CLEARANCE 7"
WHEELBASE 8' 10.5"
FRONT TRACK 5' 6.7"
REAR TRACK 5' 3.7"

Test Scorecard

(Average of scoring by
Autocar Road Test team)

Ratings: 6 Excellent
5 Good
4 Above average
3 Below average
2 Poor
1 Bad

PERFORMANCE	4.83
STEERING AND HANDLING	3.00
BRAKES	3.20
COMFORT IN FRONT	3.58
COMFORT IN BACK	3.14
DRIVERS AIDS	3.25
(instruments, lights, wipers, visibility etc.)	
CONTROLS	4.14
NOISE	4.17
STOWAGE	3.50
ROUTINE SERVICE	3.30
(under-bonnet access, dipstick etc.)	
EASE OF DRIVING	4.00
OVERALL RATING	**3.61**

Comparisons

	Price (£)	max mph	0.60 (sec)	overall mpg	capacity (c.c.)	power (bhp)	wheelbase (in.)	length (in.)	width (in.)	kerb weight (lb.)	fuel (gal)	tyre size
Chevrolet Blazer	**9,009**	**90**	**14.5** (13.1 in low)	**10.6**	**5,733**	**165**	**107.0**	**184.0**	**80.0**	**5,152**	**26.0**	**H78-15B**
Range Rover	8,008	99	14.6	14.1	3,528	130	100.0	176.0	70.0	3,965	19.0	205-16
Jeep CJ6	5,237	82	16.5	13.7	3,799	101	84.0	139.0	72.0	2,515	12.3	F78-15
Peugeot 504 Estate	4,578	99	14.1	20.9	1,971	93	114.0	189.0	66.5	2,930	13.2	185-14
Volvo 245 DL Estate	5,357	106	11.4	21.3	2,127	97	104.0	193.0	67.0	3,073	13.2	185-14
Jeep Cherokee Chief	9,489	—	—	—	5,900	175	108.0	183.0	67.0	3,875	18.3	H78-15B

Mud is thrown into the engine compartment, but kept out of the engine by an oil bath air cleaner. Fluid levels are easy to check, but otherwise maintenance is naturally rather awkward due to the height of the Blazer

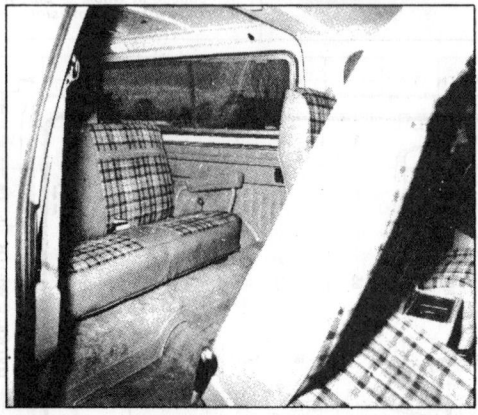

Access to the rear is only via the tipping front passenger's seat. Installed there, one sits rather high up. Lap straps are provided for the rear passengers

Above: Dirt collects on the sills, and on passengers' clothes if they are not careful. Lurid scrolled door trim panels complement the US style interior. There are three air conditioning vents on the dash, and two in the doors

Right: Repositioning the spare wheel would be the first priority for the serious load carrier; and once down the tailgate is kept level by flimsy straps

to rely on the door mirrors, as long as they have not been knocked slightly out of position. For a vehicle offering such creature comforts, we find it extraordinary that only a bottle jack should have been provided. Known for their inability to function in mud and difficult terrain generally, there surely could have been a better provision for wheel-changing. Located under the bonnet, the jack and wheelbrace are the only tools provided, and we would imagine that most owners would want to have their servicing done professionally; however, they might take note of the price of spares. A windscreen is over £220, and a front wing in excess of £150.

Engine accessibility in general is good for checking levels and so on, but there are occasions when a stool to stand on might be something of an advantage.

In conclusion

At the price, and with very high running costs, we cannot imagine the hard-headed farmer, boatbuilder, or even landowner giving this vehicle serious consideration, unless he is something of an extrovert. Perhaps it was for that reason that most who drove it enjoyed the Blazer and the effect it had on their egos. The fact is the Chevrolet Blazer is too large and unwieldy for our crowded roads, though it does cruise down motorways effortlessly. Off the road it has ample power to go anywhere but we would think it much less wieldy than the opposition. Its overall size is not reflected in internal carrying capacity, and it badly needs some means of improving rearward visibility while on the move. Without the excellent automatic transmission and light steering the Blazer would be very tedious to drive, but as it is we are sure that there will be a limited market for such a dramatic and robust looking vehicle which, with some improvements made to the braking, would make an excellent tow wagon.

MANUFACTURER:
Chevrolet Motor Division
General Motors Corporation
Detroit
Michigan 48202

UK CONCESSIONAIRES:
Lendrum and Hartman
(Motor Services Ltd)
122-124 King Street
Hammersmith W6 0RH

PRICES

Basic	£7,700.00
Special Car Tax	£614.67
VAT	£667.33
Total (in GB)	**£9,009.00**
Seat belts	standard
Licence	£50.00
Delivery charge (London)	£60.00
Number plates	£15.00
Total on the Road (exc. insurance)	**£9,134.00**
Insurance	Group 7

EXTRAS (inc. VAT)
None listed

TOTAL AS TESTED ON THE ROAD	**£9,134.00**

I N THIS ISSUE we are publishing our first vehicle owner survey. This particular one is about the Chevy Blazer/GMC Jimmy and we're sure you'll find it interesting—and revealing. The purpose of this introduction is to tell you what we've done, how we've done it and what we hope to accomplish. In other words, the methodology and the rationale.

We started with a four-page questionnaire in the October '78 issue. Most of the 53 questions contained therein were about the vehicle itself, the equipment that was on it and the owner's experience with its reliability and dependability. In addition, we included questions that would provide us with some basic demographic information about the owners themselves (age, sex, job, income, etc.) and we also included shorter sections about tires, headers and suspension systems. The purpose of these extra questions was to get specific details about the experience owners had had with particular makes. Also, for our own edification, we included a question about the editorial contents of the magazine, asking whether the reader would like more, less or about the same amount of several different categories of editorial material.

The questionnaire was bound into every copy of the magazine so the response would include subscribers as well as readers who bought the magazine on the newsstand.

The questionnaire was designed as a self-mailer so that after filling it out, the respondent could fold it and drop it into the mail—we paid the return postage. One of the reasons we paid the postage was to get as large a return as possible and in this we were successful. Next time we may not

pay the tab—just in the hope it will reduce the volume somewhat. (Have you ever considered the hours required just to open and sort several thousand questionnaires? Especially ones that have been sealed with everything from a dozen crooked staples to a yard of racer's tape?)

What we got was a response that was far larger than we required to get valid results—980 completed questionnaires from Blazer/Jimmy owners. Because of this we were able to be more selective in the vehicles to be included in the sample. After sorting the questionnaires we tabulated a sample that included vehicles going back to 1973, when the current model came on the scene, and analyzed the results. The most important fact we learned from this was that Blazer owners who bought their vehicles new had a different story to tell than those who bought a used one. The used-vehicle owner generally couldn't report on what had happened before he owned it, obviously, and with the luxury of the very large sample we were able to exclude all except those who had their vehicle's complete history, adding considerably to the completeness of the results.

With the large sample we were also able to restrict our survey to only the most recent vehicles. One of the primary purposes of these surveys is to provide information to those who may be considering the same kind of vehicle. The newer the vehicles in the survey, the more accurately the results will reflect what the buyer of a new machine can expect. With the Blazer/Jimmy we were able to include only 1976 and later models, which adds much to its usefulness. It is true, however, that with some of our less popular models we aren't going to have a sufficient number of ques-

tionnaires to let us do this and for these we'll have to go back farther until we get what we believe to be a suitable sample.

In our experimental tabulation, we also discovered that machines that had covered less than 10,000 miles hadn't really been around long enough for the results to be significant. So we excluded all vehicles that had covered less than 10,000 miles.

So what we have in this first survey are one-owner recent models that have covered at least 10,000 miles. We had a total of 383 questionnaires that fit this criteria. Not all future surveys will include this many vehicles since, with this one, we actually did more than were needed in order to find out the minimum number from which we can expect valid results. To do this, we tabulated the first 150 and then totaled the results again after 200, 250, 300 and so on. The maximum variation we found between doing 150 and the whole 383 was less than five percent—and this was on one of those questions about the other kinds of vehicles in the household. For those types of questions directly related to the machine—which we regard as much more important—the variation was less than three percent, which is as close as can be expected in a survey of this type. So, in the future, if we have a good sample of 150, we'll be confident that the results are typical of the whole group.

How good is this kind of survey? And by "good," we mean how close would the results of a survey done in this way be to a pure sample where some given number of truly random owners were asked the same questions? Before we can answer that, you▶

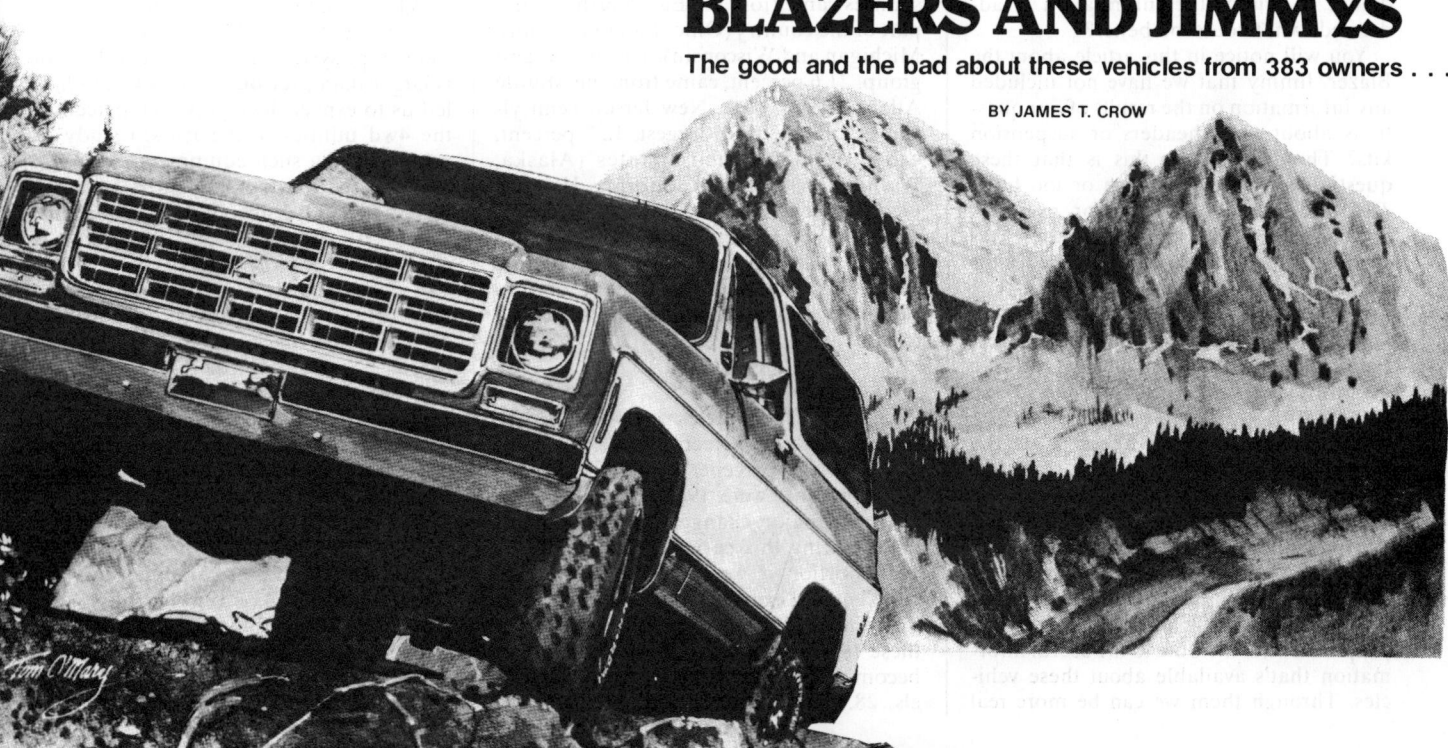

PV4 Owner's Survey:

BLAZERS AND JIMMYS

The good and the bad about these vehicles from 383 owners . . .

BY JAMES T. CROW

have to understand that what we have here is a highly specialized sample rather than a cross-section of everybody who has bought a Blazer/Jimmy since 1976. The people who participated in this survey, first of all, are readers of this magazine. And, right off, this keeps them from being a true random sample since, traditionally, only a small, non-typical percentage of vehicle owners actually read car magazines.

This is not a serious limitation on the survey's validity, however, since we can demonstrate that the Blazer/Jimmy owners who participated are typical of PV4 readership—and those people, by other means, have been defined. This is important. We can do this by comparing the basic demographic data in our survey with the results of a study done earlier this year by Leslie A. Riffkin and Associates of New York. When this comparison is made, it is obvious that our participants are typical of our subscribers. The results are too close to be coincidental. (The actual numbers are included in the Blazer/Jimmy survey, in case you're interested.)

So, to answer the question, what we have here are results that are valid for readers of this magazine. And since that's the audience to whom the information is addressed, what could be better?

You will notice in this article about the Blazer/Jimmy that we have not included any information on the results of our questions about tires, headers or suspension kits? The reasons for this is that these questions gave us too much or too little. The question about tires, for example, elicited more of a response than there was space to write in. Consequently, the results are garbled and probably useless. The responses for the headers and suspension kits look good, however, and we'll be getting around to those later when we have accumulated sufficient numbers to be meaningful.

As for the question about what the respondents would like to see more, less or about the same of in the magazine, we're keeping track of those and the editor is worrying about what it all means. How can he do more of everything?

Okay, then, the last question to be answered is why we're doing this. Our real purpose is to contribute to the useful information that's available about these vehicles. Through them we can be more real

help to our readers than we've been able to be in the past. Our vehicle tests can only provide so much information—and always about a vehicle that's brand new. Now, through these surveys, we can provide information about what they're like after the new wears off. We'll find out about their abilities—and their liabilities.

And if these surveys also provide us with a way of bringing some things out in the open that should be brought out in the open—then that's a bonus for all of us, isn't it?

DEMOGRAPHICS

Our respondents provided us with demographic information as well as details about their vehicles. In general, we found that our Blazer/Jimmy owners are male, young, well educated and relatively affluent. Specifically, we found that 99.2 percent of the Blazer/Jimmy owners participating in this survey are male, that they averaged 32.4 years of age and that 72.3 percent are married. We also learned that 65.9 percent had either attended or graduated from college and that their annual household income averages $27,515.

Several of these figures are very, very close to results reported for all PV4 subscribers in a recent study conducted by Leslie A. Riffkin & Associates. For example, the Riffkin study showed PV4 subscribers to be 99.2 percent male, 32.0 years old and 73.3 percent married (compared to results showing 99.2 percent, 32.4 years and 72.3 percent in this survey). In education and income, however, the Blazer/Jimmy owners are different from the typical PV4 subscriber in that more have been to college (65.9 percent vs. 59.9 percent) and have a higher annual household income ($27,515 vs. $21,711).

Altogether, 23.5 percent of our responses came from the East North Central part of the country (Ohio, Indiana, Illinois, Michigan and Wisconsin). The next largest group, 21.6 percent, came from the Middle Atlantic (New York, New Jersey, Pennsylvania) and the third largest, 12.7 percent, came from the Pacific states (Alaska, Washington, Oregon, California, Hawaii). Geographic location of the respondents is not believed to be of significance since our analysis showed there was no discernible differences in either equipment or mechanical problems that could be attributed to this factor.

THE VEHICLES

Of the 383 vehicles included in the survey, 136 (35.6 percent) were 1976 models, 184 (48.0 percent) were 1977s and 63 (16.4 percent) were 1978s. As there have been no major changes—and few minor ones—during this period, there should be no distortion if we consider all these as "one" model except where we can discover differences or trends. For example, one of these trends show that the 400-cid V-8 is becoming more popular. Of the 1976 models, 28.7 percent were 400s. In 1977 this

increased to 32.6 percent and in 1978 to 38.1 percent.

As expected, the 350 V-8 was the engine owned by the largest number—63.4 percent overall—and in the entire group just 4.4 percent were equipped with the 305 V-8. Out of the 383 vehicles, there was only one with the standard-equipment 250-cid in-line Six.

Overall, 77.6 percent of the vehicles had automatic transmissions, 21.4 percent had the 4-speed manual and only one percent had the standard-equipment 3-speed.

As for full-time and part-time four-wheel drive, the vehicles with automatic transmissions had full-time and those with manual gearboxes had part-time. In percentages, these were 77.6 percent and 22.4 percent, respectively.

The most popular factory option—after the 350 V-8 and automatic transmission—was heavy-duty suspension, a total of 62.4 percent having chosen it. Air conditioning was the next most popular (60.3 percent), followed by limited-slip differential (43.6 percent), AM/FM radio (40.5 percent) and special wheels (37.1 percent).

EQUIPMENT BOUGHT LATER

The accessory added more often than any other single item was, you guessed it, a CB radio. An average of 72.3 percent of all our Blazer/Jimmy owners added a CB but there's a clear indication that the boom is over since 79 percent of the 1976s were so equipped but this figure diminished to just 62 percent with the '78s.

Larger-than-standard tires came next on the list of equipment bought later (65.5 percent) and next, something of a surprise, came driving lights (53.3 percent). This is much higher than the average for all 4wd utility vehicles (29.1 percent) reported by the Riffkin study mentioned earlier.

Wheels came next in overall numbers (51.2 percent), and then another surprise, stereo tape systems (50.4 percent). This too is larger than previous surveys would have led us to expect since only 23.6 percent of the 4wd utilities in the Riffkin study reported having such equipment. Also very high among equipment added later was heavy-duty shock absorbers (45.7 percent).

USE OF VEHICLES

As you might expect, our respondents report that their Blazers are combination work and play machines. The largest single use, 85.1 percent, is for daily transportation but in addition 75.7 percent are used for off-pavement recreational driving, 74.2 percent for vacation and travel, 55.4 percent for on-pavement funtrucking and 48.6 percent for work or business.

The activities in which the owners participate are also fairly predictable and include such things as camping (66.3 percent), fishing (55.4 percent), hunting (54.0 percent), photography (30.5 percent) and motorcycling (22.5 percent). Only 15.9 percent of our Blazer/Jimmy owners belong to an off-road club of any description

and less than half of these actively participate in any of the club's activities.

Overall, the 383 Blazer/Jimmys had covered an average of 26,128 miles each at the time their owners filled out these questionnaires. The mileages varied depending on the model year, the '76s having traveled an average of 34,051 miles while the '77s had gone 22,649 and the '78s just 16,912. The owners also told us they drive an average of 14,165 miles-per-year and indicated that about 20 percent of this is done off pavement. This last figure is suspect inasmuch as our questionnaire did not include a blank for any percentages between zero and 10, and many respondents noted that they did do some off-pavement driving but this averaged far less than 10 percent of the total. The Riffkin study referred to above indicates that about a third of PV4's subscribers spend about five percent of their time off pavement and that the overall average for off-pavement mileage is 10 percent.

TROUBLES

Of the many subjects covered in our questionnaire, the most interesting—and most important—have to do with the problems encountered by the owners. Until we have accumulated information on other makes we will not be able to make comparisons regarding reliability between makes but even this first survey provides some fascinating results.

Overall, we found that there was one problem that was shared by more than 10 percent of our Blazer/Jimmy owners and that there were eight trouble areas shared by 5-10 percent.

The parts that accounted for more repairs and replacements than any other were universal joints, a total of 19.1 percent of our owners having replaced one or more. The average mileage at which U-joint trouble first happened was 19,360 and our results bear this out since only 9.5 percent of our 1978 models had had a failure compared to 20.7 percent of the 1977s. (You'll recall that the average '78 in our survey had covered 16,912 miles whereas the '77s had an average of 22,649 miles on them.)

Is there anything the owner can do to reduce the likelihood of U-joint failure? If so, our survey does not show it. The only cause for failure that could be identified

were instances where the problems appeared to be related to the installation of suspension lift kits. It is known that increasing drive shaft angles puts additional strain on U-joints but the percentage of owners having suspension kits *and* U-joint trouble was insignificant compared to those who had the problem but did not have a suspension kit. We'll put this question to Chevrolet engineering and report on it later.

In the meantime we'll point out an area where the factory did do something to improve a part with a high failure rate. Of the 1976 models in our survey, a total of 14.7 percent had fuel pump problems within the first 20,000 miles. It is clear that something was done about this since only 3.2 percent of 1977 models were reported as having the same trouble. So the factory does pay attention to failure rates—especially those that take place within the warranty period, one suspects.

Another part whose failure rate was improved was the alternator belt. In 1977, a total of 13 percent of these required replacement within the first 20,000 miles and several owners added gratuitous remarks about its quality. Among the '78s, however, the number reporting defective alternator belts was less than three percent.

It is pleasant to be able to report that there were very few engine problems of a serious nature with the Blazer/Jimmy. In all our 383 vehicles there was not a single report of a broken crankshaft, connecting rod or piston. Altogether, only 2.9 percent of all engines had a problem sufficiently serious to require removal of the heads or some equally serious disassembly and these were completely random in nature, no particular part accounting for as much as one percent of the total.

The transmission did not enjoy the same freedom from difficulties; however, a total of 8.9 percent of our owners reported a variety of problems that ranged all the way from persistent leaks to complete failure. Several owners took this opportunity to make derogatory remarks about the Turbo Hydra-matic 350, one asking, "Shouldn't a vehicle like this have the Turbo 400?" With the number of problems reported, we're inclined to agree. Admittedly, some of the transmission problems came as the result of abuse, a few owners saying things like, "Tranny gave up while I was pulling others out of the snow last winter," or "Blew transmission while buried in the mud."

Summing up the whole list of problems encountered by five percent or more of the owners, 19.1 percent had problems with U-joints, 8.9 percent reported transmission trouble, 8.9 percent had to replace rear brakes within the first 30,000 miles, 7.6 percent (average for the three years) had a fuel pump problem, seven percent had carburetor trouble, 6.3 percent reported trouble with front springs, 5.5 percent had something go wrong with the heater (usually leaks in the core), 5.5 percent also had front brakes replaced before 30,000 miles

and 5.1 percent had one problem or another with the transfer case.

As another criterion against which to measure the Blazer/Jimmy's reliability, we also tabulated the number that reported no troubles beyond normal replacements and maintenance. Those reporting no troubles totaled 28.7 percent and this, considering the way in which the typical Blazer/Jimmy is used, has to be a remarkable testimony to its overall excellence.

Perhaps the most surprising result in our survey was to learn that 21 percent of all the Blazer/Jimmys had been out of service for a day or longer while awaiting parts. ▷

BLAZER/JIMMY OWNER SURVEY

Models Included
1976—35.6%
1977—48.0%
1978—16.4%

Engines
250 Six—0.03%
305 V-8—4.4%
350 V-8—63.4%
400 V-8—32.2%

Transmissions
3-speed manual—1.0%
4-speed manual—21.4%
Automatic—77.6%

Full-time 4wd—77.6%
Part-time 4wd—22.4%

Most Common Factory Options
350 V-8 engine—63.4%
Automatic transmission—77.6%
Heavy-duty suspension—62.4%
Air conditioning—60.3%
Limited-slip differential—43.6%
AM/FM radio—40.5%
Special wheels—37.1%

Most Popular Aftermarket Equipment
CB radio—72.3%
Larger tires—65.5%
Driving lights—53.3%
Special wheels—51.2%
Stereo tape—50.4%

Most Common Uses
Daily transportation—85.1%
Off-pavement recreation—75.5%
Travel/vacation—74.2%
On-pavement funtrucking—55.4%
Work/business—48.6%

Most Common Activities
Camping—66.3%
Fishing—55.4%
Hunting—54.0%
Boating—38.4%
Photography—30.5%
Motorcycling—22.5%

Who Performs Routine Maintenance & Repairs?
Dealer—18.4%
Independent garage—17.8%
Owner—77.8%

Curiously, there seemed to be no pattern to this—while one owner waited for three days for his air conditioning to be fixed, another waited a week for a front drive shaft and still another took five weeks to get a new side window. The only characteristic these seemed to have in common was that virtually all were parts that had a low failure rate. Obviously, if it fails with some sort of predictable regularity, the parts supply system is ready for it. If you happen to own the only vehicle that ever had a particular problem, you could wait weeks for replacement parts!

It was nevertheless surprising to learn that more than a fifth of our owners had their vehicles laid up while waiting for parts. When we gain more experience with other vehicles in these surveys it will be interesting to find out whether the Blazer/ Jimmy experience is typical or whether it is as unusual as it seems.

BESTS AND WORSTS

After going through all the questionnaires it is obvious that Blazer/Jimmy owners like their vehicles very much. For example, we listed 10 different qualities for the owners to choose among as the "best" features of their machines. All but one of these was marked by more than 40 percent of the owners. And the one that wasn't? Fuel economy!

Overall, a total of 85.9 percent regard the "go anywhere, anytime" character as one of the Blazer/Jimmy's best features. Also listed by more than 50 percent of the owners were "fun to drive" (75.5 percent), reliability (59.5 percent), durability (55.4 percent) and luxuriousness compared to other 4wds (53.2 percent).

We also asked the owners to tell us what they considered the worst features of their vehicles. There was general agreement (by 69.7 percent) that fuel consumption was its least endearing characteristic, which is not surprising. After fuel consumption there were no outstanding "worsts" but the list included poor dealer service (30.5 percent), lack of power (21.4 percent), noisy (16.7 percent) and rough highway ride (16.7 percent).

The fact that Blazer/Jimmy owners are well pleased with their machines was also confirmed by the fact that 81.2 percent of the owners say they would consider buying another vehicle of the same make.

We also asked the owners to rate the service they have received from their dealers and it will probably be a surprise to the 24.5 percent who rated their dealers as "poor" to learn that more than half (58.1 percent) thought that their dealers were either good or excellent.

CONCLUSIONS

After processing these 383 questionnaires, our overall conclusions are that the Blazer/Jimmy is reliable (more than a quarter had no problems at all), satisfying to own (shown by the high percentage of "bests" marked by the owners) and that a comparatively small number of buyers have been disappointed in their selection (four out of five would consider buying another Chevy/GMC).

Areas we have questions about include the reliability of the universal joints (can the factory do nothing about this?) and whether it is normal for a fifth of a three-year production run to be laid up a day or more while awaiting parts.

Answers to these—and other—questions will perhaps become apparent as we process more of these surveys and learn what has happened to others.

Next month: International Scout II ●

BLAZER / JIMMY PROBLEMS / TROUBLES

Troubles Encountered by More than 10% of Owners
Universal joints—19.1%

Troubles Reported by 5–10% of Owners
Transmission—8.9%
Rear brakes—8.9%
Fuel pump—7.6%
Carburetor—7.0%
Heater—5.5%
Front brakes—5.5%
Transfer case—5.1%

Ever Out of Service While Awaiting Parts?
Yes—21.0%

Owners Reporting No Troubles—28.7%

Dealer Ratings
Excellent—24.0%
Good—34.1%
Fair—17.3%
Poor—24.6%

Three Best Features
Go anywhere, anytime—85.9%
Fun to drive—75.5%
Reliability—59.5%

Three Worst Features
Fuel consumption—69.7%
Dealer service—30.5%
Lack of power—21.4%

By Another of Same Make?
Yes—81.2%
No—6.3%
Undecided—12.5%

CHEVROLET BLAZER 350

*(Continued from page **16**)*

Nevertheless, the Blazer is a good machine and deserves consideration from anybody who is planning a purchase in the recreational car field. To begin with, it can be bought in less elegant trim, without carpets, air-conditioning, etc., if one is seeking a really functional piece of machinery. In a more stark configuration it becomes pure truck, a point that is driven home to the owner the first time he has to climb up on the radiator in order to reach the oil dip stick. Then again, one has to recall that this machine is a tentative gesture—a move by Chevy to test the market.

One of these days somebody is going to bust this particular market wide open. For example a 4wd van-type vehicle (with a suspension setup that doesn't make it as tall as a tractor-trailer) has to offer tremendous potential in terms of carrying capacity, small outside size and off-the-road capability. At the same time, it seems as if hydraulic suspensions are an obvious choice for machinery of this type. Then, in the best Citroën tradition, one could operate on the highway with a lowered suspension and jack things up when the going gets more rugged. All 4wd systems must become more flexible too, in the fashion that the Blazer has used so effectively. The idea that 4wd can only be operated by ex-tank commanders and veteran truck drivers keeps many average motorists away and it must be made effortless to operate before it will become a factor in the market. This may come to pass, simply because the recreational vehicle market is going to get bigger. As modern man becomes more frantic in his search for refuge among the natural surroundings that he himself is destroying, he will be increasingly attracted to vehicles that carry him to these venues. And those vehicles will not be trucks trying to be automobiles or automobiles pretending to be trucks. They will be a brand of vehicle from a new and distinctive genre, unlike anything we have seen so far.

In a personal sense, the Blazer has been a blast. Its traction, its toughness and the brand of raw enthusiasm it exudes has given me an entirely new perspective on driving. Rather than fret over foul weather reports, I move freely, regardless of the conditions. It is a friendly, eager vehicle and I am willing to overlook its deficiencies in favor of its mobility and its flexibility. Off-road vehicles are a whole new thing to a lot of us who have been locked up with high-performance road cars, and I look forward to warmer days when I can thrash the Blazer through the countryside chasing Pileated Woodpeckers, or whatever else one does off the road. Recreational vehicles are here to stay, and I consider the Blazer not only a beginning for Chevrolet but for myself as well. ●

"Quick Doctor, A Horsepower Injection:"
CHEVROLET BLAZER 4X4
All things to all men, but oh, those shocks...

PV4 TEST

The first thing test crewmen asked after driving the '79 version of Chevrolet's Blazer was—Where has all the performance gone? Equipped with the 400-cid V-8, the largest engine offered by Chevy in a 4x4, test personnel expected better than average performance, based on previous tests of GM vehicles fitted with this powerplant.

The 400 V-8 equipped '79 Blazer isn't grossly underpowered, mind you, but it's a long way from delivering the kind of horsepower the 400 was putting out just a short two years ago. In a few

moments we'll get into how well this vehicle did in acceleration tests as compared to the last 400-inch V-8-powered Blazer we tested, and an explanation from Chevrolet engineering as to why the loss of power seems so apparent.

Chevy's Blazer takes a back seat to no one in terms of cosmetic appeal. But this appeal can take several forms. In the base package, the Blazer has the looks of a good surburban cruiser, capable of transporting the family to various outings, shopping at the local supermarket or getting to and from work during adverse weather conditions. Another image, and one that has grown steadily over the years, is the macho look. Outfitted properly, the

Blazer looks for all the world like an indestructable machine capable of leaping tall buildings and can thoroughly impress friends and neighbors who are unfortunate enough not to own such a weapon.

The truth is, however, the Blazer is somewhere in between these images, and if accepted in that vein, it has been and still is a good all-around vehicle filling the needs and wants of approximately 85,000 folks each model year.

The test Blazer was splendid in exterior appearance with a coat of Dark Carmine red (new for '79) and a black fiberglass hardtop. The vehicle was shod with 10 x 15 Uniroyal Land Trac raised white letter tires mounted on▷

BLAZER

Rally 15 x 8 wheels. The top-of-the-line Cheyenne trim package contributed chrome bumpers, upper and lower side moldings, bright tailgate appliqué and various bright trim on windshield, side windows, upper and lower tailgate, wheel openings, etc.

Looking inside the Blazer discloses more Cheyenne trim pieces such as custom cloth high-backed bucket seats, console, full instrumentation, custom steering wheel, special body insulation, headliners with trim moldings, door trim panels with storage pockets, rear sidewall trim panels and cut-pile carpets in the front section. If the folding rear bench seat is specified, as it was in the test vehicle, the rear section has floor and wheelhouse carpeting. The inside mounted spare tire is also fitted with a vinyl cover. Total cost of the Cheyenne package is $748 without the rear seat and $1030 with. The Cheyenne option transforms a basic utility Blazer into a very plush country club-type vehicle.

But this is all cosmetics. The test Blazer had another $3600 worth of options, some cosmetics, but mostly convenience, comfort and mechanical. Air conditioning and an AM/FM radio with

rear seat speaker along with standard power steering and power brakes insured convenience and comfort, while the 400 V-8, automatic transmission, full-time four-wheel drive and locking rear differential satisfied the mechanical requirements. Tallying up all the extras resulted in a price tag of $11,597 not including $494 freight charges to the West Coast. From the base F.O.B. Detroit price of $6884 for a six-cylinder Blazer, the prospective buyer can "go for it," as the in-crowd says it these days. These options separate this vehicle into its various images but that's only the tip of the iceberg. The Chevy option book contains many more items and the aftermarket contains more stick-ons and bolt-ons for the Blazer than perhaps any other vehicle—truck or automobile.

The four-wheel-drive Blazer comes in only one Gross Vehicle Weight Rating (GVWR)—6200 pounds. There is a heavy-duty front spring option (also includes heavy-duty shocks front and rear) but it is recommended for snow-plow-type use only. For some reason known only to Chevrolet, you can't order heavy-duty shocks without getting the optional front spring. This is difficult to understand because Chevy allows a customer to specify either the heavy-duty springs *or* heavy-duty

shock absorbers on the K-10 half-ton pickup, which is very similar to the Blazer. It's too bad really because the test Blazer could have benefited from some heavy-duty snubbers—both on and off the pavement.

The Dark Carmine paint job with the black fiberglass top is very compatible. Seems most Blazers are fitted with a white top no matter what the body color. This gives the impression the top is a separate piece (which it is, of course) but the black top blends in to give the appearance of an integral piece. Although the top is removable, reader mail doesn't indicate that removing the top is a common occurrence. That's probably the biggest reason that Chevrolet came out with the vinyl top Blazer in late '76. The vinyl top looks good, fits snug and for those folk who like the open air, the soft top can be rolled up on the sides or removed in short order. Besides, you can save a hundred bucks by opting for the vinyl top.

Perhaps the single most disappointing feature of the Blazer, noted by all who drove it, was the bucket seats. This has been a regular complaint in all Chevy trucks since the short-backed bucket seats were dropped after the '77 model year (with the exception of the vinyl buckets in Chevy vans, which are much better). The high-back seats do not offer sufficient lower back support nor do they have the proper angle to the lower seat cushion. The seat cushion is high on the front side and low to the rear, forming a cavity where it joins the seatback. This makes for premature driver fatigue on trips of any length at all. Rearward visibility is also restricted with the high-backs. The high-back seats in Chevy vans taper toward the top thereby not restricting driver visibility nearly as much. The cloth insets of the buckets, however, were very comfortable and attractive. Could be that GM would be smart to make short buckets standard with the high buckets optional unless, of course, there's a federal safety standard that says the seats must have high-backs. If there is such a standard, test crewmen are not aware of it.

The folding rear bench introduced last year is a good thing. For those times when a seat isn't necessary and extra cargo space is needed, the seat folds up against the front seat with a positive latching device. If more space is required, the seat can be removed.

Quality control on the Blazer was above average for a GM truck. Trim moldings aligned properly, paint was applied evenly with no runs or orange peel, and the body was tight with no squeaks or rattles, even off pavement. Even the doors could be shut without slamming.

Some new features for '79 include a wider vent window post for better anti-theft protection, concealed fuel filler door, minor grille and headlamp bezel modifications, and more extensive use of rust deterrent metals. Coatings, cosmetics, convenience, quality control, overall appearance—all good and desirable characteristics for the prospective purchaser of a four-wheel-drive sport utility truck. But in the final analysis, it's how the vehicle performs that counts.

The '79 Blazer does very well in most all departments. Certainly it more than

Need more load space than this? If so, you can displace the back seat.

satisfies those qualities outlined in the previous paragraph. Performance is the only question mark. In the area of handling and driveability, the Blazer scores well in city and freeway driving. Idle is smooth and warmup takes a minimal amount of time. The ride is on the soft side for a 4wd, which is no bad thing; on certain sections of concrete freeways where the surface has become somewhat lumpy, however, the Blazer begins to develop a chop that causes the tires to bounce as if they were badly out of balance. This condition is mostly attributable to inadequate damping by the stock shock absorbers. It's possible that the optional factory heavy-duty shocks would be capable of diminishing this undesirable trait, but as mentioned earlier, the shocks can't be had without the heavy-duty front springs.

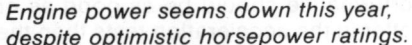

Engine power seems down this year, despite optimistic horsepower ratings.

Flinging the Blazer into a sweeping turn at legal speed would result in a slight wallowing but the steering remained mostly neutral unless pushed really hard, and then the vehicle would develop a degree of oversteer. Feedback through the steering wheel is minimal but not vague. Only a light touch is required to activate the power steering pump; however, the unit retains a feel of the road for good directional control. One of the test crewmen voiced an opinion that he would prefer the steering to be less sensitive—in other words, to require more effort to turn the steering wheel, while others liked the quick steering that the Saginaw variable ratio gearbox offers. The optional tilt steering wheel is worth the extra cost of $78, especially if several people of various heights and arm lengths drive the vehicle. Even with just one principal driver, the tilt wheel helps prevent driver fatigue on long trips by varying the seating and arm position. Kinda like the relief one gets by driving with the shoes off for a short period of time.

Flow-through ventilation is very good when the fiberglass top is equipped with the optional sliding side windows and glass wind deflectors. But at a cost of $176, they can't be considered a necessary option. At $105 the rear roll bar is a good investment, however.

With the windows all up and cruising the freeways, the Blazer is one of the quieter 4wds around. The aggressive treaded Uniroyal Land Tracs could be detected above other vehicle sounds but would not be considered a noisy tire at least during the first few thousand miles of tread wear. The polyester cord used in the construction offered ade-▷

quate sidewall flex and, of course, did not flat spot after sitting overnight as most nylon cord-constructed tires do. Ground clearance at the differentials is more than eight inches thanks to the Uniroyals.

Street running the Blazer is fun, but off pavement is where it's at. The Blazer did a commendable job here but the soft shocks proved even less effective in the outback. Running on smooth trails with just an occasional chuck hole or whoop-de-doo was duck soup for the big Chevy. The ride was good with no objectionable jounce or rebound but into the rough stuff, the ride and handling deteriorated. The Blazer would pitch and wallow if pushed hard where the bumps were closer together. The shocks just could not keep the tires in contact with the undulating terrain and as they heated up, they were even less effective.

Visibility is only fair-to-good off pavement. The broad hood obscures the terrain directly in front of the vehicle, especially when topping a rise. It seems forever before a view of the ground becomes visible to the driver as the vehicle drops down the other side of the rise. Short hooded 4wds like Jeeps and Scouts have a big advantage here. Even though the Blazer is large by 4wd standards, it's still very nimble in the outback and can hustle at speed with the best of them. Of course, the width of the Blazer dictates just where it can be driven but with a turning diameter of just 37 feet, it can be maneuvered around just about anything.

Although the temperature was only about 75 degrees during the off-pavement testing program, it was necessary to use the air conditioner to bring the interior to a comfortable temperature. That's with the windows up to prevent

Map pouches on the Blazer's door panels are a handy detail trim item.

The Blazer's dash, like that of most of the rest of the trucks in the GM line, is quite easily read and contains controls which are handily placed.

dust from covering the interior of the Blazer. The air vent alone with the windows up would just not offset the heat generated by the catalytic converter even on such a pleasant day. Test crewmen have also experienced this in other Chevys equipped with catalytic converters, especially pickups. This won't be as much of a hassle in areas that don't have a dust problem as the heat isn't so noticeable with the windows down. We would recommend the air conditioner in dusty areas however.

Getting back to the question of what's happened to the performance of the Blazer and the 400 V-8 in particular, there seems to be only one logical reason: the addition of a catalytic converter and a single exhaust in place of the previously used dual exhausts. Horsepower ratings as released by Chevrolet do not indicate any significant changes within or on the engine itself. For instance, the 1977 horsepower and torque rating for the 400 were 175 hp at 3600 rpm and 290 lb-ft at 2800 rpm. The '79 California certified 400 as tested was 170 hp at 3600 rpm and 305 lb-ft at 1600 rpm. This shows a drop of five horsepower but a gain of 15 lb-ft of torque at 1200 rpm less for the '79 version. This would indicate that performance should be as good as or better in the acceleration tests than the '77. Not so! Back in February of 1977, PV4 tested a Blazer Chalet, the short-lived entry by Chevrolet in the recreational vehicle market. The Chalet weighed just over 1000 pounds more than the '79 Blazer and was fitted with the 400 V-8 and 3.07 axle ratios. Not only was the Chalet a half-ton heavier but it presented a larger frontal area for added wind drag and tall 3.07 gears vs. 3.40 gears on the '79 Blazer. But would you believe the acceleration runs were almost identical? The Chalet did zero to 60 mph in 13.3 seconds and the quarter mile in 19.2 at 71 mph. The '79 was only fractionally quicker to 60 at 13.1 seconds, but had a quarter-mile elapsed time and speed exactly to that of the Chalet. There's no way the two engines could be putting at the same horsepower, especially considering the heavier vehicle also had taller gears.

So where has the power gone? In test crewmen's opinion it has to be mostly attributable to the single exhaust system and back pressure of the catalytic converter. It's surprising that the horsepower figures as released by Chevy don't reflect this drop in horsepower. As the test procedures used by Chevy engineers states: "These (hp and torque) curves represent full-throttle performance as obtained from a dynamometer test simulating actual operating conditions when the engine is in the vehicle." Any drop in power from '77 to the present should be reflected in lower engine ratings but as pointed out earlier, they're basically the same.

Chevy engineering was unable to explain the reason for the drop in performance other than mentioning the ever tightening emission controls which will result in less performance from engines now and in the future. But still the fact remains that if indeed the engine is putting out less horsepower (which must be the case or else performance wouldn't be down) then this should be reflected in lower factory horsepower ratings such as Ford has listed for the ratings of the 351 and 400 V-8 in its '79 pickups. Ford's engines reflect a loss of approximately 25 horsepower due to a camshaft change, along with other minor modifications.

Fuel economy still isn't a strong point with the Blazer but at 11.7 mpg, it's in the ballpark with similar vehicles of this type and bulk. If and when (and perhaps when will be 1981 for GM) the Blazer is downsized, fuel economy will no doubt improve but at what sacrifice remains to be seen. Certainly the full-time 4wd system as used in the test Blazer will be gone. This alone could improve gas mileage by up to 10 percent. Extensive work is going on involving automatic locking hubs to replace the full-time feature, plus many other areas of redesign and improvement. But until that time comes, the current Blazer is a solid vehicle, has a strong cosmetic and macho appeal second to no other vehicle, and is comfortable to drive, with more than adequate people and cargo hauling capacity. There's still a lot of demand for such a vehicle. ●

CHEVY BLAZER
SPECIFICATIONS AND PERFORMANCE

PRICES

Basic list, FOB, Detroit
Blazer Hardtop Six $6884
Blazer Vinyl Top Six $6784

Standard Equipment ....250-cid in-line Six (350 V-8 in Calif.), 3-spd manual transmission, 2-spd transfer case, free-running front hubs, front bucket seats, power front disc/rear drum brakes, power steering, heater, defroster, 2-spd electric wiper washers, painted front and rear bumpers, removable fiberglass hardtop or vinyl convertible top (vinyl top is $100 less than hardtop), H78 x 15 tires

GENERAL

Curb weight, lb (test model) 4900
Weight distribution, %, front/rear 55/45
GVWR (test model) 6200
Optional GVWRs ....none

Wheelbase, in. (test model) 106.5
Track, front/rear 65.8/62.7
Overall length 184.4
Overall height 72
Overall width 79.6
Overhang, front/rear 33.4/44.5

Approach angle, degrees 33
Departure angle, degrees 23

Ground clearances (test model):
Front axle 8.2
Rear axle 8.5
Oil pan 16
Transfer case.....................................11*
Fuel tank 15.5*
Exhaust system (lowest point) 10.6
*To skidplate

Fuel tank capacity (U.S. gal.).................25
Auxiliary ....31-gal. replacement tank, $33

ACCOMMODATION

Standard seats ....front bucket seats
Optional seats ....folding rear bench seat, $260
Headroom, in. 37.5
Accelerator pedal to seatback, max 44
Steering wheel to seatback, max...........17
Seat to ground 34
Floor to ground 22.5

Unobstructed load space (length x width x height):
With seats in place ....36 x 47 x 42
Rear folded or removed ....59 x 47 x 42
Tailgate (width x height) ....65.5 x 37

INSTRUMENTATION

Instruments ....speedometer/odometer, fuel gauge
Warning lights............alternator, oil pressure, water temp, parking brake/service brake warning, seat belt, transfer case lock, hazard
Optional ....oil pressure gauge, voltmeter and water temp, $29; tachometer (with gauges), $87

ENGINES

Standard ....250-cid in-line Six*
Bore x stroke, in...........................3.87 x 3.53
Compression ratio 8.3:1
Net horsepower @ rpm ....130 @ 4000
Net torque @ rpm, lb-ft ....210 @ 2000
Type fuel required ....unleaded
*Not available in Calif.

Optional 305-cid V-8, $240*
Bore x stroke, in...........................3.74 x 3.48

Compression ratio 8.4:1
Net horsepower @ rpm ....140 @ 4000
Net torque @ rpm, lb-ft ....240 @ 2000
Type fuel required ....unleaded
*Not available in Calif.

Optional 350-cid V-8, $365*
Bore x stroke, in...........................4.00 x 3.48
Compression ratio 8.2:1
Net horsepower @ rpm ....165 @ 3600**
Net torque @ rpm, lb-ft ....270 @ 2000**
Type fuel required ....unleaded
*Standard engine for Calif.
**For Calif. rating is: 155 hp @ 3600, 260 lb-ft @ 2000

Optional 400-cid V-8, $535*
Bore x stroke, in...........................4.125 x 3.75
Compression ratio 8.2:1
Net horsepower @ rpm ....185 @ 3600*
Net torque @ rpm, lb-ft ....300 @ 2400*
Type fuel required ....unleaded
*For Calif. rating is: 170 hp @ 3600, 305 lb-ft @ 1600

DRIVETRAIN

Standard transmission ....3-spd manual
Clutch dia., in. 11
Transmission ratios: 3rd 1.00:1
2nd...1.75:1
1st...2.99:1
Synchromesh ....all forward gears

Optional ....4-spd manual, $164*
Transmission ratios: 4th 1.00:1
3rd...1.70:1
2nd...3.58:1
1st...6.56:1
Synchromesh ....2nd, 3rd and 4th gears
*Not available with 400 V-8

Optional ....3-spd automatic, $370
Transmission ratios: 3rd 1.00:1
2nd...1.52:1
1st...2.52:1
Rear axle type ....semi-floating hypoid beam
Final drive ratios 2.76, 3.07, 3.40, 3.73, 4.11

Free-running front hubs ....std with part-time 4wd
Limited slip differential $185
Transfer case ....NP 205 2-spd (part-time 4wd) NP203 2-spd (full-time 4wd)
Transfer case ratios ....1.96:1, 1.00:1 (NP 205); 2.00:1, 1.00:1, (NP 203)

CHASSIS & BODY

Body/frame ....ladder-type frame with separate steel body
Brakes (std)................front, 11.86-in. dia. disc; rear, 11.15 x 2.75-in. drum
Brake swept area, sq in. 431
Swept area/ton (max load)....................139
Power brakes ....std

Steering type (std) ....recirculating ball
Power steering ....std
Power steering ratio.............variable 16/13:1
Turning circle, ft 37
Wheel size (std) ....15 x 6
Optional wheel sizes ....15 x 8 rally, 15 x 8 steel spoke, 16 x 5 steel disc
Tire size (std) ....H78 x 15B
Optional tire sizes ....L78 x 15B, LR78 x 15C, 10 x 15B, 7.00 x 15C, 6.50 x 16C

SUSPENSION

Front suspension ....semi-elliptic leaf springs on live axle, anti-roll bar and tube shocks

Front axle capacity, lb 3600
Optional..none
Rear suspension ....semi-elliptic leaf springs on live axle and tube shocks
Rear axle capacity, lb 3750
Optional..none

Additional suspension options...........HD front springs (includes HD front and rear shocks), $71, recommended for snowplow-type usage only

TEST MODEL

Blazer with hardtop, 400-cid engine, automatic transmission, Cheyenne trim pkg., air conditioning, chrome front and rear bumpers, Calif. emission certification; tachometer, tinted glass, sliding side windows in hardtop, below eyeline mirrors, fuel tank skidplate, AM/FM radio, rear roll bar, folding rear seat, rear seat speaker, tilt steering wheel, 31-gal. fuel tank, towing hooks, 3.40 axle ratios, locking rear differential, 10 x 15B tires, rally wheels
West Coast list price ....(includes $494 freight) $11,597

ACCELERATION

Time to speed, sec:
0–30 mph 4
0–45 mph 7.6
0–60 mph 13.1
0–70 mph 19
Standing start, ¼-mile, sec. 19.2
Speed at end, mph 71

SPEED IN GEARS

High range, 3rd (3500 rpm) 84
2nd (4000 rpm) 69
1st (4000 rpm) 42
Low range, 3rd (4000 rpm) 48
2nd (4000 rpm) 35
1st (4000 rpm) 21
Engine rpm @ 55 mph 2300

BRAKE TESTS

Pedal pressure required for ½-g deceleration rate from 60 mph, lb 36
Stopping distance from 60 mph, ft 167
Fade: Percent increase in pedal pressure for 6 stops from 60 mph 42
Overall brake rating ....very good

INTERIOR NOISE

Idle in neutral, dbA 54.5
Maximum during acceleration 74
At steady 60 mph cruising speed 76

OFF PAVEMENT

Hillclimbing ability ....excellent
Maneuverability.............................very good
Turnaround capability ....very good
Driver visibility ....fair/good
Handling ....very good
Ride..good

Handling ....very good
Ride...very good
Driver comfort ....good
Engine response ....good

FUEL CONSUMPTION

City/freeway driving, mpg 11.7
Off pavement 7.9
Range, city/freeway driving, miles..........292*
Range, off pavement 197*
*Range is 362 city/freeway and 245 off pavement with 31-gal. replacement tank

Prowling the back-blocks with rapacious ease, the low-volume import Chevy Blazer is the most expensive 4WD currently on sale in Australia. Text and photography: Michael Richardson

Below: giant Blazer looks like demon machine from sci-fi comics.
Right: trim and finish are first-rate for an American 4WD. Windows are power-operated . . .
Bottom . . . as is tailgate. Blazer back is long enough to sleep in with seat removed.
Opposite: long wheel travel, excellent low-down torque gives Blazer good off-highway performance.

IT'S HARD to get *really* excited about the 1979 Chevy Blazer. And that's despite the quite exciting standard features of the Blazer — at $22,500, the most expensive standard four-wheel-drive sold in Australia.

Is it perhaps because we're jaded by a diet of look-alike Yank Tanks from Ford, GM, Jeep and International? Perhaps — but then again we were pleasantly surprised by the off-highway capability of the Jeep Cherokee (tested OL, November).

So let's put it down to a case of deja vu. We've already seen heavyweight vehicles with seating for five, full-time four-wheel-drive, disc front brakes, and automatic transmission. What would have made the Blazer different would have been coil spring or independent suspension, a diesel engine, or diff locks. Without one or all of these features, the Blazer is a less able 4WD vehicle than the ten-year-old Range Rover — at a $3000 higher price-tag.

For the *macho* man, of course, the Blazer has everything. It shares its front end with the K20 4x4 — and that puts it in the Giant Class. Our test vehicle, prepared by the importer's "unofficial Queensland agent", TJM Products, had been raised 50mm all round, giving it an even meaner appearance. Remember those awesome science fiction comic books from your childhood, with giant man-eating machines that scoured the countryside, munching up men, women and children? At first sight, from ground level, the Blazer inspires the same sort of feeling.

THE PEOPLE MUNCHER

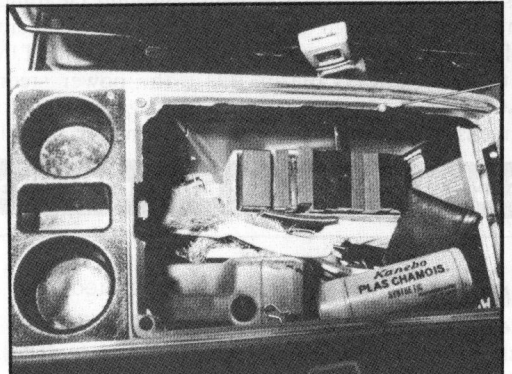

Above: Comprehensive instrumentation is marred by poorly positioned A/C controls.

Above, right: enormous amount of rear leg-room is matched at front. Cloth trim inserts are standard; Recaros are not.

Right: enormous centre bin is versatile bonus for overlanding.

Far right: 6.5L V8 engine is biggest in Australian four-wheel-driving.

Australian importer Ron Hoskins, of Melbourne's South Pacific Imports, is only bringing in Chevvy K5 Cheyennes. This is the luxury, up-market version of the Blazer which, in standard form in the US, has a 4.1L, six-cylinder engine, three-speed manual gearbox and a conventional 4WD power train.

Correctly reading that Australian consumers would not be interested in this pretty basic vehicle for perhaps $18,000, SPI's Ron Hoskins has opted for the luxury up-market model, with full-time 4WD, an enormous 6.6L V8 engine, full carpeting throughout, centre console, cloth trim seats, radio, auto trans, heavy-duty battery, alternator and cooling system, integrated air and (wonder of wonders) three power-operated windows.

It's this last touch that finally puts the Cheyenne into the luxury vehicle class. After all, even the Jeep Cherokee only has a power-operated tailgate window. The Cheyenne driver (is he also a Red Indian?) can open and shut three windows from his seat by remote control! This is a wonderful feature if you happen not to like your passenger. At the appropriate moment, you can open his window and let him cop a faceful of mud, wind, water, dust — anything your heart desires. We could play with it for hours.

Hoskins converts the vehicles to RHD in Melbourne, using a locally available Chev C20 dash to give a totally integrated appearance. The finish and overall appearance of the Blazer is superior to its

American counterparts, the Scout and the Cherokee, and at least on a par with the Ford F100.

The list of standard features on this vehicle seems endless: everything the $4000 cheaper Cherokee has except a CB radio.

But our test vehicle supplier, TJM Products of Brisbane, was still not satisfied in a number of areas. TJM's Lloyd Taylor pointed out that the standard Cheyenne 'heavy duty' suspension has only three leaves at the front and six at the rear. The K20 (tested OL, November '78) has a similar suspension system with an extra leaf at the rear, and tramps appallingly on washboard surfaces. TJM added one spring all round, bolted Koni shocks on the rear and dual OME Rough Country shocks on the front and boosted the ground clearance by 50 mm — partly by fitting 12 x 15 BF Goodrich All-Terrain Radial tyres.

And, as if the standard 117L tank were not enough, TJM bolted a 64L auxiliary tank under between the chassis rails and both door sills, giving a total fuel capacity of 244L.

A 59L aluminium water tank, tow-bar, Panther CB Radio, Super Snooper detector and Recaro seats rounded off TJM's modifications. As an eye-catcher the Blazer certainly made an impression on Brisbane city streets, but we were more interested in its overall performance.

On the Road

Our initial impression of the vehicle was

that it was sluggish. Now it may be able to out-accelerate Range Rovers, Land Cruisers and perhaps even Scouts, but it certainly didn't feel like it. We felt that a 6.6L motor (bigger than anything currently fitted to a 4WD in Australia) should have performed better.

The problem was not entirely of Chevrolet's making. TJM's 12 x 15 radials increase standard rolling diameter by 15 per cent, making the gearing too tall for the motor. Our test vehicle had 3.73:1 diffs; optional are 4.11:1 diffs which would be a better bet with the larger tyres. (Other ratios are 3.40, 3.07 and 2.76).

The net result was that acceleration for overtaking from 100 km/h was poor, although with encouragement the auto trans would kick down to second at 80 km/h. Top speed, with standard or accessory tyres, was 160 km/h.

Of course, power-robbing also occurs in the emission control equipment, the power steering, the air conditioning, and in the sheer mass of the thing — 2200 kg. Not to mention the full-time 4WD.

Now the Yanks seem to have taken to full-time 4WD with the same fervour they did Coca-Cola and central heating. Unknown in the US before the early 1970s, it is now offered as a top-of-the-line option by every US 4WD manufacturer. Naturally, it's supplied in combination with auto trans and power steering. You don't have to drive your 4WD: just sit back and let it drive you.

The Blazer system is no better or worse

than Jeep's Quadratrac, although Jeep claim superiority because of their limited slip third diff. For on-road use, of course, this doesn't matter a hoot. And our test Cheyenne was equipped with a limited slip *rear* diff which, when the centre diff was locked, gave it an advantage off-highway over the Cherokee.

While the Blazer/TJM ride was acceptable (most of the pitching and tramping over bumps being eliminated by the suspension mods) we feel sceptical about the vehicle's ability to travel quickly and safely over rough roads in standard trim. To the Americans, our Outback highways are rugged four-wheel-drive tracks, and this is precisely why so many of their 4WDs don't stand up to Australian conditions. Even with the reduced body roll, stiffened suspension and radial tyres, the Blazer oversteered noticeably and rolled on the corners. Its primary safety was further reduced by poor brakes (front discs notwithstanding).

As we expected, fuel economy was poor — around 21.8L/100km (13mpg) at fast highway speeds. Careful drivers could expect up to 17.8L/100km. Sluggish performance from a 6.6L motor inevitably adds up to poor economy.

But the Americans have never been too concerned about handling and economy. Ninety-nine out of a hundred Americans would prefer the Blazer to, say, a Toyota diesel. What they would be sold on would be its *machismo* appeal — and creature comforts.

Now no-one could deny that the Blazer is a comfortable vehicle. The standard seats are soft and cloth upholstered and offer reasonable lateral support on bitumen roads. They adjust fore-and-aft but not for rake. The steering column is six-way adjustable so you can virtually dial in your driving position. Add the Recaros fitted to our test vehicle, and Australia's your oyster.

The back seat holds three people and there are four inertia reel belts and one lap belt. One thing that will appeal to family overlanders is the enormous amount of leg-room, front and back — more than in any four-wheel-drive we have tested. Yet space is wasted. Around the back seat, for example. And in the body panels. This vehicle could be 20 per cent smaller without sacrificing any usable space.

For the long-distance traveller there's a centre console big enough to carry a week's groceries, plus map pockets on both front doors. Tinted glass windows and a truly excellent air conditioning unit are standard equipment. There's a push-button radio, which is more than can be said for the Range Rover. And it's so quiet inside! The Yanks would love it!

The dash is neatly stitched and upholstered and full of useful-looking dials. Things like oil pressure and water temperature gauges and a voltmeter. No tripmeter, though. The washer/wiper switch is

oddly designed but does incorporate an intermittent control. (In Queensland's balmy winter climate, who needs it?)

If the washer wiper control seems odd, how about this: the column auto shift and blinker control have been transposed. Now that takes some familiarisation. It becomes particularly annoying if you stall the engine: unlike most automatics, the Blazer cannot be started in Neutral, only in Park.

Which brings us to another point: the foot-operated parking brake. We've always hated 'em, but they really do make good sense on an automatic. Yet fit one to a manual and unless you're Jake the Peg you're in big trouble. Remember those awful CJ-5s and 6s?

Security is pretty lax. The quarter vent catches don't lock, although there is a steering column lock. Perhaps no-one would want to steal a Chevvy Blazer. It is, after all, distinctive.

But who needs to stop when you can let

the good times roll? In perfect harmony with your surroundings, radio blaring advertising jingles, a trail of pollutants spewing from the dual exhaust system, the horizon seems limitless. No wonder TJM fitted extra fuel tanks: even at 23.5L/100 km, the range is 1000 km. Perhaps the centre console could double as a money safe to pay for the fuel.

In the rough

Bouncing into the bush with that 228 mm ground clearance made us forget about the centre-mounted rear diff and 18.5:1 low, low gear ratio. And with good reason.

Set up as our test vehicle was, there were no problems whatsoever with ground clearance. Moreover, the Blazer has an excellent turning circle of 9.4 m (11.6 m with TJM's big tyres) which, with the power steering, tends to make you forget you're driving a big vehicle.

In fact, the Blazer is only 17 mm wider

SPECIFICATIONS: Chevy Blazer K5 Cheyenne

ENGINE
Type: Chevrolet small-block V8, cast-iron block
Bore x stroke: 104.7 x 95.2 mm
Displacement: 6556 cm³
Compression ratio: 8.5:1
Claimed max. power: 130 kW at 3600 rpm
Claimed max. torque: 394 Nm at 2500 rpm

TRANSMISSION
Internal ratios: 1st: 2.48; 2nd: 1.48; 3rd: 1.00; Rev: 2.10.
High range: 1:1; low range: 2:1
Diff ratio: 3.73:1 (optional: 4.11; 3.40; 3.07; 2.76)
Gearchange: column-mounted auto shift; single transfer diff lock lever (full-time 4WD)
Clutch: torque converter

SYSTEMS
Fuel: Mechanical fuel pump feeding 4bbl Rochester from 117L rear-mounted tank
Lubrication: wet sump, 4.8L capacity
Cooling: 19.3L water jacket/radiator; 8-blade viscostatic steel fan
Air filtration: pleated paper element
Electrical: 85Ah no-maintenance battery; 63A alternator; QI headlights

RUNNING GEAR
Wheels and Tyres: (standard) H78-15B highway or Tracker A/T tyres on 15 x 6 six-stud 'spokers'
Brakes (front): 297 mm discs; (rear): 283 mm ventilated sls drums, system power-boosted. Parking: cable-operated, rear drums only

STEERING
Type: recirculating ball, power assisted, steering damper
Turning circle: 9.4 m
Turns lock to lock: 4.25

SUSPENSION
Front: 3 semi-elliptic leaf springs, tele shocks; stabiliser bar
Rear: six semi-elliptic leaf springs, tele shocks

GENERAL
L x W x H: 4683 x 2021 x 1829 mm
Kerb mass: 2200 kg. Payload: 1020 kg
Wheelbase: 2705 mm
Ground clearance: 178 mm (under diffs)
Track (F&R): 1694/1618 mm
Fuel consumption: 21.8L/100km (on-road) Range: 535km.
Special equipment fitted: two 64L auxiliary fuel tanks; 55L aluminium water tank; bull-bar; 150W KC Daylighters; transmission cooler; suspension pack; 12 x 15 BF Goodrich All-Terrain T/A Radials on 15x10 rims; Super Panther CB radio; Super Snooper radar detector; Recaro seats; tow-bar.
Options available: varying diff ratios; (1980 models) LPG dual/fuel system; part-time 4WD with FWH
Supplier: TJM Products P/L, Morrisby St, Geebung, Brisbane 4034
Importer: South Pacific Auto Imports Pty Ltd, 468 Canterbury Rd, Forest Hill, Vic 3131.

and 23 mm longer than a Cherokee. It's substantially smaller overall then the Ford F100 4WD and has a 5.2 m tighter turning circle in standard trim.

This makes it competitive with other US-built 4WDs and it suffers from the same sorts of advantages and disabilities.

It has power to burn, but effective gearing can give the same sorts of results from a smaller motor. This is where the Americans have forgotten the lessons of WWII. They have yet to build a better off-road vehicle than the GPW Jeep.

Yet, perhaps because of the limited slip rear diff, it was possible to drive lots of places in 4H without locking the centre diff. The fire trails and other terrain we traversed would, we imagine, be roughly comparable to the American experience. The transfer lever pattern is Lo-Loc, Lo, N, Hi, Hi-Loc — unlike the Jeep and Range-Rover there is no separate diff lock control.

Suspension travel and chassis flex were good. The hardtop Cheyenne has a fibreglass reinforced plastic hardtop that bolts onto the body and is almost unbreakable. Traction was at no time limited by lifting wheels (with 2.2 tonnes plus load pressing down on the springs, that's not so surprising).

We were eventually stopped by a loose-loamed hill that offered no traction for the All-Terrain Radials. Amazingly, the rear wheels only   hand brake worked perfectly on the slope (the door locks did not). The full-time 4WD system with auto trans locks all four wheels — another reason for US 4WDs not having a tailshaft parking brake.

Once turned around (in difficult circumstances — the low C of G gives a good rollover angle) the *bete noir* of all automatic 4WDs immediately showed up: lack of engine braking. A quick comparison of

the Blazer's with other vehicles' gearbox ratios shows why. At 18.5:1, the Blazer's low-low ratio is only marginally better than the frankly awful Scout Traveltop's 17.6:1; the Jeep Cherokee, at 22.5:1 is a clear winner in the auto stakes. And the manual Range Rover; at 48:1, is beyond comparison.

Better control of a vehicle can be retained downhill under engine braking. A real danger in using the foot brake is that the engine may stall, cutting out the power booster; the sudden decrease in pedal effectiveness can cause an unwary driver to crash.

However, shod with high-flotation tyres and with all that power under the bonnet the Blazer would make excellent holiday transport to Fraser Island or the Red Centre. Most components are tucked up inside the chassis rails, with a bash-plate under the transfer case to protect those that are not. Front and rear overhang are not excessive despite the high length/wheelbase ratio — partly through TJM's suspension mods. We scraped the tow-bar only once.

Suspension kits are available in the US to raise the suspension by up to 125 mm. We shudder to think what the Blazer would look like!

A viscostatic, eight-blade steel fan makes for safe water crossings, although we did experience some trouble with water entering the air filter and stalling the engine. (Surprisingly, not with the standard paper air filter, but using an oil foam "off-road" type).

Would the engine overheat in an Australian summer? Probably not — the heavy-duty cooling capacity is 19.3L — as much as any 4WD on the market. For tough summer off-road work, though, we feel a transmission cooler could be an advantage.

With the rear seat removed (undo four bolts), there's enough room for two six-footers to sleep side-by-side in comfort — if they bolster the rear floor and mount the spare wheel on an external carrier. Ventilation would be provided by the sliding side windows. Alternatively, you can carry a tonne of equipment, although we wouldn't like to try it without TJM's suspension mods. How GM can claim that "No additional suspension equipment is required on Blazer for off-road use" is beyond us. We wouldn't like to put anything heavier than a sleeping bag on the chromed tube roof-rack, either.

Maintenance should present no real problems, provided you carry a step-ladder to help you into the engine bay. The Blazer is unencumbered by much of the pollution equipment festooning many 4WDs. Its 6.6L motor is a standard Chevvy small-block V8, albeit slightly larger than the biggest Holden motor ever marketed in Australia. The open CV joint front axle looks identical to the Chevvy K20's, as do the front body panels. Other parts can be supplied by South Pacific Imports within a day or two. (The company's back-up, we understand, is good).

In retrospect, the Blazer would make a pretty good round-Australia vehicle. It's got comfort, towing and carrying capacity, reasonable dust-proofing and a fair turn of speed. Add TJM's suspension mods, underbody water tank and long-range fuel tanks (the gauge mounts in the ashtray) and you'll get to all the top scenic spots without difficulty.

New for 1980 will be an optional dual fuel system with the LPG tanks concealed underneath the vehicle. This, suggests Ron Hoskins, should offset the only real stumbling block to Blazer sales: poor fuel consumption. ☼

The Great RV Binge

CONTINUED FROM PAGE 27

CONTINUED FROM PAGE 27

transmission and power steering. Ford should offer these two items as options; they are well worth the extra money.

The Jeepster? Well, it just trundled along, going where the others went but with a great deal more effort. It was hindered by too-soft suspension, with ground rated spring capacities of 945 pounds in front and 1,185 pounds in the rear, resulting in a ground clearance of only 7.5 inches. Despite the inclusion of a front stabilizer bar, body roll was undue, and when driving in sand the car slid until the tires would dig in and throw you in the opposite direction. It was sort of a thrill but not recommended. With a medium-length wheelbase, 101 inches, and a narrow width, 65.2 inches, the Jeepster was maneuvered fairly easily; but when in rocky country more often than not the suspension would bottom out, slamming the unprotected gas tank down on some awaiting boulder. Of the three vehicles on the trip, the Jeepster was the only one to get stuck, although for a very short period. Again, insufficient ground clearance was the villain.

Adequate passenger comfort is also important to the off-roader since rough country can lead to driver fatigue and here the Blazer won out. Its bucket seats were very good, providing excellent lateral support and just enough padding to absorb blows to the rump. Legroom was sufficient and armroom adequate despite

a huge steering wheel that stared you in the face. The Jeepster rates second, again on the strength of its comfortable bucket seats, but legroom was lacking and occasionally the car rocking motion would cause a leg to sharply strike the steering column. Bench seats, totally inadequate legroom and a generally awkward driving position relegate the Bronco to last place in comfort. Perhaps the wagon version improves on this situation — we would hope so — but some advancement is definitely needed in this area.

The conclusions? In our little contest the Blazer wins hands down with the Bronco a distant second. Both are decent off-road vehicles and while the Ford requires improvement in several important areas, Chevrolet seems to have the inside track on what it takes to achieve its purpose, with a smattering of style. The Jeepster needs to decide whether it wants to be a street automobile or an off-road machine. In its present, compromise configuration it is not really well suited to either.

But no matter what we have said about these three particular vehicles, one inescapable fact remains: off-road driving is fun and exciting. If we came away with any definitive statement after our three-day desert bash it was, if you want to escape the pressures of the civilization, off-roading is the way to do it. No other means we know of allows you to reach the "way back" country, free of smog and urban congestion, in the relative comfort of an automobile seat. Now we know why recreational vehicles are so popular, but we wonder how long it will last. After all, there's only so much open land left. /MT

Suspension Modifications and their Effects

What do you get when you upgrade your vehicle's suspension system?

BY JAMES T. CROW

IS THERE ANY off-road driver who hasn't wondered what difference it would make if he were to modify the suspension of his vehicle? How much better would it be if he put on a set of high-performance off-road shocks? What would be the effect of changing springs as well? What would a whole replacement system—springs, lift blocks, shocks—do? How much difference would genuine racing shocks make? How different would the ride be? How much faster could you expect to go?

I know I've asked myself questions like these, several times. And even after I did put on new front springs, a rear-end lift kit and high-performance off-road shocks all around, I still didn't have any handle on

the percentage of improvement I'd gotten. The seat of my pants told me my truck's performance was better than before. I knew too that I had better ground clearance and that my vehicle didn't slam down against the bump stops nearly so easily as it had before. But how much faster? I didn't have any real idea.

So it was with great anticipation that I loaded the back end of a pickup with camping gear and headed out for the back country to participate in a series of tests that would answer these questions.

It was possible to carry out this program only because Lonnie Woods of Rough Country, Inc., El Cajon, Calif., volunteered to furnish the necessary parts and

labor if we would perform the tests. "It's an educational program, as far as I'm concerned," Lonnie said. "Like you, I know there's a difference but I've never documented it. This way we can do that."

Greg Smith and Ty Tipton came along from Rough Country to do the wrenching and from their experiences in off-road racing, were able to set up a highly efficient operation out there in the boonies. Lonnie was there to enjoy the outing, supervise the modifications and answer questions. From the magazine came Don E. Brown, who would do the driving, photo chief Brian Blades, to take the pictures, and myself, who would ride along doing the timing and putting the notes together.

Here is how we planned to do it: Using a 1979 Chevy Blazer, we would drive over a 14.95-mile trail that included a wide variety of road conditions—everything from slow to fast, rough to smooth, soft sand to hard rock. This distance was divided into five sections, depending on the type of terrain; we would time the Blazer through each section. The same driver and observer would make all the runs and the driver would run at the fastest possible controlled speed commensurate with not damaging the vehicle. We'd make the run in box-stock condition and also after various modifications, and when we were through we should have a solid handle on the differences each change would make.

SUSPENSION

For the first run we would use standard springs along with a set of worn-out original-equipment shocks. These shocks were originally put on for use during the course familiarization runs to save wear and tear on those that came with the vehicle, but we decided to make a full run with them and include the results since we believed this would be typical of the suspension at the point an owner would decide he had to do something about them.

Next we'd put on the near-new standard (not heavy-duty) factory-equipment shocks which at that time had covered approximately 2400 miles. This would tell us about the effectiveness of the standard system as it comes from the factory, providing us with a baseline from which to measure in both directions. They would also tell an owner about what he could expect in the way of improvement if he were to replace his worn-out shocks with another set of OEM-type shocks.

This would be followed with a run using a single Rough Country replacement shock on each wheel. These are perhaps the best known of all the specialized off-road shocks. They have about 50 percent more oil capacity than original-equipment shocks and have a Freon cell to pressurize the oil and prevent foaming. They are pretty much state-of-the-art so far as bolt-on replacement shocks are concerned, and as such should represent what the typical Blazer owner could expect by installing a set of shocks of this type. The retail price for a set of four of these shocks is $130.

For the fourth run a complete suspension kit would be installed—new springs at the front, lift blocks at the rear and a single shock absorber at each wheel. This is Rough Country's Phase I standard suspension system. With it the vehicle is raised approximately 3½ inches and the springs have a rate of approximately 600 lbs/in. compared to the standard Blazer's rate of approximately 425 lbs/in. All the parts in this system are bolt-on, requiring no welding or metalwork, and the retail price for everything, including four shocks, is $335.95.

The final configuration would be what Rough Country markets as its Phase III suspension system. This uses the same front springs and rear lift blocks as described above but uses three of Rough Country's B Mark V racing shocks on each front wheel and two on each rear. These shocks are designed for racing applications and while they are also of the Freon cell type they also have very special velocity-sensitive valving specifically tailored to this multi-shock installation. Where all previous modifications were pure bolt-ons, this one requires that the inner fenderwell be trimmed away to make room for the bolt-on steel hoop to which the upper ends of the triple front shocks are anchored. The retail price for the Phase III system, including the 10 B Mark V shock absorbers, is approximately $900.

The road we used, which is part of a course used for off-road racing, was a total of 14.95 miles in length and included several different types of terrain. The first section was over a hard-packed sandy road that was mostly hard-pounding whoop-de-dos. These limited the speed which could be attained, pitching the vehicle nose and tail in hobby-horse fashion, but there were also a couple of short stretches where it was possible to accelerate up to 40 mph or so before having to brake again for the next series of whoops. This section was 3.60 miles long.

The second section was slightly longer, 3.65 miles, but quicker. It too was sand, but much smoother and faster. Here the ultimate velocity was limited by the twists and turns rather than road surface. This section was also characterized by deep-worn ruts and a high center.

Next was the longest section, 4.65 miles, and it combined several types of terrain. It started with a series of vicious whoops, smoothed out for a short distance, then began a transition from sand to mixed sand and rock. After a rough, broad wash with several sharp cuts, there was a quick upward pitch, a narrow plateau, then two deep canyons to be crossed.

This brought us to a flat stretch where the road was hard-packed shingle over dirt. This section, 1.50 miles long, was the fastest stretch of the entire distance though a series of flat twisting bends somewhat restricted the speed which could be achieved. This section ended with a twisting drop into another canyon and the start of the last section, 1.55 miles in length. This was the roughest, slowest section and was made up of canyons, cuts, wash-outs and generally confused terrain where it was impossible to establish any rhythm and where there was no good section where any comfortable running could be done.

Immediately after crossing the finish line we stopped to record the temperature of the right-front shock absorber, to which was attached a thermocouple. That was the procedure used for each configuration.

The first run was made with standard factory springs and worn-out shocks. Although there was some damping action in the first section, they faded completely less than halfway through the second, and thereafter offered virtually no resistance in either the bump or rebound direction. This resulted in the vehicle bottoming heavily if too much speed were attempted, and the oscillations that were set up over even the gentlest bump made it necessary to hold the speed down simply to retain control.

Our overall conclusion was that nobody should go anywhere with shocks as bad as these.

For the next run we replaced the worn-out shocks with the standard factory-equipment units that came with the Blazer. At this time they had been in use for approximately 2400 miles and there had been no appreciable deterioration since new.

These offered reasonably good damping through the whoops of the first section, still provided some control over the fast sand roads of the second but began to fade badly by the time we reached the initial canyon crossing in the third. As we skittered across the fast shingle in section four the driver estimated that they had lost 75 percent of their effectiveness; it was necessary to pussyfoot through the rough terrain of the final stage to prevent bottoming and retain control. The temperature of the right front shock at the end of the run was 240 degrees F.

As we returned to base on the highway the shocks recovered as their temperatures dropped and by the time we got back to camp they were working reasonably well again, having regained approximately 90 percent of their original effectiveness.

What we learned from this run was that the stock shocks weren't much and that, in fact, they weren't capable of doing an acceptable job off road for more than a short distance. The 240-degree temperature noted at the end of the run also indicates that these stock shocks will be short-lived when given hard use. The fact that they did not make a 100 percent recovery after cooling off demonstrates that the temperatures reached were sufficient to begin a deterioration that will be progressive as the shocks are overheated again and again.

Overall, we concluded that stock shocks ▷

How to tell just how much difference each change in suspension configuration made was the problem; that was solved by timing the test Blazer's progress over a measured course with the watch Jim Crow has his hand on here. Next to the watch is the thermocouple readout.

SUSPENSION

are better than worn-out shocks but still leave much to be desired, especially if any serious long-distance off-road driving is done since the chances of damaging the vehicle are greatly increased when the shocks overheat.

Our next run was also made with stock springs but now the Blazer was fitted with Rough Country bolt-on replacement shocks. It was immediately apparent to both driver and passenger that the suspension was under much better control, which let the driver go faster in both fast and slow terrain. One of the reasons we were faster was that the damping was far more positive, making it possible to get back on the gas sooner after a bump. Now the wheels seemed to stick to the ground, the vehicle landing and squatting, ready to shoot ahead rather than continuing to oscillate up and down on the springs as we had with the worn-out and the overheated stock shocks.

In later sections we did note some loss of effectiveness and this was estimated to be approximately 25 percent, compared to roughly a 75 percent loss with the stock shocks. Now it was possible to bottom the

suspension over a bump where, earlier, we had not had this problem to worry about. At the end of the run the shock temperature was 210 degrees, compared to 240 degrees for the stock shocks, and this was after going a lot faster, working the shocks a lot harder. The lower temperature is at least partially explained by these shocks having a greater oil capacity than the standard units. A temperature of 210 degrees is still enough to cause deterioration, however, and no shock can continue to operate at such a temperature without some loss in effectiveness. These quickly recovered when they cooled off and by the time we returned to camp we could detect no reduction in damping ability.

Our overall conclusion was that these shocks did a remarkably good job. They let us drive faster through every section and for the whole distance we averaged 28.9 mph where, with stock shocks and worn-out shocks, we had averaged 25.6 and 23.1 mph, respectively. This is a 10 percent increase in speed over the stock suspension, which is really remarkable considering that it involves nothing except the bolt-on replacement of four shock absorbers.

The next phase involved replacement of the front springs with Rough Country's Phase I suspension system which includes

front springs, rear lift blocks and one shock per wheel.

By this time we had become accustomed to rather large increases in speed. In three stages we had gained more than five mph, which is a big jump at the speeds we're talking about. It was something of a surprise, then, when this configuration resulted in a net loss in overall speed.

This requires analysis, especially when you realize that no loss in shock effectiveness could be detected; this was confirmed by the fact that the shock temperature at the end of the run was just 125 degrees F. Also, with this suspension, the vehicle felt absolutely bulletproof and there was a feeling that nothing you could do, short of crashing, could hurt the suspension in the least. No bottoming, never, no matter what bumps we hit. The only complaint about the handling came from the increased height. With the higher center of gravity and the short wheelbase, the Blazer began to feel slightly "tippy" through the fast bends and was harder to place exactly where the driver wanted it.

But why slower overall? Several reasons. The springs were considerably stiffer and from the very first whoops the Blazer wanted to pitch back and forth, hobby-horse style. Too, we had stock seats in the▷

On its first run past PV4's photo location (top), the Blazer was equipped with stock suspension; extreme suspension deflection, resulting in the vehicle hobby-horsing, is quite evident. This kind of behavior keeps speeds down and can result in broken suspension components. The last run (bottom), with the full kit comprised of heavy-duty springs and 10 shock absorbers, illustrated how much more stable the Blazer was.

SUSPENSION PROGRAM SUMMARY

A 1979 Chevrolet Blazer was run over a 14.95-mile off-road course divided into five sections as follows:
1. 3.60 miles. Mostly hard-packed sand with whoop-de-dos. Fastest of the slow sections.
2. 3.65 miles. Hard-packed double-rut sand with high center. Next-to-fastest stretch.
3. 4.65 miles. Transition from sand to rock-and-sand, then two rough canyon crossings. Next-to-slowest stage.
4. 1.50 miles. Hard-packed shingle over dirt. Fastest stage.
5. 1.55 miles. Rough canyon crossing and cuts. Slowest of all.

The purpose of this program was to measure the difference that can be expected by making changes to the vehicle's suspension system. To do this, the vehicle was run through the test course at the quickest possible controlled speed in stock condition, and after various changes were made. The same driver (and observer) made all the runs. Using an electronic stopwatch with interval timing capability, the time for each section was recorded on tape and transcribed, along with other pertinent notes, at the end of each run.

The configurations and the order in which they were run were:
1. Standard springs, worn-out shocks of unknown history and mileage.
2. Standard springs, stock shocks with about 2400 miles of use.
3. Standard springs, single Rough Country shock on each wheel.
4. Rough Country Phase I system (replacement springs in front, lift blocks in rear, single shock on each wheel).
5. Rough Country Stage III suspension system (springs and lift blocks as above but using B Mark V racing shocks, three per wheel in front, two per wheel in rear).

A thermocouple was attached to the right front shock absorber on runs two, three, four and five, and the shock temperature recorded immediately after the end of the run.

SUSPENSION STUDY
Average Speed (in mph)

Run Number	1	2	3	4	5	Total
Standard springs, worn-out shocks	24.0	29.8	20.6	28.7	16.1	23.1
Standard springs, stock shocks	26.2	31.7	23.3	35.1	17.2	25.6
Standard springs, replacement shocks	30.1	34.0	26.3	38.0	20.9	28.9
Replacement springs, lift blocks, single shocks	31.3	35.1	24.0*	37.2*	19.9*	28.1*
Replacement springs, lift blocks, multiple racing shocks	32.8	35.3	26.4	40.3	22.7	30.2

Slower than previous run, see text for discussion

Shock Temperatures at End of Each Run

Stock springs, worn-out shocks	240 degrees F
Stock springs, replacement shocks	210 degrees F
Replacement springs, lift blocks, single shocks	125 degrees F
Replacement springs, lift blocks, multiple racing shocks	110 degrees F

SUSPENSION

Blazer, along with standard seat belts, and these were simply inadequate for keeping the driver and passenger in place in anything resembling comfort. Also, the front springs, being brand new, had not had a chance to work in—which they would have done after a few hours' running—and the comparatively brief run wasn't long enough to let the occupants become accustomed to the stiffer ride—which they would have, of course. An additional factor was that the Blazer was still running on factory seven-inch wheels and 10 x 15 tires. A suspension system such as this permits the use of much bigger tires and these would have not only improved the directional stability but also helped to cushion some of the harshness resulting from the stiffer springs.

There was also an additional complication which may have affected the speed. I had been having trouble with my tape recorder on this run and in looking down, looking up, looking down, looking up, I got sick and had to ask Don to stop and let me lean out the door and throw up. I punched the "time out" button on the watch so the time wasn't screwed up, but it's possible that after that Don took it slightly easier than he would have if my breakfast had stayed in place.

Over the first two sections, the Blazer was faster than it had been before (31.3 vs. 30.1 and 35.1 vs. 34 mph) but the third section, the one in which I got sick, was slower, as were the last two. Overall, we averaged 0.7 mph slower than on the earlier run.

I don't think there is any doubt that it would have been faster all the way through if I hadn't gotten sick, would have been a lot faster yet if the suspension had been broken in and we had been used to it, and even faster still had we been on something like 12 x 15 Goodrich radial T/As.

One other note about this suspension configuration. As noted earlier, the shock temperature at the end of the run was just 125 degrees, indicating that these shocks would last indefinitely. The reasons for the much lower temperature (with standard springs the same type of shock has registered 210 degrees) was that these springs, being stiffer, were now doing much of the work that previously had to be done by the shocks.

For the final run the 3½-inch springs and lift blocks were left in place and the single-shock arrangement replaced by the B Mark V racing shocks, so there were now three on each front wheel and two on each rear.

With these racing shocks, much of the harshness noted on the previous run was absent. The ride was still firmer than with standard springs but the multiple shocks were damping the harsher action of the springs, making the ride much better.

The Blazer was fastest of all with this suspension—faster in every section and faster overall. There was still some hobby-horsing over bad bumps but this was not nearly so violent as with the single-shock arrangment. And, again, had the springs had a longer time to work themselves in, the occupants sufficient time to become accustomed to the ride, and had bigger wheels and tires been installed, the Phase III system would have been considerably faster than it was. It also should be noted that the shock temperature at the end of this run was just 110 degrees, indicating that you probably couldn't ever run fast enough to overheat these shocks.

The overall average for the 14.95 miles was 30.2 mph, more than seven mph faster than with the worn-out shocks and 4.6 mph faster than with stock suspension. These are impressive numbers, considering the low average speed, and would perhaps be more meaningful if expressed as a percentage. If you look at it that way, the final configuration was 18 percent faster than the stock vehicle and 31 percent quicker than when equipped with worn-out shocks. Those are impressive improvements!

There was also more to it than pure speed. With the multi-shock Phase III setup, the Blazer could not be bottomed, felt absolutely bulletproof and the shocks never got warm enough to cause any fade

KRUNCH! PV4's test Blazer, running with stock suspension components, lands hard after hitting a rise and being launched in the air. This is the sort of thing which blows out tires and bends wheels. Fortunately, both tire and wheel survived unscathed.

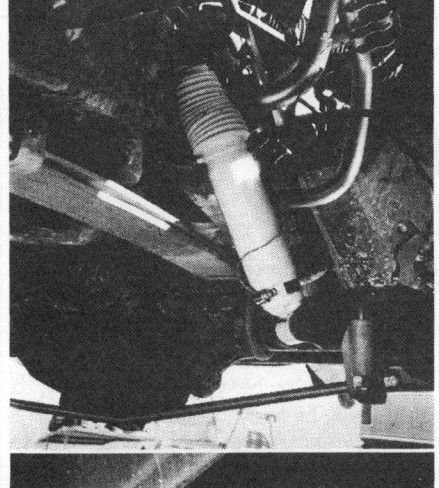

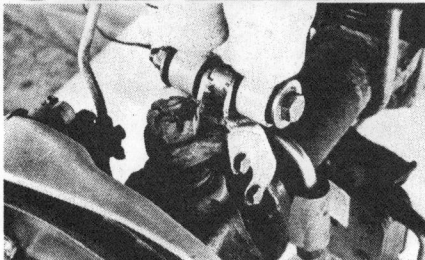

From top to bottom, the photos show: stock suspension, single aftermarket shock up front; rear suspension with double shocks and lift block; front suspension, killer triple shock set-up; the mount points for two of three front shocks.

Hard at work in the desert: The PV4 crew sets about turning the stock Blazer into a hard-running desert speedster by virtue of improved suspension.

at all. So we could have gone on at maximum speed all day, eating up the miles and not having to worry that we were going to break the machine. Which wasn't the way we felt with the stock suspension. With that we were down to a careful creep, comparatively, trying to keep it off the bump stops and worrying about breaking something.

So what did we learn from all this? A lot. Perhaps the most important single thing we learned was that bolting in a set of high-performance off-road shocks is the single, easiest, quickest, least expensive change you can make to realize a large improvement in your suspension. It isn't the ultimate—it's still possible to bottom out and the temperatures the shocks work at assure that they won't last forever—but it's still the most you can get for your dollar.

It needs to be kept in mind, however, that not all suspension is like that of our '79 Blazer. If your particular vehicle's standard springs don't provide enough travel to let the shocks work, then you'd better get some more travel by using a suspension system designed for off-road performance.

Now that we've finished the program I can look back and think of other things I wish we had done. I wish we had put on a set of bigger, better tires. They would have helped all the way through and would also have allowed the complete suspension systems to more nearly demonstrate their full potential.

Also, now that it's too late, I wish we'd have also used double shocks in front with the standard springs and with the 3½-inch front springs. You'll recall that with the single Rough Country shocks and standard springs the shock temperature got up to 210 degrees and that this was sufficient to cause them to begin to lose some of their effectiveness. So it would be good to know what effect double shocking would have had on this. It's logical to assume that the temperatures would have been lower than with the singles, that the damping action

would have been even more positive and that there would have been less fade. Unfortunately, my hindsight is better than my foresight.

Maybe we should lay on a disclaimer. Before we started we made sure that Rough Country's Lonnie Woods understood that we were going to treat this as an educational program rather than a puff piece for a particular kind of equipment. Lonnie agreed to that, saying, "Call 'em as you see 'em. I wouldn't want it any other way."

We've done that but we think it also needs to be pointed out that what we've reported here we know to be true only for Rough Country equipment, the '79 Blazer and the conditions we described. We think you'd get generally comparable results if you ran the same tests using high-quality components from another manufacturer. Not an exact duplication, of course, but what I'm trying to say is that what we learned were general truths rather than ones that apply only to one particular brand.

And what exactly was it we learned?

1. Worn-out shocks cause you to go slower and increase the odds of damaging your vehicle.

2. Stock shocks lose their effectiveness very quickly once you begin to ask much from them.

3. The greatest improvement you can make per dollar is to bolt in a set of high-performance off-road replacement shocks.

4. Adding a complete suspension system improves the vehicle by giving you greater ground clearance, more suspension travel and making the vehicle less likely to damage itself—but the ride may be worse, depending on the spring rate.

5. For ultimate speed, the whole system must be very carefully engineered. In this particular instance, the 10 B Mark V racing shocks worked very well but it cannot be assumed that 10 shocks (unless specifically designed for that purpose) are the answer.

Fair enough?

●

GMC Jimmy
The venerable six-in-a-row is still with us, and offers performance and mileage surprises...

PV4 TEST

What vehicle is responsible for taking more families off road, in comfort than any other?

There're probably as many arguable answers to that one as there are to the question, which is the best off-road tire? We'd guess, however, that the Chevy Blazer/ GMC Jimmy would rank right up there towards the top of most peoples' lists.

And why not? The Blazer/Jimmy (they're really the very same vehicle; just the nameplates are different; they're even built on the same assembly line) offers an option list as long as the Ayahtollah's beard, they're as comfortable as

your water bed, and while not as maneuverable as your favorite CJ, they're still pretty comfortable.

And maybe best of all, thanks to the venerable Chevy small-block engine, they usually have plenty of power—at least early ones did, until the reality of air pollution control and fuel economy mandates began taking its sorry toll.

Since that has happened, neither Blazers/Jimmys in particular nor light pickups in general have been either particularly powerful nor particularly economical.

Ah, but that's with V-8 power. What would happen if you stuck a Chevy Six into such a vehicle? We'd been wondering about that, and indeed such a combination has not been readily available for a while. But it is now, and we've road

98

tested a Jimmy equipped with the 250-cid Six and heavy-duty 4-speed transmission. Power? Well, we knew better than to expect much in that department. Economy? We had our hopes. The verdict? Read on.

What we thought, upon first climbing inside the orange Jimmy and driving off, was that we'd gotten the wrong truck. Usual procedure when beginning to evaluate a vehicle is to pop the hood and generally take a look around before we do anything else. We didn't do that until we drove the vehicle home the first day, and all the way along that drive we found ourselves wondering how come we'd gotten a V-8-powered Jimmy when we'd specifically asked for one equipped with the Six. We figured that when we reached the office the next day, we'd call the GMC guy who operates the press pool fleet from which road test vehicles come and really raise hell with him.

For sure the thing was no rocket, but it seemed pretty clear that whatever it was living under that sloping hood, it certain was no whimpy six-cylinder engine.

Wrong again.

The 250-cid six-cylinder engine now being supplied as the base powerplant in many GM trucks is a development of the famous stove-bolt Six built by Chevrolet since the late '20s. It has been steadily improved and refined to the point where while it remains very like that original engine, it is, in practical terms, quite different from it.

A case probably could be made that because of emissions and economy regulations, the Six has been, for the last few years, a shadow of its former self.

That is true no longer. In its 1981 form, at least as evaluated in this particular test vehicle, and in fact in several other test trucks as well, the Six has proven to be robust, smooth, and reasonably economical.

The nature of the Six, in this particular test vehicle, was helped a great deal by the fact that it was pulling against fairly short gears—3.73s. Because of Detroit's emphasis on economy these days, we just don't see ratios like that very often—more likely gear sets in test vehicles will have numbers ranging from 2.56:1 to 3.2:1 or so.

But what we're talking about here is a fairly small engine, one which makes 115 horsepower at 3600 rpm and 200 lb-ft of torque at 2000 rpm, pulling around a vehicle which weighs in at 4600 pounds. So gear ratios of this particular magnitude

If we had our druthers that spare would go out back on a carrier. Nevertheless you can cram all sorts of recreational gear in here. The rear floor and intruding wheelwells were upholstered in material color-keyed to the exterior: in our case bright orange.

are not only called for, they're very nearly mandatory if any sort of performance is to be extracted from the truck.

But there's performance and then there's performance. At least partly because of the transmission's stiff-shifting nature, this is not the most pleasant around-town rig. That point is driven home by the relatively modest level of the Six's power. Still, on-road performance isn't really all that bad. The Jimmy had no trouble at all keeping up with traffic, either on the freeway or in town, and was never in anybody else's way. Once on the highway, it was completely content to cruise at speeds well in excess of the speed limit.

Out in the dirt, the truck's character undergoes a bit of a change, particularly when a bit of acceleration is needed and there's a grade ahead, and you're maybe at 5000 feet elevation or more—in other words, a taxing situation.

It's then that the driver can't help but notice, for instance, that there's rather a gap between second and third ratios.

Third isn't short enough to pull the vehicle, second is so short that it's possible to rev the engine right to its limit. So you make do with modest throttle and with second gear, the only choice.

The little Six is at a bit of a disadvantage in the dirt even on level surfaces—at least when you're driving briskly, sliding the corners just a bit. You can pitch the chassis sideways all you care to, but the engine just doesn't have the oomph to carry the slide 'round the arc.

In the really rough stuff, however, the areas in which you have to travel very slowly, this particular power train really shines. And as often as not, off roaders are more interested in going slowly, very slowly, than in going very quickly.

With its extra low-ratio first gear, the heavy-duty 4-speed trans in this test truck filled this particular bill very nicely indeed. The transmission is the SM-465, built by General Motors in its Muncie, Indiana gearbox plant. It is very much a working 4-speed, as opposed to a sporting 4-speed. In most situations you use it as though it was a 3-speed, ignoring low gear, which with its 6.56:1 ratio is very much a grannie gear. Shifting the box is a bit stiff and notchy, but the throws are short and the detents positive, so while the transmission does take some getting used to, it isn't hard to get the hang of it.

Once you do get things figured out and get yourself and the truck into the outback, shift into low range and point the beast at the rough country, you find yourself working with some pretty wild gear ratios. Consider that the differential ratios are 3.73:1, the transfer case low-range ratio is 2.61:1 and the first gear ratio is 6.56:1. That means that when all the low gears have been selected, the vehicle's final lowest ratio available is an incredible 64.1:1.

What this means is that even with the engine idling, the Jimmy would climb any slope where it could find traction with no trouble at all. It might just be one of the slowest vehicles we've ever tested, at least in this particular frame of reference, and that ought to be music to the ears of many off roaders.

Less melodic to those same ears will be the news that this is not the base transmission with this vehicle—a three-on-the-tree is what you get unless you order differently; probably not the world's best transmission for off roading. The SM-465 will set you back an extra $141, but in our estimation that's money well spent.

While we're on the subject, we should point out that the Six is the base engine, and won't cost you anything extra. If you choose to order the V-8, you can have any V-8 you want as long as its the 305/ ESC engine (see PV4, March, '81, for a test of a Jimmy equipped with this engine). Unless you live in California, in which case you get a 350 V-8. The 305 will set you back an extra $345, will run a bit more strongly, and won't deliver quite the fuel economy. You pays yer money, and you takes yer choice.

In any case, this vehicle, sitting as it was with a modest trim level—that means it was neither a stripper nor a full dresser—tipped the dollar scale with a list price of $11,863. Base price for a complete stripper is $8842, which means there were $3000 worth of options built in there somewhere. You could probably do some creative price paring and get the total down a bit from that.

If it was us, we'd keep the heavy-duty double-front-shock suspension. We'd lose the Delco AM/FM/stereo, though, and plug in a good aftermarket unit. And so on, tailoring the unit to personal needs. In any case, it should be reasona-

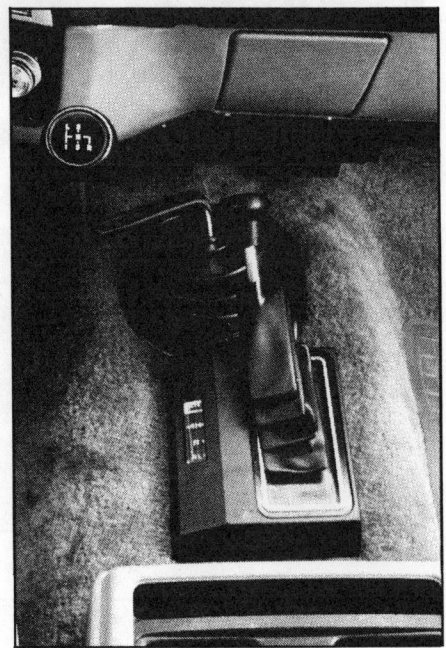

No fumbling at night to distinguish between the transfer case and shift lever as on some other 4x4s; placement is good.

bly easy to get the price of a comparable vehicle down below 10 grand, as long as you're willing to give up a few luxuries.

Anyway, you're no doubt wondering about the relative economy of this vehicle—as mentioned, so were we. As recorded by our electronic fuel flow meter over a 20-percent city/80-percent freeway loop, it recorded 17 mpg. Real world economy, measured by the fill-and-refill method out during normal everyday driving, showed us an average of 14.5 mpg, with a low of 13.8 mpg—that's the tankful we used during our off-road testing, so it's naturally lower than the rest.

By comparison, the last Ford Bronco we tested with a Six and a 4-speed trans

gave us 15.9 mpg as measured on the electronic equipment, and 13 to 14 mpg out on the road in real driving. This was a 1980 model, now; mayhaps an '81 would do a bit better.

The rest of the Jimmy was about what we've come to expect—comfortable, cloth-covered bucket seats, good visibility, and marginal paint.

A word about that visibility: it's enhanced by the new nose on GM light trucks this year, which slopes rather more than last year's nose. This means that when cresting off-road rises, seeing what's ahead of you over the rise is a bit easier than it has been in the past. You'll still find situations where you absolutely must get out and take a look-see, but things in this area are better than they've been in the past.

As mentioned, the interior was up to its usual comfort levels—which are very high. We did find one thing to complain about, however. GM wires the clutches on its equipment through the starter circuit so that the vehicle can be started only if the clutch pedal is fully depressed.

There are times, off road, when you want to be able to start the vehicle in gear without a clutch. If this was our vehicle, one of the first things we'd do is bypass this puny attempt to protect us from ourselves. Besides the fact that some of the gauges are obscured by the steering wheel, we can think of little else, in the way of the vehicle's interior, to bitch about.

Mostly, we think a Jimmy like this one is a pretty darned acceptable truck. It gets the job done quite nicely and is in the upper end of its class in the fuel economy department.

Pretty hard to beat twin qualifications like that. ●

The Six has come a long way since GM introduced it fifty years ago. It's hardly the same engine except for its in-line configuration. Loaded here with all the amenities required by emissions regulations, it's hard to find the Stove-bolt under all those hoses, but it's a stump-puller and delivers good fuel economy.